EMPIRE OF RESENTMENT

Also by Lawrence Rosenthal

The New Nationalism and the First World War
(co-edited with Vesna Rodic)

Steep: The Precipitous Rise of the Tea Party
(co-edited with Christine Trost)

Empire of
RESENTMENT

**POPULISM'S TOXIC EMBRACE
OF NATIONALISM**

LAWRENCE ROSENTHAL

THE
NEW
PRESS

NEW YORK
LONDON

Requests for permission to reproduce selections from this book should be made
through our website: https://thenewpress.com/contact.

"The Times They Are a-Changin'," written by Bob Dylan. Copyright © 1963,
1964 by Warner Bros. Inc.; renewed 1991, 1992 by Special Rider Music. All rights
reserved. International copyright secured. Reprinted by permission.

Published in the United States by The New Press, New York, 2020
Distributed by Two Rivers Distribution

ISBN 978-1-62097-510-7 (hc)
ISBN 978-1-62097-511-4 (ebook)
CIP data is available

The New Press publishes books that promote and enrich public discussion and
understanding of the issues vital to our democracy and to a more equitable world.
These books are made possible by the enthusiasm of our readers; the support
of a committed group of donors, large and small; the collaboration of our many
partners in the independent media and the not-for-profit sector; booksellers, who
often hand-sell New Press books; librarians; and above all by our authors.

www.thenewpress.com

Book design and composition by Bookbright Media
This book was set in Adobe Garamond and Univers

Printed in the United States of America

10 9 8 7 6 5 4 3 2 1

CONTENTS

To Sasha and Theo
and to their generation

EMPIRE OF RESENTMENT

1

The Ideological Migration of 2016

In a celebrated exchange during one of their presidential debates, Hillary Clinton sought to distinguish herself from Donald Trump in terms of her greater readiness to take on the job of the nation's chief executive. "I prepared to be president," she stated, and her implication was clear: Trump had never prepared himself to be president.

Clinton was certainly right. Trump was expecting to act as president as he had acquitted himself throughout his life in business: he was going to improvise. But, like many other observers, she missed the fact that Trump had prepared himself for his *run* for the presidency.

How?

Trump had immersed himself in right-wing media. This included Fox News on cable television, which Trump personally followed on a daily, if not hourly, basis. With the help of aides his practice included attending to talk radio personalities—the likes of Rush Limbaugh, Michael Savage, and Sean Hannity—monitoring Tea Party websites and discussions, and following right-wing news sites like the Drudge Report and Breitbart News.[1]

The substance of Trump's presidential campaign, the issues he thundered about in rallies and debates, was the direct result of what he found in these right-wing media.

What he found there was a populist revolt.

This revolt was congenial to him in terms of his own politics and, even more so, in terms of his vulgar, over-the-top style.

Donald Trump won the 2016 election by convincing America's right-wing populists to migrate ideologically—from the Tea Party's free-market fundamentalism to Trump's anti-immigrant, America-First nationalism.

This book is the story of that migration.

It is also the story of where it might be heading.

Right populism's migration to Trumpian nationalism ignited momentous political changes. As its predominant voting bloc, the right populists' migration exerted a gravitational pull on the (rest of) the Republican Party. From a starting point that was at once ideologically opposed and morally aghast, the Republican establishment and mainstream Republican voters moved toward Trumpian nationalism and unflinching defense of Trump's scofflaw approach to American political traditions and the limitations of the office of the presidency. Ideologically, the Republican Party came not only to resemble the anti-immigrant parties that have existed in Western Europe for a couple of decades, and which themselves had flourished since the European refugee crisis of 2015, but to have leapfrogged its Western predecessors into becoming the first such party to control a major Western democracy.

As Trumpian nationalism established itself as the novel ideological direction of one of America's two major political parties, the tenor and substance of national political discourse in the United States mutated. Vulgarity, mockery and insults, combined with an overweening sensitivity to criticism, had pride of place in Donald Trump's presentation of himself as candidate and as president—and these traits rallied a following that was primed with resentment toward his targets. Beyond the populists, voices long confined to the fringes of American political life now had a place in mainstream American debate. The "alt-right," steeped in America's historical currents of white supremacy, resonated with Trump's attacks on immigrants, and commanded a platform unseen at the national level for eighty years. Trump's winning the presidency gave these voices legitimacy. So too did the international illiberal zeitgeist, which had already set down roots in Eastern Europe and Asia, and was now setting liberal democracy back on its heels in the West. Donald Trump's electoral victory was a beacon for illiberalism internationally and at home he embodied the age's challenge to the liberal democracy Americans had taken for granted as their political patrimony.

Populism and Resentment

The populist revolt Trump discovered was less about the *emergence* of populism than its *transformation* in the Obama years.

Few topics have been bandied about as much in the past few years as populism. But too often populism is presented as a novelty emerging with the rise of Trump's anti-immigrant politics in the United States or anti-refugee movements in Europe. "Populism" was crowned Cambridge University Press's "Word of the Year" in 2017. But Cambridge defined the word simply by the populist concerns that roiled the globe in 2016:

> What sets populism apart from all these other words is that it represents a phenomenon that's both truly local and truly global, as populations and their leaders across the world wrestle with issues of immigration and trade, resurgent nationalism, and economic discontent.[2]

Yet on either side of the Atlantic populism has been alive and well since at least the end of the Cold War. The populist politics of Silvio Berlusconi, for example, had dominated Italian politics for almost a generation by 2010. In the United States, Tea Party populism had held sway in national politics throughout Barack

Obama's presidency. But these were populisms whose ideological and policy concerns were not the same as the populist issues of 2016.

Emotion is the prime mover of populist politics. In general, the essence of populism is group resentment, powerfully felt, toward a perceived elite. From the populist point of view, these elites are understood to be corrupt, powerful, and ideologically suspect. In the United States, populism of the left has typically focused its resentment on financial elites. Populism of the right, on the other hand, focuses on cultural elites—Hollywood, university professors, urban life, the "mainstream media," and much more. The elitists right populists resent are "un-American" individuals and institutions that they regard as looking down on them—the people who, in their view, think they know better than they do and want to tell them how to run their lives.[3] Both Tea Party voters and Trump voters have been acutely aware of the attitude in the liberal world that regards them as the backward, almost premodern, fraction of American society.

In political terms, the enduring object of right populist resentment is American liberalism. The dominant political figures are the Democratic Party and its "client base"—the "takers," largely minorities, who support the party for its "giveaways"—plus the Democrats' "elite" urban donors and voters, and the "mainstream media," whose "liberal bias" has long been a certain conviction on the populist right. Resentment does not stop with the political positions the liberals stand for. Rather it is continuous with resentment on how those actors think and live their lives—on the perceived culture of liberals' lives. In French social theorist Pierre Bourdieu's terms, the object of resentment is liberals' "cultural capital," and it is often expressed by attacking or ridiculing liberals' "symbolic goods."[4] Lifestyle, finally, becomes indistinguishable from politics.

The Club for Growth is a free-market political-action committee that frequently supported Tea Party candidates. In 2004,
the club ran a famous advertisement attacking presidential
candidate Howard Dean. In the ad, a couple, white seniors, in
front of their plainly nonurban house—this would turn out to
be the core Tea Party demographic—is asked by an announc-
er what they think of Dean's tax policies. Notice how the
couple's political resentment elides effortlessly into cultural
resentment—in this case, indignation largely about patterns of
"liberal" consumption, what liberals eat and drink and drive
and more:

> Man: What do I think? Well, I think Howard Dean should take
> his tax-hiking, government-expanding, latte-drinking,
> sushi-eating, Volvo-driving, *New York Times*–reading . . .
>
> Woman: . . . body-piercing, Hollywood-loving, left-wing freak
> show back to Vermont where it belongs.
>
> Man: Got it?[5]

Alcohol and Evolution

The history of American populism suggests that in order for
populist resentment to become a serious national political factor, in order for it to coalesce into a movement with national
consequence, the populists' resentment needs to attach itself
to an ideology. Currently evangelical Christians make up
the stable cornerstone of Donald Trump's populist support.
Political commentator and former George W. Bush speech-
writer Michael Gerson observed in 2018 that evangelicals constitute "the single largest religious demographic in the United
States—representing about half the Republican political coalition." But Gerson recognized that to be politically effective as

a national force, evangelicals have historically needed to align themselves in coalitions with other political forces.

> The evangelical political agenda, moreover, has been narrowed by its supremely reactive nature. Rather than choosing their own agendas, evangelicals have been pulled into a series of social and political debates started by others.[6]

In 2016, America's right-wing populists detached themselves from the extreme free-market agenda that had held sway in the Tea Party and reconnected to a different one—the America-First nationalism of Donald Trump.

Both the Tea Party and the Trump movement are descendants of other notable uprisings of right-wing U.S. populism. For example, right-wing populists were central to the imposition of Prohibition, the ban on the sale of alcohol in the United States between 1919 and 1933. In the nineteenth century "demon rum" explained the layabout drunk in small-town America. With the rise of immigration, urbanization, and the industrialized mill town, alcohol continued to explain to right-wing populists the dysfunctions of modernizing U.S. society. But it was only when a powerful class of wealthy captains of industry concluded that banning alcohol would help control a new working class that needed to learn such demands of modernity as showing up reliably for a scheduled workweek that Prohibition developed the political heft to become the Eighteenth Amendment and for Congress to pass the Volstead Act to implement Prohibition over President Woodrow Wilson's veto.[7] The same capitalist class turned against Prohibition in the 1920s as a reaction against generalized lawlessness and the federal income tax (hoping to move back to dependency on taxes on alcohol). Repeal of Prohibition followed with the presidential election of Franklin Roosevelt in 1933.

Right populism also rose up against the teaching of evolution in the public schools, as this contradicted the fundamentalist—that is, the literalist's word-for-word—interpretation of the Bible. Although the famous 1925 Scopes "monkey trial" returned a conviction for the prosecution, the decision was overturned at the state level. The trial itself, which pioneered film and radio coverage as well as attracting both the national and international press, occasioned a level of derision of fundamentalist religion and its populist practitioners that has remained current for a century.[8] There is a straight line between H.L. Mencken's characterization of the "yokels" and "booboisie" of the anti-evolution movement and, say, Bill Maher's relentless characterization of American right populists as ignorant and superstitious on his cable TV program and in his film, *Religulous*.[9]

With the repeal of Prohibition and the reversal of the Scopes decision—triumphs that felt taken away—right-wing populism was humiliated and lay largely dormant for decades on the national stage. However, it remained significant at the local and state level in the United States, especially in the South, Midwest, and, later, in the Sunbelt. In these places, right-wing populism often consolidated institutionally as a continuing force in regional politics. Gerson observes:

> The fundamentalists were not passive in their exile. They created a web of institutions—radio stations, religious schools, outreach ministries—that eventually constituted a healthy subculture . . . [10]

This subculture was in readiness for a resurrection of right-wing populism as a national force, a situation that would come thirty years later when the sixties upset traditional norms and institutions in America.[11]

The Dance of Resentment and Contempt

Emotion—more than ideology or dogma—is the motor force of populism. The classic emotion associated with populist movements is resentment. Resentment is anger directed at those perceived as above oneself or one's class. The inverse of resentment is contempt. Contempt is anger directed at those people or classes seen as below one's class. Since Trump's election America's liberals have been admonished repeatedly not only for having lost the traditional working-class base of the Democratic party, but as well for having conveyed contempt for the Americans who have been "left behind." Some of the most influential books among liberals have been on-site examinations of the grievances of Tea Party and Trump supporters. Arlie Hochschild's *Strangers in Their Own Land* offered a deeply empathetic understanding of rural Louisianans who staunchly supported the Tea Party and rejected Democrats despite living in conditions of grotesque environmental damage brought on by the oil and gas industry.[12] In *The Politics of Resentment*, Katherine J. Cramer investigated the depth of feeling in rural Wisconsin against "urban elites" in a state whose narrow swing to Trump was fundamental to his electoral victory.[13] J.D. Vance's unflinching first-person account in *Hillbilly Elegy* highlighted the ingrained social history of Appalachian American that would resonate with Donald Trump's candidacy.[14]

What is a good deal less well known than the charge of liberal contempt is that among themselves—on social media, on right-wing news sites like Breitbart, on radio talk shows—right-wing populists talk in a way that is a mirror image of this perceived contempt from the left. Nothing, absolutely nothing, is more common in these exchanges than expressions of the stupidity of the liberal world. That the "libtards" are hopelessly unintelligent or imbecilic, naïve, brainwashed, and ultimately laughable—or even mentally ill—is both a taken-for-granted reality and a favored expressive trope when right populists are talking among themselves.[15]

Like many elements of populist thinking, the premise of the stupidity of liberals is a vulgarization of the thinking of conservative intellectuals, both contemporary and historical. (This is a theme that will occur throughout the course of this book.) In a 2002 column, Charles Krauthammer gave voice to this tradition.[16] "To understand the workings of American politics," he wrote, "you have to understand this fundamental law: Conservatives think liberals are stupid." Krauthammer moderates his patronizing view of liberals with noblesse oblige or, as he calls it, "compassionate condescension." He attributes the intellectual shortcomings of liberals to their philosophical anthropology, or how they look at human nature.

> Liberals tend to be nice, and they believe—here is where they go stupid—that most everybody else is nice too. . . . Liberals believe that human nature is fundamentally good. . . . Liberals suffer incurably from naivete, the stupidity of the good heart.

In populist vulgarization of this thinking, the good heart has been lost. Looking down on liberals in populist hands is suffused with anger. Compassionate condescension has turned into contempt.

In America, much of the one-up/one-down tally takes place over questions of both intelligence and education. Trump asserts over and over that he and his followers are smarter than his competition—either Democratic or Republican. Of many examples: Trump declared in 2018 "that China has total respect for Donald Trump and for Donald Trump's very, very large brain."[17] Earlier that year, he famously tweeted of himself, "I think that would qualify [me] as not smart, but genius . . . and a very stable genius at that!"[18]

Turning the tables on the educated liberal elite by claiming superior intelligence is a long-established trope on the right among talk-show opinion leaders who have developed extremely loyal followings. Rush Limbaugh, long the master of this medium, regularly offers his listeners (his "dittoheads") variations on the following:

> Greetings, conversationalists across the fruited plain, this is Rush Limbaugh, the most dangerous man in America, with the largest hypothalamus in North America, serving humanity simply by opening my mouth . . . doing this show with half my brain tied behind my back just to make it fair because I have talent on loan from . . . God.[19]

But this is more than a celebrity trope. One of the dynamics of a populist mobilization—when populism on the right becomes a political force or a political movement or when it has been roused by a demagogue—is that the populists' sense of resentment is transformed into contempt. The looked-down-upon now collectively feel themselves looking down. The populists together become contemptuous of the elite. This is the social psychological step, the flip-flop, that's needed to turn populist sentiment into a political mobilization. It is emotionally transformative at both the organizational and individual levels, empowering the movement to act, to cure the pervasive and festering one-down sensitivity that is resentment's characteristic mood. Resentment does not fade away—it abides, especially as a feeling on the individual level; but now resentment sits alongside contempt, an effervescent feeling that arises especially in group situations. Here is how Marine Le Pen expressed this on December 7, 2015, when, in the first round of regional elections,

France's Trump-like National Front scored an historic electoral breakthrough, outpolling both of the established conservative and socialist parties.

> I believe that the National Front's incredible results are the revolt of the people against the elite. The people no longer support the disdain they have been [subjected to] for years by a political class defending its own interests.[20]

At times, Trump makes explicit this feeling of flipping the populists' relation to the "elite" from one down to one up. This often takes place at his political rallies where Trump and his most ardent populist supporters participate in a call-and-response that energizes both leader and followers. Here is Elaine Ganley's reportage of Trump at a rally in June 2018:

> "I hate it," Trump moaned to the crowd in North Dakota. "I meet these people they call them 'the elite.' These people. I look at them, I say, 'That's elite?' We got more money, we got more brains, we got better houses, apartments, we got nicer boats, we're smarter than they are, and they say they're elite? *We're* the elite. *You're* the elite. We're the elite."
>
> And he wasn't even finished! "So I said the other day, let's keep calling these people—and let's face it, they've been stone-cold losers, the elite, the elite—so let them keep calling themselves the elite," he continued. "But we're going to call ourselves—and remember you are indeed, you work harder, but you are indeed smarter than them—let's call ourselves from now on the super-elite. We're the super-elite."[21]

The Tea Party began as an organized movement in February 2009, merely a month after Barack Obama's inauguration as president. The prequel to the Tea Party's populism was the 2008 vice-presidential campaign of Sarah Palin. In retrospect, Palin's impact was extraordinary, given the brevity of her candidacy: she was introduced as John McCain's running mate just before the Republican convention in early September and was on the campaign trail only two months. Palin's rallies prefigured Donald Trump's rallies both as a candidate and as president. Palin rallies were raucous occasions, where attendees evoked a devotion to the candidate nowhere to be found at rallies for John McCain at the head of the ticket. Palin as a speaker, like Trump, had a stream-of-consciousness style that evoked a fervid call-and-response among the rally-goers. She swiftly became a lightning rod in the populist dance of resentment and contempt, a stature that would remain with her for years to come. (Maher, on birtherism in 2009: "I'll show you Obama's birth certificate when you show me Sarah Palin's high school diploma."[22])

Tea Party websites never tired of recalling with resentment a 2008 remark then-candidate Obama uttered at a fundraiser in that most liberal quarter of the United States, San Francisco, to characterize what happened to people in deindustrialized small towns in America: "They get bitter, they cling to guns or religion or antipathy to people who aren't like them or anti-immigrant sentiment or antitrade sentiment as a way to explain their frustrations."[23] In January 2016, Palin became the earliest big-name Republican politician to endorse Trump.[24] Even sympathetic observers found her endorsement speech rambling, bizarre, and often incoherent.[25] In a particularly noticed passage, Palin referred back to Obama's remark, turning a trope of resentment into one of contempt, in this case directed at the Republican establishment, then firmly in opposition to Trump's candidacy.

> Now they're concerned about this ideological purity? Give me a break! Who are they to say that? Oh, and tell some-

body like Phyllis Schlafly. She is the Republican, conservative movement icon and hero and a Trump supporter. Tell her
she's not conservative. How about the rest of us? Right win-
gin', bitter, clingin', proud clingers of our guns, our God and
our religions, and our Constitution. Tell us that we're not red
enough? Yeah, coming from the establishment. Right.

Back on the National Stage: The Sixties and Beyond

After the humiliations of Prohibition and the Scopes trial, right
populism was dormant as a political force on the national scene
for a generation and a half. But the sixties reawakened it. For the
populists, the traditional world, the world as they had known
it, began to tremble beneath their feet in the 1960s. Political
developments in that decade threatened taken-for-granted and
bedrock premises of American social hierarchy and power relations as never before: race relations were challenged by the civil
rights movement; gender relations challenged by the women's
movement and the gay rights movement; patriotism challenged
by the antiwar movement; the place of religion challenged by
banning prayer in public schools and the 1973 legalization of
abortion; traditional morality challenged by the "drugs, sex, and
rock and roll" of the youth counterculture.

As before, for populism to become a national force meant
forming a political coalition and marrying the resentment that
is the motor force of populism with an ideology. Populism
aligned itself with the burgeoning conservative New Right, a
movement that self-consciously "fused" social conservatism,
"the social issues," with economic free-market conservatism
and anti-communist foreign policy.[26] This was the movement
that was brokered beginning in the 1950s by William F. Buckley

and his group at the *National Review,* which would come to power with the presidency of Ronald Reagan in 1980 and dominate American politics for the next quarter century. In various incarnations—"Reagan Democrats," "values voters," Christian conservatives—and through a succession of leaders and leading movements—Newt Gingrich, Tom DeLay, George W. Bush, the Tea Party—right populist voters have constituted the crucial voting base of the Republican Party. Conservative writer Jeffrey Bell argued this pointedly in 2012—a view that was summarized in a *Wall Street Journal* column by James Taranto:

> Social conservatism, Mr. Bell argues in . . . "The Case for Polarized Politics," has a winning track record for the GOP. "Social issues were nonexistent in the period 1932 to 1964," he observes. "The Republican Party won two presidential elections out of nine, and they had the Congress for all of four years in that entire period. . . . When social issues came into the mix—I would date it from the 1968 election . . . the Republican Party won seven out of 11 presidential elections."[27]

Throughout this period, right-wing populism was nurtured by a succession of new media: first in talk radio, then on cable TV (Fox News especially), and finally online in social media and outlets like the Drudge Report and Breitbart News. From the start, right populist politicians made prodigious progress on local and state levels. They often ran for positions like school boards and agitated for issues like inclusion of "intelligent design" in textbooks and curricula. Perhaps the most famous of the schoolbook controversies took place in Kanawha County, West Virginia, in 1974. Fierce populist mobilization against the appearance in textbooks of feminist thinking and what would come to be called multiculturalist ideas escalated into substantial parental boycott of schools and violent attacks and bombings. Feminism and multiculturalism would become the two mainstays of the right's attack on "political correctness," a charge that became a watchword in Tea Party discourse and finally a mainstay of Donald Trump's presidential campaign in which he frequently charged:

> I think the big problem this country has is being politically correct, I don't, frankly, have time for total political correctness, and to be honest with you, this country doesn't have time, either.[28]

The Kanawha County schoolbook controversy prefigured how the populist right would mobilize going forward, through both the Tea Party and the Trump eras. As Carol Mason observed, "The tactics of [Kanawha] coalition building would become the script the Right would follow for decades to come."[29]

The enduring issues of the modern populist right have been gun rights, opposing the gay rights movement, and, above all, opposing abortion—"Guns, God, and Gays" in the famous phrase attributed to the Oklahoma senator James Inhofe. The New Right coming to national power in the United States via the presidential election of Ronald Reagan coincided with the Republican Party's adoption of the populists' maximalist position, which called for a constitutional amendment to ban abortion. Before 1976, the party platform made no mention of abortion. In 1976, abortion was mentioned but with a big-tent approach that allowed for differing views. By 1980, this changed for good. Note the difference between the Republican platform on the abortion question in 1976 and its position in 1980:

> **1976.** The question of abortion is one of the most difficult and controversial of our time. It is undoubtedly a moral and personal issue but it also involves complex questions relating to

medical science and criminal justice. There are those in our
Party who favor complete support for the Supreme Court
decision which permits abortion on demand. There are others who share sincere convictions that the Supreme Court's
decision must be changed by a constitutional amendment
prohibiting all abortions. Others have yet to take a position,
or they have assumed a stance somewhere in between polar
positions.

1980. There can be no doubt that the question of abortion,
despite the complex nature of its various issues, is ultimately
concerned with equality of rights under the law. While we
recognize differing views on this question among Americans
in general—and in our own Party—we affirm our support of a
constitutional amendment to restore protection of the right to
life for unborn children. We also support the Congressional
efforts to restrict the use of taxpayers' dollars for abortion.[30]

Support for what came to be called the "human life amendment" has remained a staple of Republican platforms ever
since, and right-wing populists have established themselves as
the party's electoral base. Yet despite their impact on the party's platform and the party's dependence on their votes, much
of the party's populist base has consistently suffered from a
slow boil—the persistent feeling that the party has taken their
votes for granted, that in campaigns for the presidency, and
for House and Senate seats, Republican candidates pledge to
act on the social issues, but once in office what they deliver is
felt to be inadequate, and their efforts marked by indifference.
In this way, right-wing populists have maintained their sense
of themselves as an insurgency within the party even as their
votes brought Republican victories over the years. In the Obama

years, Tea Party voters sent representative after representative to the House, with the explicit mandate to overturn Obamacare which, of course, never came to pass. In time, Tea Party resentment, the primal energy of populist politics, came to encompass disappointing Republican politicians, whom they dubbed RINOs (Republicans in Name Only) as well as Democratic liberals. Grouping the RINOs with the liberals—collectively they became the "globalists"—was the seed of the populist revolt and the opening toward nationalism that animated Donald Trump's run for the presidency.

Epidermic Ideology

In their excellent study of the 2016 election John Sides and his collaborators observe: "The idea that ordinary Americans are not orthodox ideologues is well established in political science."[31] It is important to avoid the trap of calling ideologues those who are merely angry and strident in expressing their views. They can be, but that is not what makes them ideologues. An ideologue is one who believes he or she has a key—an idea, or a set of ideas—that explains everything. An extreme example: In 1994 before investigation of the incident, Newt Gingrich blamed what turned out to be a South Carolina woman drowning her children to get out of her marriage on the decline of morals owing to the welfare state and the counterculture.[32] In the end, an ideologue is someone who, without knowing the facts of a situation, has all the answers. It is the métier of the propagandist.

The right populist is a different kind of political actor. When these populists align with an ideology, their passion comes with them, but not the commitment of an ideologue to a key principle. What made the Tea Party unique in the march of modern

American conservatism was that the passions of the populist right, the uncompromising, expressive side of the American right, were brought to bear in the name of the doctrines of fiscal extremists. The zeal and the vitriol brought to opposing abortion or the gay agenda were being directed as well against Keynesian stimulus legislation, cap-and-trade climate legislation, economic regulation, taxation, and, above all, expansion of health insurance coverage to millions of uninsured Americans.

And yet this ideology was shed in 2016, when the populists migrated from Tea Party fiscal fundamentalism to Trump's America-First nationalism—once again bringing their passion with them. Defying Republican Party leadership in the name of "debt crises," in 2011 Tea Party members of Congress put the U.S. government at risk of default—tempting international financial emergency—by refusing to raise the debt limit and also threatened a government shutdown; in 2013 they again played chicken with defaulting on the debt and actually did shut the government.[33] Six years later, having migrated to America-First nationalism, along with much of the Republican Party, right populists were indifferent to the prodigious leap in the national debt under Trump.[34] And they cheered closing the government in the name of building a wall on the U.S. border with Mexico.

This transformation is not unusual in the annals of populism. Quite the contrary. No matter the passion they bring to the tenets of a coalition party's principles, when populists align themselves with an ideology beyond their stable core (like "God, guns, and gays" in America) they hold these adopted ideologies (like free-market fundamentalism) only lightly. For populists, the grip coalition ideology has over them is epidermic. It only goes skin deep. It is fungible.[35]

In 2018, Silvio Berlusconi planned his return to the controlling heights of Italian politics by building a coalition with other right parties. That had been his strategy during his twenty-year run as leader of the right until his conviction for tax fraud in 2013. Berlusconi's populism was a secular version of the prosperity gospel—you too can become like Silvio, Italy's richest man—cut with a garish, Eurotrashy, Dolce Vita-ish disposition toward the consumption of media, goods, and women.[36] Among the four small parties Berlusconi aligned his Forza Italia party with in 2018 was the League, Matteo Salvini's anti-immigrant, Italy-First party, which had tallied 6.2 percent of the vote in 2014 (when still running as the Northern League), compared to Forza Italia's 16.8 percent of the vote. But as in America, the Italian right populists had moved on, had shed Berlusconi populism for Salvini populism. The League shot to 17.4 percent of the vote in 2018, handily beating Forza Italia's 14 percent.[37] Salvini became the leader of the right, deputy prime minister and the most powerful figure in Italian politics. Like extreme free-market ideology in 2016 America, Berlusconi's appeal proved fungible. His ideological hold was epidermic.

Othering and Identity

Anti-immigrant ideology operates by defining immigrants as the Other. Sociologically, the Other is a group or individual in some fundamental way different from one's own group. Implicitly, one's own group acts as the taken-for-granted norm, or mainstream. The Other violates the culture or status (like ethnicity or nationality) of the in-group. And in this, the Other also betokens a hierarchy: the in-group sees itself as dominant and the Other inferior and subordinate.

The very process of defining others out of the mainstream, the process of *othering*, is critical for the in-group's sense of its own identity. The antithesis of othering is *belonging*, feeling yourself part of a group, having a social or political identity.[38] Othering is often, in fact, the very touchstone of the in-group's identity formation: defining the group that is Other is at one and the same time defining the group to which one belongs. British sociologist Yiannis Gabriel's definition of othering highlights the built-in connection between identity and othering:

> Othering is the process of casting a group, or individual, or an object into the role of the other and *establishing one own identity* through opposition to and, frequently, vilification of this Other [emphasis added].[39]

A potential Other may be around for some time and regarded with relative indifference, even noblesse oblige. It is only when that potential Other emerges as a perceived threat to in-group status that what was previously a tacit apprehension of dominance and subordination crystallizes into the stratified hard edges of othering. It is also when the in-group's identity becomes self-conscious. This process of populist identity formation has been of decisive significance in the Tea Party and the Trump eras.

This is an historically familiar pattern. In his 1929 study *Ideology and Utopia*, Karl Mannheim attributed the historical emergence of conservatism itself to this interplay of status threat and othering. Mannheim called conservative thought "the expression of a feudal tradition become self-conscious."[40] Political power in the Middle Ages lay with the church, the army, the crown and aristocracy, and the landowning classes. These forces would become the backbone of classical conservatism in Europe. But it was not until the rise of capitalist wealth and liberal political thought that they came to regard themselves—to identify—as "conservatives." Mannheim's feudal tradition was tacit, a taken-for-granted but not spelled-out understanding of the world, until it was challenged by new rising powers.

The conservative doctrine that emerged emphasized that the

state was an organic entity beyond the grasp of the rational mind. What liberalism had to offer—rational decision-making—was fine for administration, for the management of discrete social organizations. But rulership was another matter. It depended on "traditionally inherited instincts"—what only breeding in the traditional ruling classes could cultivate; these arts and instincts for handling human affairs constitute, in Mannheim's phrase, the "je ne sais quoi element in politics."[41] These classes had been ruling all along, but their identity as the (proper) ruling classes became explicit, or self-conscious, according to Mannheim, only when liberalism presented itself as a threat to that status.

In a recent study, Ashley Jardina makes a parallel case for the nature of white identity—that for many whites the development of white identity in contemporary politics derives not from pre-existing racist views, but from the changing national demographic, which now confronts whites with a coming majority-minority population. Jardina's expression for this—"making the invisible visible"—resonates with Mannheim's "tradition become self-conscious." Jardina writes:

> Whites have the luxury of not thinking about their racial group . . . when their status at the top of the racial hierarchy is secure. . . . Dominant group identities can become salient and politically meaningful . . . when the group believes that its status is sincerely challenged.[42]

There are a number of strains of American conservatism. The one that hews most closely to the classical conservative tradition often goes by the name "paleoconservatism." This is a name the paleos gave themselves, to distinguish themselves, not without irony, from neoconservatives. They are also distinct from free-market conservatism. Paleoconservatism is the strain that most closely foreshadowed Trump's America-First anti-immigrant ideology. On their *American Conservative* website they sum up this pattern in the course of explaining themselves: "A people only begins to discover conservatism when it becomes aware of something it has lost."[43]

The New Identity Politics

"Identity politics" has been a catchphrase in American political discourse for several decades. It connotes a politics, sometimes a movement, based on race, ethnicity, religion, or sexuality. Identity movements in the United States have typically been the province of women or minority constituencies. In effect, these paradigmatic identity movements have demanded a seat at the table—they seek to redress the condition and the experience of themselves as systematically locked out of the seats of power and well-being and justice that others—those at the American table—have taken for granted. These movements have been habitually criticized over the years from both left and right. From the left, critics argue that identity politics deprives progressivism of its universalistic appeal that "can still stir the general public."[44] From the right, critics have most often seen identity politics as pleas for special privileges.

In her vice-presidential run, Sarah Palin stirred her followers by calling them the "real Americans." In this she gave a name to an identity that would carry this constituency into the Tea Party era and beyond. Palin implicitly contrasted her constituency with the urban elites (versus "small-town, everyday Americans") who have been the right populists' long-standing source of resentment.

> We believe that the best of America is in these small towns
> that we get to visit, and in these wonderful little pockets of
> what I call the real America, being here with all of you hard

working very patriotic, um, very, um, pro-America areas of this great nation. This is where we find the kindness and the goodness and the courage of everyday Americans.[45]

With the electoral loss to the Democrats and the coming of the Obama presidency, the emotional urgency of this resentment—the un-Americans were now in power—mushroomed into the populist mobilization that overnight turned into the Tea Party. The quality of the resentment that blossomed after the election reprised a similar pattern on the previous occasion a Democrat had taken the White House. At the start of Bill Clinton's administration in 1993, Rush Limbaugh, whose national influence on the populist right would grow immensely in the Clinton years, began his daily radio program by parodying the distinctive opening of the TV show *Nightline*. *Nightline* began broadcasting as a nightly report on the Iranian hostage crisis—the 444-day seizure of fifty-two Americans from the U.S. embassy in Tehran. Each episode of *Nightline* began by announcing the numbered day of the hostage crisis. By flaunting this opening, Limbaugh went to the heart of what Clinton and the Democrats in power felt like to the right populists: the country was now in un-American, if not enemy, hands. It felt like being in a country that had been occupied.

In 2013, the Department of Defense under President Obama planned military exercises called Jade Helm, which were to take place in a number of southern and western states. In these exercises, special forces (Green Berets, Navy Seals, and others) were to play the roles of occupying and resistance forces. The Republican governor of Texas, Greg Abbott, his party already in thrall to the Tea Party, called up the Texas State Guard to protect against what seemed to half of Tea Party supporters an imminent or possible invasion of Texas under the guise of Jade Helm.[46] Among the many rumors that spread about the "invasion" was that "patriots"—like Tea Party supporters—were going to be rounded up and placed in FEMA internment camps or abandoned Walmarts.

An occupied country indeed.

What Palin had ushered in in 2008 was an inverted version of conventional identity politics, a version that would ramify and establish itself as the core of the Tea Party movement, and would then become radicalized as the core of the Trump movement and racialized by the alt-right in its rallying around both the Trump campaign and his presidency. For the Trump movement, the Other would be immigrants. For the Tea Party it would be the "undeserving." For the alt-right it would be the nonwhite population. In each case, the Other was seen as backed by the liberal establishment and their pro-multicultural and pro-feminist "politically correct" elites.

The Tea Party, the Trump movement, and the alt-right are all identity movements. The difference between the traditional identity movements and these identity movements is the difference between *deprivation* and *dispossession*. While the traditional identity movements felt themselves deprived of a seat at the table, these new movements feel themselves dispossessed of their seat at the table. Tea Partiers objected to how the new-fangled presence of the Other at the table made them feel—that they and their values had become marginalized; that they had lost their long-established seat at the table, and lost those seats to people who were not "real Americans." The Tea Party's most enduring expression of their political mission, which also prefigured Trumpism and the alt-right, was "taking our country back."[47]

The resentment that feeds these movements is far more acid than what has motivated conventional identity politics. The anger is fiercer and more directly vectored—the force that has taken their place is plain to see; it is the Other. Back in early sixteenth-century Florence, in *The Prince*, Machiavelli warned that the most murderous political enemy the ruler can make is one whose patrimony he has stolen.

> . . . but above all [the Prince] must abstain from taking the property of others, for men forget more easily the death of their father than the loss of their patrimony.[48]

In politics, patrimony can be about status as well as property. A central element in the national debate about the Tea Party, Trumpism, and the alt-right has focused on whether the movements are a response to economic displacement or cultural displacement. Studies like *Identity Crisis* have convincingly demonstrated the primacy of cultural displacement.[49] The fierceness of the new identity movements is more about status lost than property lost. It is a loss so profoundly felt that it has generated a fierceness powerful enough to transform U.S. politics—and much of world politics—into a new era.

2

The Tea Party

Right Populism with a Koch-Brothers Mask

The Tea Party died on May 26, 2016. This was the day Donald Trump clinched the Republican nomination for the presidency.[1] The cause of death? Trump had won over the party's largest voting base, its right-wing populists, in a primary battle against sixteen other contenders for the nomination. His opponents all stood for either Republican ideological orthodoxy, or its more extreme variant, the free-market fundamentalism that had galvanized the Tea Party populists. Uniquely, Trump stood for an America-First nationalist ideology that, in its disdain for immigration reform, free trade, and international trade deals, stood both Republican orthodoxy and extremism (as well as orthodox Republican foreign policy) on their heads.

There were dramatic parallels between the candidacy of Donald Trump and the emergence of the Tea Party: Both were utterly unexpected, and both were driven by a wave of anger that seemed explosive in its intensity. More than that, each was received beginning at its outset by a kind of split-screen America. On one screen, the Tea Party and Trump were met with dismissal and ridicule. To both the Republican and Democratic establishments, Tea Party and Trump rhetoric and substantive positions appeared beyond the rules and norms of accepted political behavior and thinking. The establishments' inability to counter the Tea Party and Trump phenomena rested finally in their inability to recognize that something indeed novel was afoot, and the attempt to analyze and contest it using their received political standards was doomed. The morning after Donald Trump announced his candidacy, his hometown tabloid, the New York *Daily News*, overlaid Trump's photograph with a clown's red nose and lips and ran it on its cover with the headline "Clown Runs for Prez."[2] To much of America, and certainly to liberal America, Tea Party proponents in 2009, like Trump in 2015, were offering up what seemed like a parade of gaffe after political gaffe—certainly not ideas that could win national elections.

On the other split screen, the Tea Party and Trump were truth tellers. And not simple truth tellers. They were tellers of the truths that lay behind what the other politicians were selling. These were often singular truths—truths that pushed the boundaries of true versus false. Assertions that were commonplace—treated as established facts—on Tea Party websites seemed to outsiders like reality upended in the name of what one wished reality to be: Hillary Clinton was sure to be jailed; Barack Obama's elections were rigged; Obama was a Muslim; sharia law was taking over in American courts; Obama was born in Kenya. America's split-screen reality in the Tea Party era built on foundations laid by talk radio in the Bill Clinton years and was institutionalized during the presidency of George W. Bush.[3] It would grow into nothing short of an epistemological crisis under Donald Trump. Ronald Reagan's son, Michael Reagan, got to the heart of how participants on the populist side of the split-screen reality experience their alternative truths when he said in the early days of Trump's campaign that Trump was just "saying what all of us are thinking."[4] It resonated intuitively. The same was true of the Tea Party experience. These were the alternative truths that mobilized right-wing populism in twenty-first-century America. And the truths that seemed incomprehensible on the other split screen of America, to whom they were nothing but gaffes. But as Boris Johnson, Britain's most Trump-like politician put it,

"When people say you are making a gaffe, what you are really doing is saying something that is true and necessary."[5]

Which of the split screens in the Tea Party's appearance ruled? By the first election in the Tea Party era, Scott Brown, a Tea Party Republican, won the Senate seat of deceased liberal icon Ted Kennedy in the bluest of states, Massachusetts. In the midterms of 2010, the Republicans picked up sixty-three seats and control of the House of Representatives—forty-seven of these sixty-three winners had presented themselves as Tea Party candidates. Already the Tea Party had established its two main tactics: primarying "inadequately conservative" Republican officeholders and obstructionism in the House and Senate.

As for 2016, Trump won the Republican nomination as the Republican establishment looked on as if suffering the mood of a Greek tragedy, living through a growing sense of baleful inevitability. As for the general election, a stunned liberal America woke up under a lowering cloud the morning after election day, a cloud that would not dissipate.

An Enemy and a Foil

The Tea Party was not simply a populist movement. Rather it was a blend of populism with free-market fundamentalism.[6] Free-market fundamentalism arose, especially among conservative corporate elites, in opposition to the policies of the New Deal under Franklin Roosevelt. It has formed the economic ideology of an implacable conservative doctrine that has worked since the 1930s to dominate the Republican Party and change the direction of social policy in the United States away from New Deal liberalism and its successors. In the 1930s the most prominent free-market fundamentalist names were the DuPont brothers of the Liberty League. In this era, the most prominent names are the Koch Brothers, whose network, now called Stand

Together (formerly Freedom Partners), functions like a shadow Republican Party, independently financed, which recruits candidates, underwrites think tanks, introduces policy proposals, and lobbies, lobbies, lobbies.[7]

In 1980 free-market conservatism came to power with the election of Ronald Reagan and remained Republican Party orthodoxy until Donald Trump's victory in the 2016 primaries. The policy issues of free-market *fundamentalism* track those of free-market *conservatism*: opposition to the welfare state, unions, taxes, regulation; the conviction that welfare programs are moral hazards that develop a culture of dependency; the goal to replace Keynesian economics with the doctrines of Mises, von Hayek, and, more latterly, the supply-side doctrine of Arthur Laffer. But the free-market fundamentalists' views were more radical than those of the orthodox conservatives who ruled Republican national politics. It was not enough for the fundamentalists to hold the line or trim back programs like Social Security or Medicare. Their goal was to roll them back entirely. It was to return the U.S. economy to its pre–New Deal condition. For some it was to return even further back, prior to the introduction of the federal income tax and the Federal Reserve. It was to go back to the USA of William McKinley.

Despite their role in the conservative movement's success in American politics since 1980, free-market fundamentalists found themselves consistently unhappy with the concessions and compromises of conservative politicians in power, maintaining their sense of themselves as insurgents within the party. The rump of the Tea Party in the House of Representatives that remained committed to free-market fundamentalism beyond the Tea Party's demise, which coincided with Trump's victory in the 2016 primaries, wound up in the Freedom Caucus. In 2017 the Freedom Caucus, using Tea Party obstructionist tactics, forced House speaker Paul Ryan to withdraw Donald Trump's bill to replace Obamacare with the American Health Care Act (AHCA). The bill was criticized by Freedom Caucus member Mo Brooks of Texas using rhetoric virtually unchanged from 1930s free-market fundamentalist anti–New Deal rhetoric:

> [AHCA is] the largest welfare program that Republicans have sponsored in the history of the Republican Party and as such it's going to undermine the work ethic, it's going to increase taxes, and it's going to increase the deficit which in turn is going to increase our risk of suffering from a debilitating insolvency and bankruptcy.[8]

The abiding free-market fundamentalist sentiment—that they represented a perpetually unsatisfied insurgency in the Republican Party—parallels resentment among right populists, like evangelical Christians, who complained that the Republican Party pandered to their views in electoral campaigns but rarely delivered on their issues once in office. In the final analysis, free-market fundamentalism and right-wing populism share two antagonists, one an enemy and one a foil. The enemy is liberalism—for the populists from a cultural point of view; for the free-market fundamentalists, from the point of view of political economy. The foil is the Republican establishment, which each one feels leans together with them like a successful motorcycle racer during political campaigns but offers more lip service than their cherished results once in power.

Conservatism's Premature Obituary

For both the free-market fundamentalists and the right populists, the fall of 2008 was a dismal season. A general mood loomed over that year's presidential election, one that suggested that American conservatism, after its thirty-year run in power, seemed fatally to have run aground. As Sam Tanenhaus argued in his book, *The Death of Conservatism*, conservatism's historical momentum was spent, its ideology worn out and incapable of innovation, its electoral chances evaporating.[9]

The reasons for this thinking were not hard to fathom. After eight years under George W. Bush, the most conservative president in memory—who enjoyed a Republican majority in Congress during six of those years—things had not only gone wrong, they had gone catastrophically wrong, in social policy, in foreign affairs, and in management of the economy. The Republican candidate for president in 2008, John McCain, ran his campaign with virtually no mention of the president or the Bush administration.

The Bush administration's credibility as the country's domestic steward was swept away with the winds and floods of Hurricane Katrina in late August 2005. Americans watched as one of their major cities was felled in a way no one had ever seen or perhaps even imagined before. During Katrina, the fecklessness, if not indifference, of Bush's government stood out in tragic relief.

Bush's foreign policy was dominated by the war his administration launched in Iraq in March 2003. But everything the administration had said about the war—its cost, its duration, the reasons for starting it, and even a stagy early declaration of victory—had turned out to be wrong. The photographs out of Abu Ghraib had shamed American armed forces and the politicians who had sent them. And, while it was rarely mentioned by polite company, this country's most disastrous foreign attack on its own soil, on September 11, 2001, had taken place on the administration's watch. (It would take the brazenness of Donald

Trump, during an attack on Bush's brother Jeb, to call this out in a Republican debate in 2016.[10])

But it was Bush's performance on the economy that seemed to seal conservatism's doom. Bush's policy of tax cuts had not only turned financial surplus into severe national debt, it had created a yawning divide between rich and poor with a dwindling middle class that rendered the country less and less like the one Americans believed was the country's promise.[11] While this could be covered up rhetorically, the financial crisis that hit in the fall of 2008 could not. Suddenly—the out-of-the-blue quality cannot be overstated—the administration announced that the country's financial system was on the verge of collapse. The word *depression*, as in the Great Depression, made a startling reappearance. Not since the 1930s had there been an economic emergency anything like this. John McCain unilaterally suspended his presidential campaign to deal with it. Only the oldest generation of Americans had any experience of the Great Depression. Never in the lifetimes of younger Americans had the word been pulled out of mothballs to chronicle the nation's economic predicament. There was no precedent for the extraordinary financial bailout measures the administration pushed through Congress to avoid what government officials promised would be "total financial collapse."

Conservatism, if not dead, certainly appeared to be on the ropes.

The Second Shock

The economic crisis was but the first of two shocks to right populists and free-market fundamentalists in the fall of 2008. The second was the election result. John McCain, the candidate these constituencies felt was hand-picked by the

Republican establishment to succeed George Bush, was beaten by a Democrat—and an African American Democrat at that. The moment seemed more than a simple triumph of the Democratic Party. It seemed historic. "Transformative" became a catchword for the incoming presidential administration of Barack Obama. The eclipse of conservatism had liberals talking about a second coming of the New Deal.

For the populists and the free-market fundamentalists, each in their own way, this put the wolf at the door. The specter of redistribution now threatened to accompany economic collapse. For the free-market fundamentalists, the scourge of the welfare state, it felt like their roll-back agenda would be eclipsed by a new New Deal they might never recover from. They swiftly seized on the tea party theme, which conjured up identification with the country's founding patriots as well as furnishing a neat acronym of Taxed Enough Already; the free-market fundamentalists created national networks, often internet-based, which convened regularly and coordinated with conservative mass media in the United States.[12] As grassroots Tea Party groups sprung up by the thousands across the country, the free-market fundamentalists operated through such organizations as Americans for Prosperity and FreedomWorks (both groups founded by the Koch Brothers), which offered financial, strategic, and political assistance to many of these fledgling chapters, and helped raise some local leaders (especially those focused on fiscal issues) to national prominence.

The populist constituency of the Tea Party was overwhelmingly white, upper middle class, and late middle-aged (in their fifties, sixties, or seventies). These were the people who attended Tea Party meetings, participated in Tea Party websites, and who were the Republican Party's most dedicated primary voters. As the "real Americans," Tea Partiers saw themselves as those who had worked hard all their lives and earned everything they had.

They viewed liberals, unions, and often minorities as forces trying to take away what they possessed and redistribute it to the "undeserving," the poor who hadn't worked hard.[13] They had long been the hard right of the Republican Party, whose votes were driven by social issues.

One of the most devastating effects of the financial crisis was a huge drop in the residential real estate market. Homeowners expecting the values of their homes to continue the upward spiral that had turned out to be a housing bubble suddenly found themselves underwater—owing more on their home mortgages than the diminished value of their homes. For aging homeowners with a relatively stable and secure economic condition, like the Tea Party populists, this was the stuff of panic. If the new government tried to address this, they felt certain, the only way to fix it would be to take from them.

This wildly heightened fear altered the focus of what would become the Tea Party's populist base from its decades-long preoccupation with social issues, like abortion or the "gay agenda," to economic issues. In this way right-wing populism's alarm matched that of the free-market absolutists, and aligned them with one another as never before. The dynamism of the Tea Party's meteoric rise, which was unlike anything seen for decades, was in large measure due to these two forces of the American right—right populism and free-market absolutism—putting aside their historical divergences and turning into a lockstep ideological juggernaut.

The rise of the Tea Party upended the gathering conventional wisdom of conservatism's decline. Any notion of the right fading into the sunset dissolved overnight. Instead, the right, or this subset of the right, was louder than ever, swiftly becoming the outstanding political phenomenon of the Obama presidency. In breathtakingly short order, American conservatism not only failed to fade away, but regrouped and moved decisively further to the right. The Tea Party resurrected themes that mainstream conservatism had rejected as too radical forty years earlier, themes that had survived on the fringes of establishment Republican conservatism.

The Tea Party's Fatal Contradiction

But the two diverse routes the populists and the free-market fundamentalists took to the Tea Party were of lasting significance. One route, the free-market fundamentalist route, was purely ideological. The other, the populist route, was reactive. At its heart it was continuous with the resentment that liberalism had long elicited from the populists. But their adoption of free-market fundamentalism, however fiercely it was embraced, was situational. It gave focus to the moment's dominant fear. The contrast to the free-market fundamentalist true believers' embrace of the Tea Party was obscured by the collective passion and solidarity that gave the movement its fiery blastoff. But this contradiction present at the Tea Party's creation would fester and eventually become untenable.

Organizationally the Tea Party remained largely inchoate on an everyday national level. Yet on three occasions, the movement spoke, indeed roared, with a single national voice. The first occasion, Tea Party 1.0—and what put them on the map as a political force—was the movement's fierce opposition to Obamacare. In the summer of 2009, during the congressional recess, Tea Party members intimidated and overwhelmed congresspeople at town-hall meetings across the country. These tactics led directly to the movement's electoral triumphs in 2010. In Tea Party 1.0, not only were the populists and the free-market fundamentalists ferociously on the same page against Obamacare, they were also in lockstep with the Republican establishment, which had pledged unyielding resistance to Obama policies with the goal of ensuring a one-term presidency.[14]

But in the Tea Party's opposition to Obamacare, the contradiction between the free-market fundamentalists and the populists lay below the surface solidarity. Free-market fundamentalists have never renounced their goal of reversing Social Security and Medicare. They viewed Obamacare as a potentially irreversible victory of the welfare state. For the populists, Obamacare felt like a threat to their security, which *depended* on the likes of Social Security and Medicare—Obamacare was going to take these things away from them, as they saw it, and give it to the undeserving.

Tea Party 2.0 encompassed the "debt crises" of 2011 and 2013, when the movement was again focused nationally on a single issue. Tea Party representatives in Congress were prepared to take what seemed to others, including the Republican establishment, radical measures. These included threatening to default on the national debt by refusing to raise the debt ceiling (until then a matter that Congress passed routinely) and threatening to shut down the government. Tea Party obstructionism in the House in 2011 prevented a "grand bargain" negotiated by the Obama administration and the Republican leadership as the Tea Party refused the deal to cut entitlements in exchange for raising taxes on high-income Americans. The Tea Party provoked a government shutdown in 2013 by blocking passage of a continuing resolution through their insistence that such a resolution must defund Obamacare.[15] There was a Masada-like quality to Tea Party rhetoric, as though its proponents were willing to contemplate economic ruin for the country, to push it over the "fiscal cliff," believing this was a last chance to save America.[16]

The Tea Party's actions were directed at their foil, the Republican establishment, or, as Tea Partiers referred to them routinely, the Republicans in Name Only, or RINOs. For their part, the Republican establishment feared for the effects on business and international finance—and for the likely negative effects for the party electorally—of both a shutdown and a default. The free-market fundamentalists were torn. They shared the Republican establishment's fears on the economy and in politics, but their heart was with the goals of the Tea Party obstructionists.[17] Tea Party 2.0 then was an open clash between the movement and the Republican establishment—unlike their solidarity under Tea Party 1.0. For the free-market fundamentalists, Tea Party 2.0 marked a clear move away from alliance with the populists, placing them in a rather awkward position between the populists and the Republican establishment.

But by Tea Party 3.0 the free-market fundamentalists had moved decisively to the establishment's side and in opposition to the populists. Now the issue was immigration. In the last two years of the Obama administration, 2015 and 2016, immigration became the dominant preoccupation of Tea Party website discussions. And the populists' position was clear and unequivocal: "illegals" needed to be removed from America, and any version of "comprehensive immigration reform"—the sorts of thing that might offer a path to citizenship—was "amnesty." The Republican establishment meanwhile had come to the urgent conclusion that, in the face of America's changing demographics, in order to remain viable in national elections the party needed an opening to immigrants, above all Latinos. (This is covered in detail in chapter 3.) The free-market fundamentalists cleaved to the establishment based not only on the establishment's political calculation, but also because they recognized the indispensable role of immigrant workers in the American labor force.

The gulf between the populists and the establishment was irreconcilable, and resentment of the Republican establishment among Tea Party populists reached heights not seen before. This was the state of the movement, Tea Party 3.0, that Trump discovered in preparing for his run for president: The Tea Party populists were in revolt against the Republican establishment based on the immigration issue. On the same basis the Tea Party populists were in an accelerating split from their free-market fundamentalist brethren, potentially freeing them up for an ideological migration. This was the wedge that Donald Trump enlisted to sever the Tea Party coalition of populists and free-market fundamentalists, winning the populists over to the nationalist ideology that was the basis of his presidential run.

The Santelli Rant

The Tea Party movement came into being shortly after the first presidential inaugural of Barack Obama on January 20, 2009. On February 19, Rick Santelli, a television reporter on the floor of the Chicago Mercantile Exchange, was commenting on the new administration's proposed relief program for financially underwater homeowners, the Homeowners Affordability and Stability Plan (HASP), designed to help homeowners avoid foreclosure. In what almost immediately came to be called the Santelli rant, Santelli turned to the traders on the floor and held forth:

> **The government is promoting bad behavior**. . . . I have an idea. . . . Mr. President. . . . Why don't you put up a website to have people vote on the internet as a referendum to see if we really want to subsidize the losers' mortgages? Or . . . at least . . . buy a house that is in foreclosure . . . give it to people who might have a chance to actually prosper down the road and reward people that can carry the water instead of drink the water?

> This is America!

> How many people want to pay for your neighbor's mortgages that has an extra bathroom and can't pay their bills?

Raise their hand!

President Obama, are you listening?

You know Cuba used to have mansions and a relatively
decent economy. They moved from the individual to the
collective. Now they're driving '54 Chevys.

It's time for another tea party.

What we are doing in this country will make Thomas Jefferson and Benjamin Franklin roll over in their graves.

In a manner that was almost prophetic, Santelli managed not
only to light a spark that led to Tea Party groups forming across
the country like wildfire, he also encapsulated three essential
themes that would motivate the Tea Party movement throughout its run. Santelli's rant can be parsed as follows:

1. **Middle-class security.** The power of the Santelli rant was
   that in seizing upon home ownership, he was directly
   addressing the symbolic heart of the American dream.
   The alternative to ranting about HASP would have been
   ranting about TARP (the Troubled Asset Relief Program),
   which bailed out American financial institutions, and
   which passed in the fall of 2008 under President Bush.
   These were institutions that had engaged in sometimes
   predatory lending of subprime mortgages to home buy-
   ers who had been only sketchily vetted to take on the
   financial obligations they were undertaking. These institutions had also securitized mortgage loans, creating
   a huge market in financial derivatives that lost most of
   their value at the housing-market collapse, leaving banks
   and other financial institutions with devastated bal-
   ance sheets and in need of capital infusion to continue
   as credit-extending institutions. The cost of this program

was $700 billion. The cost of HASP was $70 billion. Santelli's turning his ire toward HASP rather than TARP anticipated the vector of populist Tea Party anger—directed
at the "undeserving" beneficiaries and the liberal elites
now in power who attempted to offer them some modi-
cum of relief.

2. **Identity.** Santelli's rant drew a fierce distinction between
"us" and "them." The Tea Party populists saw themselves as having *earned* their middle-class security. The
Others were those who only pretended toward middle-
class respectability—people who needed the government
to bail them out of situations they should not have been
in in the first place. They were "undeserving" of middle-
class security. As Santelli put it, they were "losers." When
the Republican Party's 2012 presidential candidate, Mitt
Romney, was appealing to the party's Tea Party base, he
would call them "takers"; and he would contrast them to
the Tea Party "makers."[18] Not only were they deserving
of what they had earned, they were also—to recall Sarah
Palin's phrase—the "real Americans." Facing the threat
they and their country were under meant it was time for
them to make a radical stand—as their real-American pa-
triot forefathers had done in Boston Harbor in 1773.

3. **Obama as anti-American.** As Santelli put it, Obama's
government was making the founding fathers "roll
over in their graves." This sentiment would find numerous expressions through the whole arc of the Tea Party
movement, often equating Obama, liberalism, and the
Democratic Party with movements seen as hostile to the
United States, like socialism, communism, or fascism.
Santelli connecting Obama's effort to help underwater
homeowners to the ideology of Communist Cuba would
be followed by the widely held Tea Party belief that
Obama's policies bordered on the treasonous. Regarding

the president himself, much of the Tea Party subscribed to the idea that Obama was not born in the United States (and therefore was an illegitimate president) and that he was a secret Muslim, tying him, in this way of thinking, to the current foreign threat to the United States.[19] Regarding the Tea Party's attitude toward his party, the Democrats, a parallel may be drawn to McCarthyism. Then, in the early 1950s, the party was assailed by McCarthyites for its "treasonous" relationship to the foreign enemy— the Soviet Union and the "international Communist conspiracy." The Tea Party regarded Democratic politicians as traitors based on their positions on domestic issues, on issues of political economy. On its website throughout its run, one of the major national Tea Party organizations, Tea Party Nation, used the phrase "the party of treason" interchangeably with the "Democratic Party," much as in political discourse one might use "GOP" interchangeably with the "Republican Party." This point of view had a long history on the far right, but it never achieved the purchase in national politics that it attained during the Tea Party's run.

Flipping the Vise

Typically, right-wing populists in America have seen themselves squeezed by forces both above and below them. This kind of populism has historically been referred to as "producerism." In Chip Berlet's account:

> [Producerism is] the idea that the real Americans are hard-working people who create goods and wealth while fighting against parasites at the top and bottom of society.[20]

This creates a classic populist self-image as a middle stratum of society caught in a vise. Before the Tea Party, this accurately described the mindset of right-wing populism in America: the liberal elitists pushing from above and their client base pushing from below. The forces felt pushing from the bottom included the poor, the working poor, welfare recipients, and, often, minorities. These people not only are regarded as not hard-working, but as people who pine in the populists' view for a life of government dependency. The liberal elite caters to them for their votes.

But this mindset changed with the Tea Party.

For the Tea Party populists, the vise was supplanted by a uniquely powerful form of perceived oppression, and this helps account for the power and success of the Tea Party. The election of a black president and the assumption of power by the liberal Democratic Party transformed the vice-like effect of producerism. Now, both the liberal elite *and* their client base, the "underclass," were on top! The experience was no longer one of being squeezed from top and bottom, but rather one of being flattened from above. The Tea Party's Other had become vastly more powerful than ever before. As one Tea Party activist put it, "The people I was looking for [as a policeman] are now running the government."[21]

Tea Party Constitutionalism

Tea Partiers loved to talk about the U.S. Constitution. Few movements ever proclaimed their fealty to the Constitution as vociferously and frequently as the Tea Party. Tea Party positions were, they insisted, directly derived from the letter of the Constitution. Nothing was more common at Tea Party rallies than handing out pocket-sized copies of the Constitution. Nothing seemed to empower Tea Party spokespeople at all levels as much as the certainty their views enjoyed a unique fidelity to word of the Constitution.

Randy Barnett, a chaired law professor at Georgetown University in Washington, DC, was instrumental in bringing an historical legal challenge to Obamacare. At the outset of the judicial challenge to the law, the national split screen was in effect: To liberal America, the legal theory behind the lawsuit against Obamacare seemed to challenge settled legal principles around the commerce clause that had been worked out in the 1930s New Deal; from this point of view, it was assumed that the courts would make quick work of dismissing the suit.[22] Instead, by distinguishing between welfare-state programs that offered aid to citizens and Obamacare's penalizing *not* buying health insurance, the lawsuit went to the Supreme Court, where Obamacare squeaked by on a five to four vote. In that decision, Chief Justice John Roberts shied away from the direct challenge to the commerce clause, which aimed at the free-market fundamentalists' historic goal of discrediting the judicial edifice on which the American welfare state stood. Instead, Roberts redefined the Obamacare penalty as a tax—an apostasy that has consigned him to RINO purgatory in populist eyes ever since.

Barnett articulated the connection between the Tea Party's ideological concerns and a doctrine of constitutional principles. After the Obamacare decision, Barnett contended that over the long run, the court's failure to defend Obamacare in the name of the commerce clause (and instead in the name of the government's power to levy taxes) would in time undermine the legal basis on which the whole of the welfare state was premised. In so doing, he put the Tea Party's rise in the historical context of free-market fundamentalism:

During the New Deal era, Americans acquiesced to an enormous expansion of federal power that they were promised would end the Great Depression. And the Supreme Court eventually expanded its interpretation of federal power accordingly. In contrast, during the Great Recession [which began in 2008], millions of Americans were appalled by government bailouts, the horrific increases in spending and debt, and the intrusion into their lives that is coming with Obamacare. They responded by demanding a return to the Constitution's constraints on federal power.[23]

The central premise of Tea Party constitutionalism is that the federal government is too big. It has expanded as a power-hungry beast beyond the Constitution's plain restrictions. This view harkens back to the oldest political fight of the Republic—the grueling reluctance of the individual states to cede authority to a centralized government. This reluctance was behind the inadequacy of the first attempt at Union in the Articles of Confederation. It underlay myriad compromises forged in the writing of the Constitution and was, finally, the motivation for the Bill of Rights, intended to ensure the prerogatives of the states and the people. States' rights has been the banner under which some of the most severe resistance to central power has expressed itself throughout the country's history and has embraced such radical doctrines as nullification and secession.[24] With the Tea Party, nullification raised its head in the form of Barnett's proposal for a Repeal Amendment to the Constitution that would permit a two-thirds majority of states to overturn federal laws they disapproved of.[25]

During the first years of the Tea Party, Glenn Beck's nightly television program on the Fox News cable channel established itself as the foremost national venue that Tea Partiers shared in common. Often emotionally overwrought, Beck would describe liberal ideas while showing old films of Nazi marchers behind him; and he expounded on extreme right-wing thinkers, like Cleon Skousen, who seemed to have been finally discredited decades before.[26] In this way he became something of the lead educator of the Tea Party, and before long began directly organizing Tea Party events.[27]

When Barnett appeared on Beck's program, he talked about both a constitutional amendment to rein in the federal government in the name of the states and the possibility of the states calling for a constitutional convention.[28] In addition, both he and other representatives of the Tea Party spoke in favor of repealing parts of the Fourteenth Amendment, and the whole of the Sixteenth and Seventeenth Amendments (which established the federal income tax and the direct election of senators), and of establishing a balanced budget amendment.[29] Most often, perhaps, the Tea Party's states'-rights conviction was expressed in the movement's passion for the Tenth Amendment:

> The powers not delegated to the United States by the Constitution, nor prohibited by it to the States, are reserved to the States, respectively, or to the people.

It was not uncommon for Tea Party activists to call themselves simply "Tenthers."[30]

"Popular Originalism" and Fundamentalism

Legal scholars characterized the Tea Party's constitutional perspective as the hybrid formulation "popular originalism."[31] Popular originalism melds the doctrine of originalism that has dominated conservative jurisprudence over the past several decades with the notion of "popular constitutionalism," which was developed, ironically, in major part by thinkers on the left.[32] Popular constitutionalism argues that interpretation of the Constitution is not properly confined to the courts. Instead, both politics, in the form of legislators at all levels including and especially state and local, as well as movements and associations in civil society, are appropriate sources of constitutional authority. Christopher Schmidt succinctly enumerated the central tenets of Tea Party constitutionalism as follows:

- The solutions to the problems facing the United States today can be found in the words of the Constitution and the insights of its framers.
- The meaning of the Constitution and the lessons of history are not obscure; in fact, they are readily accessible to American citizens who take the time to educate themselves.
- All Americans, not just lawyers and judges, have a responsibility to understand the Constitution and to act faithfully toward it.
- The overarching purpose of the Constitution is to ensure that the role of government, and particularly the federal government, is a limited one.[33]

The key to understanding the Tea Party's blend of popular constitutionalism and originalism is to be found in religious fundamentalism. For our purposes, this fundamentalism has two important characteristics: the word; and every person his or her own interpreter. We will look at these in turn.

The word: Fundamentalism, of course, originates as a particular reading of the Bible in which the text of the Bible is both unerring and complete; that is, as the direct word of God, it is word-for-word absolute truth and is all the truth that needs be known. Tea Partiers read the Constitution (and the Declaration of Independence) in this manner and rebelled against interpretation that seemed to them beyond the word. Here is a quite ordinary intervention from a participant on a well-known pro–Tea Party website, Free Republic:

> I challenge the liberal New York Times editors to find con-
> stitutional warrant for federal activities outside those specifi-
> cally authorized by the Constitution, *chapter and verse*. They
> can't find it [emphasis added].[34]

Chapter and verse: in its essence, the Tea Party's model for read-ing the Constitution was the fundamentalist Protestant reading of the Bible. A Louisiana Tea Party member "attended weekend classes on the Constitution that she compared with church Bible study."[35] Local Tea Party groups running educational programs on the Constitution that were similar to Bible classes was a Tea Party mainstay.

The practice of reading the Constitution, like studying the Bible, was important not only for retaining fidelity to the word, but also because such repetition was seen as needed to convert nonbelievers who, in the fullness of time, would come to see the light. After sixty-three new Republican congresspeople, over-whelmingly Tea Party–identified, were elected in November 2010 to the U.S. House of Representatives, making the Republicans the chamber's majority party, the opening session of the new Congress in 2011 included a spectacle unprecedented in Amer-ican history: The Constitution was read aloud word for word before the work of the Congress began.[36] The Tea Party Caucus in the House also insisted that all new bills need to make explicit reference to the passages in the Constitution that attest to their constitutional validity—in effect, citing chapter and verse.[37]

Every person his or her own interpreter: The populist element in Tea Party popular originalism—that individuals and institu-tions both in government and in civil society are as justified in interpreting the Constitution as are the courts—harkens back to the very founding of Protestantism. The hierarchy and practices of Roman Catholicism seemed to the likes of John Calvin and Martin Luther more an impediment to a believer's Godliness than a legitimate guide—and a self-serving impediment at that, benefiting a corrupt priestly bureaucracy whose major concern was its own privilege. Luther "insisted that every baptized Christian was a priest, and suggested the recruitment of clergy by popular election of 'pious and learned citizens.' "[38] The Protestant argument for an unmediated relationship between the individual and God rested on an unmediated relationship between the individual and the Word, the Bible. Popular originalism sought to empower citizens and politicians outside the judicial sphere in their unmediated relationship to the text, the word, of the Constitution; in other words, they had authority on constitutional matters. What Sanford Levinson called Protestantism's discarding of Catholicism's unwritten tradition in favor of the text foreshadowed the fundamentalist reading of the Constitution the Tea Party embraced.[39]

American Civil Religion vs. the Secular Elite

Since the 1960s sociologists like Robert Bellah have discussed what they call the tradition of "American civil religion."[40] In this understanding, American civil religion began in the hands of colonial preachers and has involved reading a particular version of the country's founding and enduring values back into biblical tradition. Civil religion has been a continuing throughline in American history between the pulpit and politics, as in the well-known example of Ronald Reagan's popularizing John Winthrop's 1630 words as he led the Puritans to Massachusetts Bay and characterized his vision of America as "a shining city on a hill."[41]

In American civil religion, the country's founding documents, the Declaration of Independence and the Constitution,
are sacred texts, the country's founders a sacred cult, lawgivers
and prophets. Veneration of these documents and these individuals demands a religious fidelity to their memory and their
writings. No movement in recent American history so embraced
this element of American civil religion as fully as the Tea Party.
Tea Party commonplaces like dressing up for political rallies in
colonial costume, complete with wigs and three-cornered hats
and re-enacting the triumphs of the founders in the persons of
Washington, Jefferson, and the like, reflected a desire not merely
to speak for the tradition of the American civil religion, but to
embody it.

Further, from the point of view of Tea Party constitutionalism, it is significant to note the point at which American civil
religion bleeds over to the view, long held on the Christian right,
that the country and its founding and values are inherently
and explicitly Christian. This conviction is a frequent thread
throughout the history of American conservatism, and enjoyed
a hearty following in Tea Party circles. In Turkey in 2009, President Obama offered the well-known constitutional view that
"one of the great strengths" of the United States is that "we do
not consider ourselves a Christian nation or a Jewish nation or a
Muslim nation. We consider ourselves a nation of citizens who
are bound by ideals and a set of values." This caused uproar in
the Tea Party, led by Michele Bachmann who, in the next Congress, would become the leader of the body's Tea Party Caucus.
This led to the submission of H.Res.397, a House resolution that
explicitly declared the religious core of American society, during the 111th Congress of 2009 to 2010.[42]

The Tea Party's most basic constitutional premise—that
the American government has wildly outstripped the docu-
ment's bounds—came complete with an explanation of how the

country arrived at this woeful pass. Beginning as early as the Progressive Era of the 1910s, a dedicated class of individuals, heavily influenced by European ideas of socialism, communism, and even fascism, labored relentlessly, as though they formed a multigenerational conspiracy, to undermine the very Americanness of the United States. This notion was the outstanding premise of Glenn Beck's ongoing history lesson that was critical for so many Tea Partiers in the early years of the movement.

Interestingly, the idea harkens back to some of the more sophisticated thinking that gave rise in the 1970s and earlier to the New Right. An important example is neoconservatism founder Irving Kristol's idea of the New Class: academics and politicians who lived far from the economic engine room of American society but sought control through their ideas of social engineering.[43] As Robert Horwitz put it in his book, *America's Right*,

> The essence of the New Class critique was that expertise was simply a masquerade for a particular kind of group self-interest. Liberal professionals in the government and non-profit sectors used their educational credentials and the language of expertise to gain power.[44]

More recently, for Angelo Codevilla, who has written extensively attacking what he perceives as this class's continuing subversion of American society, the liberal elite has "usurped" the Constitution. Codevilla simply calls them the "ruling class."[45] To move forward into the Trump era, these are the people Steve Bannon has in mind when he talks about smashing the administrative state.

In politics, this is the filter through which Tea Partiers viewed liberal social policies, such as environmental protection. Rejecting social science and, often, natural science, Tea Partiers were convinced that such policy initiatives are merely ruses that liberals employ to gain power or wealth.[46] A favorite Tea Party politician, Senator James Inhofe of Oklahoma, called global warming "the second-largest hoax ever played on the American people, after the separation of church and state."[47] Tea Party rhetoric was often quite radical in this regard, conflating liberals and their policies if not with communist or fascist tyranny then at least with European social democracy. This conflation was a taken-for-granted premise of Tea Party discourse. As one sign at a Tea Party rally in Washington put it, "Liberalism, Socialism, Communism. What's the difference?"

In its more sober statements, the right's criticism of liberalism labels its ideology "statism." Tea Party thinking embraced a view steeped in American civil religion that the liberal elite's history of subversion has functioned by replacing God with the State, and religion with secular religion. In this view, as articulated in perhaps its most sophisticated form by Robert George of Princeton University, secularism becomes effectively a competing faith-based belief system that deludes itself with its pretensions to neutrality and science.[48] This view leads to the argument that separation of church and state is a false doctrine.

A vulgarized version of such thinking animated the work of far less exacting thinkers like evangelical minister and self-styled historian David Barton, who argued that the framers of the Constitution took their ideas and their language word-for-word from the sermons of colonial preachers.[49] Barton, who was vice chair of the Texas Republican Party between 1997 and 2006, was a regular presence on Glenn Beck's program, and fellow Fox News commentator, former Arkansas governor and presidential candidate Mike Huckabee, called him America's most important historian, whose work should be taught in classrooms everywhere in the country. In 2014, Tom DeLay, former Republican congressman who was the party's House minority leader from 2003 to 2005, succinctly summarized the connection between the civil religion tradition and Tea Party constitutionalism as follows:

> I think we got off that track when we allowed our government to become a secular government, when we stopped realizing that God created this nation, that He wrote the constitution, that's based on biblical principles.[50]

"Hands Off My Medicare": Zero-Sum Thinking

It was a well-known oxymoron in the Tea Party years. Tea Partiers would show up at anti-Obamacare rallies with signs reading "Government Hands Off My Medicare."[51] Oxymoronic, plainly, because Medicare is a government program. And, inevitably, a cause for a chapter in the dance of contempt and resentment, with liberals mocking the ignorance of the message, while Tea Partiers felt it properly expressed their sense of the essential injustice of Obamacare.[52]

There was a logic behind the oxymoron. In the view of Tea Party populists, proposing to grant health insurance to tens of millions without coverage was tantamount to taking that very benefit away from them, expropriating them. Benefits, in short, are not an expandable commodity, but a zero-sum one. They are a fixed sum. The only way to offer existing benefits to a new population is to take them, at least in part, away from those who already possess them, to dispossess them.

But zero-sum thinking in American conservatism goes deeper than disputing spoils. It shows up at times that often bewilder liberals. In her hearing before the Senate Judiciary Committee, Justice Sonia Sotomayor commended the value of empathy in a judge. In response, then-senator Jeff Sessions countered, "Empathy for one party is always prejudice against another."[53] At its most general level, zero-sum thinking is the logic behind the very idea of liberty in right-wing thinking.

Robert Bork was, perhaps, the American right's grand legal theorist of the zero-sum view of liberty. Bork was famous for arguing that the 1964 Civil Rights Act was based on a principle of "unsurpassed ugliness."[54] His reasoning in this regard was particularly well-known in the matter of public accommodations. The idea that lunch-counter owners could not deny service based on race took away the owners' freedom to deal only with whom they wished. Giving blacks the right to sit at that counter—expanding their liberty—came at the counter-owners' expense. The counter owners were dispossessed of their freedom. Tea Party Republican candidate Rand Paul reiterated this view in 2010 during his campaign to be U.S. senator from Kentucky.

Implied in Bork's position on the Civil Rights Act was the equivalence of positive and negative rights. There was nothing inherently superior in the black person's right to be served as compared to the owner's right to deny service. Any judge who would see a superior interest in the right to be served was only relying on personal values and usurping the functions of the legislature, in Bork's thinking. Any law that would favor one or the other's freedom, whether positive or negative, was playing favorites between claims of equal standing.

So extreme was this view for Bork that during his famous, and failed, 1987 confirmation hearings for a seat on the Supreme Court, under questioning by Illinois senator Paul Simon, he was forced to carry his concept to the logical conclusion that the judiciary could not rightly call for the abolition of slavery. The freedom to hold slaves, in Borkian principle, enjoys the same protection as the freedom from slavery.

These zero-sum opinions lay at the heart of Bork's approach to constitutionalism. In these same hearings he described these views as the basis for his judicial philosophy, which he called "original intent," and we might today simply call originalism. He displayed an almost metaphysical vision of natural law that insisted that liberties cannot be created or expanded; they could only be "redistributed." He asserted this was an "arithmetic" and "indisputable" certainty. According to Bork, since every expansion of liberty in one area means taking it away elsewhere, such action calls for value judgments in which no judicial principles of right and wrong pertain.

It is often difficult for liberals to comprehend when conservatives argue that government social programs are destructive of freedom. What links the two in the American right-wing worldview is zero-sum thinking. It may seem a long way from Bork's lofty calculus of liberty to the Tea Party's furious demand that others not enjoy the health insurance protection their government assures them. But the Tea Party's feeling that something of theirs was being taken away and given to others was precisely the feeling that Robert Bork was translating into a judicial philosophy. It represents the defining element of a Tea Party constitutionalism. It was through the zero-sum principle that originalism met populism.

The Neoliberal Arc

Two years after the Tea Party's appearance, another new movement burst onto the political stage. Occupy Wall Street (OWS) emerged at the end of the Tea Party–inspired debate over the national debt in the summer of 2011. If "deservingness" was the Tea Party's central theme, a concern with "fairness" was that of the Occupiers. Rising economic inequality, the concentration of wealth in the hands of a few, and corporate greed were OWS's central complaints. The movement's slogan, "We are the 99 percent," entered the lexicon of American politics, especially as it defined its counterpart, the 1 percent.[55]

Occupy seemed to be a counter-movement to the Tea Party. Their respective activists came from opposite ends of the American cultural and political spectrum. Largely young and ethnically diverse, the ranks of the Occupiers were made up of students, veterans, unemployed workers, former homeowners, teachers, and union organizers. The contrast to the late-middle-aged, white, and buttoned-down Tea Party was stark. Instead of large one-day rallies, like Tea Party Tax Day demonstrations, OWS set up tent villages in city parks and in the shadow of financial institutions. Run by "general assemblies" and equipped with makeshift health clinics and media centers, these occupations represented a novel and infectious form of grassroots protest.[56]

But the Tea Party and OWS shared something fundamental in common. They were mirror images of one another—expressions of pain from differing points of view of the same social process. This process is the still-ongoing dismantling of American middle-class life. The financial meltdown of 2008 brought a shocking and explosive end to what had been a slow-motion process of decay. In its final stage before the financial meltdown, the erosion of middle-class life was masked by easy credit, in particular, the ability of homeowners to borrow against what seemed like the continuous upward valuations of their property. In September of 2008, this all came apart. The explosion of the financial crisis came toward the end of the working lives of most Tea Party supporters. Everything they had earned, suddenly, was insecure. The Tea Party was their furious mobilization against those they felt were poised to take it away. For the Occupy movement, the financial crisis came at the beginning of their working lives. Their prospects for housing, for adequate wages, for the mere opportunity to pay off their student loans— all this was bleak, and worse. In effect, the Tea Party was reacting to the threat that prosperity would be taken away from them. The Occupy movement was reacting to the threat that they would never have it.[57]

Mark Lilla, who grounds his political science in the history of ideas, argued that the United States underwent two "revolutions" between 1963 and 1990.[58] One was a cultural revolution, often called "the sixties." Another was a political-economic revolution, often called "the eighties," or the Reagan Revolution. Sexual mores, family life, religion, music, the use of intoxicants, all underwent radical transformation in the sixties revolution. The effect of the eighties revolution was a sea change turning against the liberal post–World War II consensus on the central questions of the welfare state, labor unions, taxation, and economic regulation, as majorities of American voters began supporting the policies of the pre-2016 Republican orthodoxy.

The Reagan Revolution withstood decades of criticism and political attack without faltering. Early on, analysts and activists on the left probed the political and economic forces of the eighties revolution and named them—neoliberalism and globalization. The left anti-globalization movement culminated in the 1999 Battle of Seattle, when tens of thousands marched against a meeting of the World Trade Organization in that city. On the right, opposition rose to the level of presidential politics. Ross Perot's presidential campaigns, in 1992 and 1996, are most memorable for his warning that the North American Free Trade Agreement (NAFTA) would lead to a massive jobs displacement to Mexico—"a giant sucking sound going south."[59] Pat Buchanan's pitchfork runs for the presidency in 1996 and 2000 acutely foreshadowed the Trump campaign of 2016 and drew upon the paleoconservative and anti-immigration wings of the conservative movement, who enjoyed little purchase at the time but would contribute major players to the Trump campaign and administration.

The potential political-liberal brake on neoliberalism and globalism never materialized. The 1992 election of a Democratic president, Bill Clinton, after a quarter century of almost uninterrupted Republican presidencies, offered no alternative vision to the Reagan political-economic revolution. Preparing for his reelection campaign in May 1996, Clinton was asked about the vision he had brought to his presidency. He responded: "I can tell you what the Evil Empire, New Deal, Fair Deal, Square Deal, New Frontier phrase will be much better when I finish with my work than I can now."[60] But he never did. The vision phrase never emerged.

Clinton's second term was better known for a sex scandal and the president's political methodology—triangulation—than it was for defining what liberalism would stand for as it crossed the "bridge to the twenty-first century," which became the motto of Clinton's fall campaign.[61] And Clinton was not alone in this. Internationally, the center left has lacked an organizing principle since before the fall of the Berlin wall. At the dawn of the age of Reagan and Thatcher and the ascendency of the New Right, François Mitterand abandoned his socialist agenda when, finally, he became president of France. Clinton's New Democrat thinking was shared internationally by the Third Way, which at one point in the nineties was a movement that met with regularity and whose members included the heads of governments in Britain, the United States, Italy, France, Spain, and Portugal. European social democracy was caught short by the end of the Cold War and the disappearance of the Soviet Union and its Eastern bloc, which had stood as the implied, and threatened, alternative to the generous European welfare states. In the end, the Third Way was more an accommodation, if not a capitulation, to the hegemonic clout of the New Right than an opposing force capable of producing a political-economic counter to neoliberalism. In the United States, the

Democrats did little to distinguish the party from the Republicans at the level of political economy. Where they did distinguish themselves was on social issues. Social issues—civil rights, gay rights, women's rights—became expressed largely as identity politics.

So certain was the sweeping dominance of neoliberalism that the most influential idea of the 1990s—the one that told the big story of the age; that announced what constituted the new fundament on the world stage—posited that capitalist liberal democracy had not merely won out over communism in the Cold War but that it faced no significant challenger on the globe. Writing from a Hegelian perspective, where history was a succession of resolving dyadic and dialectical confrontations, Francis Fukuyama concluded that with no possible challenger to the liberal democracy that had won the Cold War, we had reached "the end of history."[62] Unlike the great totalitarian ideologies liberal capitalism faced in the twentieth century, communism and Nazism, liberal democracy no longer had a dyadic adversary of historical note.

Seeing only the "total exhaustion of viable systemic alternatives," Fukuyama gave short shrift to a recurrence of nationalism.[63] It was not that Fukuyama did not see nationalism haunting corners of the globe. It was that those movements were inadequate, as worldviews and ideologies, to contend on the world stage; in this, he implied, they were doomed to futility. Nationalism no longer had the capacity to mount a challenge as it did through German National Socialism. We can use Umberto Eco's words to fill out Fukuyama's argument about what made Nazism a "viable systemic alternative" to liberal democracy:

Mein Kampf is a manifesto of a complete political program. Nazism had a theory of racism and of the Aryan chosen people, a precise notion of degenerate art, entartete Kunst,

a philosophy of the will to power and of the *Ubermensch*.
Nazism was decidedly anti-Christian and neo-pagan.[64]

In short, Fukuyama concluded, post–Cold War nationalism
lacked the ideological gravitas to once more challenge liberal
democracy.

But that is what has come to pass. Neoliberalism's seem-
ingly exclusive hold on the political economic imagination—
the indominable Reagan Revolution—showed cracks with the
financial crisis of 2008, cracks that developed further during
the near depression which followed. Beyond nationalism from
the right, there were stirrings as well from the left. A universalistic program, Obamacare, became the most important piece of
social legislation since the sixties—though the administration
was blocked from its transformative new New Deal hopes on
matters like cap-and-trade and massive infrastructure renova-
tion. By 2016 Bernie Sanders ran the first American presidential campaign using the word "socialist" since before World
War II. Sanders won twenty-three state primaries and received
over 13 million votes. His emphasis on universal health insurance, free higher education, and student loan forgiveness, curb-
ing corporate power and, perhaps above all, inveighing against
America's runaway wealth inequality recalled the energy and
demands of Occupy Wall Street's opposition of the 1 percent and
the 99 percent. By 2019, Sanders's positions were widespread not
only in the party, not only with a young generation in Congress
that seemed eager to displace what they saw as the timidity of
the Democrats in the face of corporate displeasure, his positions
were also assumed by other candidates for the Democratic presidential nomination (all of which almost instantly became grist
for a Republican counter that the Democratic Party wanted to
turn the United States into Maduro's Venezuela).

But the greater firepower to undermine the Reagan Revolution has come from the nationalist right, and it has been international in its scope. In the United States, the ideological challenge Trump presented to Republican orthodoxy was extensive: he attacked international trade agreements and the principle of free trade; he attacked international military and political agreements; and he did not share Republican hostility to the welfare state.[65] Above all, he was adamantly anti-immigration.[66]

Today there are vigorous nationalist parties in every western European country; in one, Italy, they came to power in 2018. In eastern Europe, nationalist parties have come to power in Poland and Hungary; the Hungarian strongman, Viktor Orbán, has given a name to the regime he has most successfully consolidated, "illiberal democracy." In Russia, Vladimir Putin reversed the hopes that liberal democracy would establish itself, creating an authoritarian political symbiosis with a kleptocratic oligarchy in what is often described as a "mafia state."[67] One finds similar nationalist developments as far-flung as in India, Turkey, the Philippines, and Brazil. Perhaps most telling is the post–Cold War nationalist transformation of the globe's most powerful remaining communist society, China. As Stein Ringen observed in 2015:

> China is responding with a new emphasis on ideology, but now in the form of nationalism rather than Marxism. In so doing, it is substituting narrative for delivery in the promotion of itself. Its narrative is one of national and military glory and strength . . . [68]

Internationally, the nationalist canary in the mine of the post–Cold War world was Yugoslavia. The Cold War ending was like the thawing of an ice age: Hoary nationalisms had spent decades frozen below a surface monopolized by the bipolar international politics of the East-West standoff. With the Cold War over, these pent-up nationalisms emerged with alarming ferocity. Bosnians, Croats, Serbs. Orthodox Christians, Catholics, Muslims—fellow Yugoslav citizens in the decades before were now the Other. The wars that ensued introduced the world to the ominous variant on genocide called "ethnic cleansing." Rife was the nostalgia that would be a hallmark of post–Cold War nationalism, the yearning for and assertion of a mythical golden age or a historical trauma still to be avenged—like the Serbian mobilization around their 1389 defeat in Kosovo at the hands of the Muslim Turks.[69] These Balkan wars created the greatest flood of internally displaced refugees in Europe since World War II, foreshadowing the 2015 refugee crisis that would move nationalist parties in Europe definitively into their countries' mainstreams. The fecklessness of liberal democracy, in the form of the European Union, to prevent or halt war on the European mainland foreshadowed liberalism's floundering as it has tried to resist nationalist forces since the 2016 Brexit vote in Britain. These nationalist forces constituted the post–Cold War zeitgeist that gave the USA Donald Trump's election.[70] It was Trump's election—effected by ideologically migrating America's right-wing populists from Tea Party free-market fundamentalism to anti-immigrant nationalism—that finally overturned the stranglehold of the neoliberal Reagan Revolution on political economy in the United States.

From RINOs to Globalists

In September 2012, at the Values Voter Summit, Bryan Fischer of the American Family Association offered this shot across the bow to the Republican establishment:

> If Barack Obama wins this election, the Republican Party as
> we know it is finished, it is dead, it is toast—you can stick

a fork in it. And conservatives, grassroots conservatives, are either going to start a third party or they are going to launch a hostile takeover of the Republican Party.[71]

Fischer's prognosis was prescient. By "grassroots conservatives," Fischer was referring to social-issue voters, the right-wing populists who had been the Republican Party's reliable, if unfulfilled, electoral base since the 1980 beginning of the conservative national ascendency. These were the people who had coalesced into the Tea Party after Obama's first election. They fervently believed that one of their own—not the Republican establishment's choice—would have won the 2008 election, and could win in 2012. Losing again to Obama in 2012 with Mitt Romney at the head of the ticket would have a last-straw quality to it, Fischer was telling his audience. The populists will have had it with the Republican establishment.

Unhappiness with the Republican establishment had been a constant drumbeat in the Tea Party's then four-year history. Day in and day out, in articles on Tea Party websites and exhaustive comment sections, members raised again and again what to do about the Republican Party's failure to come through for them; what to do about the party leadership's insufferable concessions to Obama and the Democrats. The Tea Party had given the Republicans the 2010 blowout election. But Obamacare still stood. Making a stand on the debt? Finally, just lip service. Fischer outlined two of the three options that appeared repeatedly in these often-heated exchanges: starting a third party and a hostile takeover of the Republican Party. The third option was hold your nose and vote Republican, ever argued as the most rational alternative (job one is to defeat the liberals), but one that had less and less appeal over time.[72]

Fischer's use of the phrase "a hostile takeover of the

Republican Party" anticipated what would become a journalistic cliché after Donald Trump's capture of the Republican nomination. Whether Fischer had Trump in mind as the political predator is unlikely, but certain signs were already available when he spoke. Trump himself had publicly considered the question of running for president in 2012. Michael Cohen, Trump's erstwhile personal attorney, had established a website called ShouldTrumpRun.com. According to a *Time* magazine interview with him on the topic in 2011, Trump had effectively readied his 2016 campaign slogan. "I can make this country great again," he said. "This country is not great. This country is a laughingstock for the rest of the world."[73]

But more than that, Trump had found his formula for cultivating the political support of American right-wing populists: he pinpointed a burning theme Tea Partiers ventilated about among themselves and, like an unrelenting poker player, he not only saw the populists on their issue, he raised them. Trump became the country's loudest and most prominent birther.[74] He talked loudly about it on national media and, with the loose relationship to fact that would be a hallmark of his presidency, he boasted he had sent "his people" to Hawaii who "have been studying it [and] they cannot believe what they're finding,"[75] Obama having been born outside the United States—exactly where perhaps uncertain; there were any number of hypotheses—was talked about inside the Tea Party as an accepted fact. What Trump did with birtherism, the formula he had discovered in 2011, he would repeat in 2015: (1) He pinpointed the most burning issue among the populists, then their inflexible opposition to immigration reform. (2) He defined himself politically as the issue's most zealous advocate. (3) He raised the stakes: he was going to build a wall.

Trump's siren song to Tea Party populists also operated on

deeper levels. He appealed to a predisposition to believe that their political opponents operated via conspiracies.[76] For people convinced that Obama's elections were fraudulent, a candidate who sounded off incessantly about "rigged" elections, a candidate who would not agree a priori to accept election results was a voice addressing their fears and fantasies. For a population open to ideas about Obama being a Manchurian candidate—cultivated from youth by domestic and international cabals to bring America to leftist ruin—Trump's allegations about the forces arrayed to stop him as a candidate or bring him down as president were continuous with ideas already heavily in play.[77] With their segue to America-First nationalist ideology, right-wing populists segued to Trump's drama of him as a president doing battle with the "deep state."

Drawing in the populist right to anti-immigrant nationalist ideology, Trump was able to transform their emotional and political landscape. Trump had found the issue on which he could effectively conflate the Tea Party's foil, the Republican establishment, with the Tea Party's enemy, the liberals and the Democrats. Trump was able to pair the resentment of liberals and Democrats that is the abiding primum mobile of right-wing populism with feelings about the Republican establishment. The Tea Party foil and the Tea Party enemy were now conflated into a single force, a single elite, the globalists. No ideology could be in starker contrast and opposition to the globalists than nationalism. Throughout his campaign, Trump heaped contempt equally on Republicans and Democrats. The liberals and the Democrats, in the right populist view, had always pandered for votes from the underclass. The crucial America-transforming underclass was now the immigrants—and the Republican establishment was joining the liberals in pandering to them with the idea of comprehensive immigration reform.

The bipolar choice of American politics was now revolution-ized. It was no longer liberal versus conservative, Democrat versus Republican. It was a conflated Establishment—Democratic and Republican as one—versus the new nationalist alternative. The American Establishment versus Donald Trump.

3

The Great Irony

*How Trump Split the Tea Party and Won
the 2016 Republican Nomination*

The Republican establishment reacted with alarm to the party's loss in the 2012 presidential election. The results brought into question the party's very viability as a national political contender. The problem? The party was living under a demographic sword of Damocles, as the population of the United States inched more and more heavily toward majority minority.

This was not a new revelation in 2012. For years the Republican establishment understood that what had happened to the Republican Party in California could happen nationally. The state that had given the nation Richard Nixon and Ronald Reagan turned reliably blue in state and national elections after the controversy over 1994's Proposition 187, which would bar "illegal aliens" from using state services including education.[1] As far back as 2009, at the very beginning of Obama's first term, the de facto head of the Republican establishment, Senate majority leader Mitch McConnell, lamented:

> We're all concerned about the fact that the very wealthy and
> the very poor, the most and least educated, and a majority
> of minority voters seem to have more or less stopped paying
> attention to us, and we should be concerned that, as a result
> of all this, the Republican Party seems to be slipping into
> a position of being more of a regional party than a nation-
> al one.[2]

Under the leadership of its chair, Reince Priebus, the Republican Party commissioned a study of what went wrong in the 2012 election and what the party needed to do to correct its problems. Formally entitled the "Growth and Opportunity Project," the study was widely called, even by Republicans, the party's "autopsy report."[3] It had a number of findings, but one stood out from all the rest. The party was marginalizing itself by alienating minority voters—especially immigrants, and Latinos, in particular.

From the point of view of the party establishment, as a political force capable of competing in elections on the national level, this was nothing short of an existential crisis: Without correction, the party would cease to exist—it would die—as a national force. Its future would be as a rump—a party reduced to a handful of regional strengths, primarily in the South and the Midwest. Urban centers, the West Coast, and the Northeast loomed as lost to Republican candidates, not merely for president but also for the U.S. Senate and much of the House of Representatives. Presenting the report, Priebus pointed out that in "the year 2050 we'll be a majority-minority country and in both 2008 and 2012 President Obama won a combined 80 percent of the votes of all minority groups."[4]

The problem as the Republican establishment understood it was that the party's base could no longer support a national majority. The party needed to expand its base. It needed to bring in new voters. There was a straightforward way to accomplish this. The party must embrace "comprehensive immigration reform." And identifying the target population was a similarly straightforward matter. The autopsy report read:

> Among the steps Republicans take in the Hispanic community and beyond must be to embrace and champion compre-

hensive immigration reform. If we do not, our Party's appeal will continue to shrink to its core constituencies only.[5]

Going into the 2016 election, comprehensive immigration reform remained the Republican Party's prime concern. The party mounted seventeen contenders for its 2016 presidential nomination. All but one—Donald Trump—embraced some form of immigration reform. Briefly among the contenders was South Carolina senator Lindsey Graham. He had summarized the party's existential dilemma in 2013:

> But if we don't pass immigration reform, if we don't get it off the table and in a reasonable, practical way, it doesn't matter who you run in 2016. We're in a *demographic death spiral as a party*. And the only way we can get back in good graces with the Hispanic community, in my view, is to pass comprehensive immigration reform. If you don't do that, it really doesn't matter who we run in my view [emphasis added].[6]

This is what I call the Great Irony of the 2016 election. On the one hand, the Republican establishment, the party's professionals, were sure that without expanding the party's base via an opening to immigrants not only could there be no national victory; the party faced existential danger. On the other hand, the lone apostate to immigration reform defeated all the other candidates and took the party's nomination. And went on to win the general election.

But the irony did not stop there. Trump did not merely do the opposite of what the Republican professionals prescribed, he did so in the most extreme manner. He alienated immigrants and Latinos as much as he possibly could. Immigrants were snakes who could never be trusted.[7] Individually and as communities, their defining attribute was crime: drugs, rape, gang violence. He would build a wall on the Mexican border. Suggestive of ethnic cleansing, he would rid the country of its 11 million "illegals." This was the candidate's political brand. By December 2015 he doubled down on Muslims, promising to ban them from entering the country.

To further the irony, Trump even managed to accomplish what the establishment had been hoping for with its goal of opening to Latinos and immigration reform. He expanded the party's base. The most talked-about voter during the campaign was the white working-class male. Trump's often repeated "I love the poorly educated" resonated with blue-collar workers and helped him cultivate their years-in-the-making migration away from the Democrats, which had accelerated in the Obama years, and lent credibility to Trump's assertion the Republicans were now the "working man's party."[8]

But Trump brought in more than the working class. He brought in the fringe of American politics. They came in two forms. One was the white supremacist right that had had no role in national politics (though some in regional politics) since the 1920s. These were the members and sympathizers of the Ku Klux Klan and neo-Nazi and similar white-power groups. The name these groups had given themselves, the alt-right, went from something known to only a handful of Americans before the presidential campaign to a matter of urgent public controversy. Trump also brought in an alienated and largely nihilistic population, chiefly of young men, who inhabited an online subculture that had largely developed out of online gaming. The border between these young men and the alt-right was blurry and as a group the young men are often referred to as the alt-lite. The essence of what the alt-lite and the alt-right share in common is the vehement conviction that discrimination in the United States has reversed: The superior stature its members once took for granted has been eroded—they have been dispossessed—and they are now the leading victims of political and cultural discrimination. For the alt-lite the new victim is the straight male. For the alt-right it is white people.

As Rachel Bitecofer has written, "Trump's 2016 path to the White House . . . was the political equivalent of getting dealt a Royal Flush in poker."[9] Though they were small in numbers, there was no gainsaying the significance of the alt-right and the alt-lite in the general election. In the three pivotal states that Clinton assumed she would win, Michigan, Wisconsin, and Pennsylvania, Trump beat her by a combined total of 77,000 votes.[10] In numbers, the alt-right and alt-lite expansion of the base might not have been many. But in an election decided by such a tiny margin, it was enough. In any case they, the alt-right, certainly believed in the significance of their vote. Andrew Anglin, the publisher of the neo-Nazi website the Daily Stormer, expressed his movement's conviction on this, the morning after the election:

> We won brothers. . . . Make no mistake about it: we did this. If it were not for us, it wouldn't have been possible.[11]

Free-Market Fundamentalist Goals for 2016

The 2016 election ambitions of the free-market fundamentalists, led by the Koch brothers' political machinery, were nothing short of breathtaking. They felt within their grasp a historical opportunity they had been dreaming about for decades: the possibility of turning back liberal institutions and customs. Things had lined up their way. Congress was in Republican hands. Thanks to the Supreme Court's *Citizens United* decision, big money, insurmountable money, could swing the party's presidential nomination their way as never before. And, at the state level, they had battle-tested their legislative game plan to roll back settled elements of environmental protections, workers' rights, progressive taxation, voting rights, criminal justice policy, and a host of social issues including abortion rights and gay rights, as well as to play fast and loose with separation of church and state. The Kochs announced plans to raise $889 million leading up to the 2016 elections.[12]

Deciding to push a ton of chips out on the table, the Kochs were motivated not only by the opportunity 2016 presented but as well by the conviction, owing to the country's demographic transformation, that their window of opportunity might be short-lived. The states where Republicans had scored a trifecta—control of the governorship and both legislative houses—had been the proving ground for the free-market fundamentalists' strategy. These states included Kansas, Ohio, Michigan, and, above all, Wisconsin. The goal in 2016 was to have a Republican trifecta at the national level—to win the presidency along with holding on to both houses of Congress. Under Wisconsin governor Scott Walker, an aggressive strategy stripped public workers' union rights, cut taxes, and severely cut funding for the University of Wisconsin as part of an overall goal of moving public-sector functions into private hands.[13] What had been accomplished in Wisconsin was to be a model reproduced on a national level.[14] The Kochs had worked closely with Walker, and endorsed him as their candidate for president.[15] He would run as the governor who stood up to the public-employee unions the way Ronald Reagan ran as the governor who stood up to campus protest and the counterculture in 1976 and 1980.[16]

Walker's was an unfortunate presidential candidacy, folding after little more than two months. This dropped the free-market fundamentalists into the same hollow as the Republican establishment: watching painfully as all their power—political for the establishment; financial for the free-market fundamentalists—proved inadequate to prevent Donald Trump's capture of the populist vote and, ultimately, the Republican nomination.[17] The Kochs notably froze Trump out of the network's financial support during the campaign.[18]

Like most of the Republican establishment, the free-market fundamentalists would embark on an arc that, over time, would take them away from fervent Never Trump positions, based on both his overturning Republican ideological orthodoxy and his prodigal moral unsoundness. Steps along the way included grudging support because "he will sign our bills" and name the right judges;[19] followed by more fulsome support as Republican candidates found their voting base had turned Trumpian.[20] Tea Party Caucus members in the House who remained loyal to the movement's free-market fundamentalist ideology realigned themselves into the "Freedom Caucus." Freedom Caucus members Mike Pompeo and Mick Mulvaney would last well into Trump's presidency, long after orthodox Republicans in their high-visibility roles (such as Rex Tillerson, secretary of state, and Reince Priebus, chief of staff) could no longer function in the administration.

The Impasse of Existential Crises

The crucial dynamic of the battle for the Republican nomination in 2016 was that the establishment's existential crisis was met with an equal and opposite existential crisis on the part of the Tea Party populists. For the establishment the existential threat was the loss of the party as a national force. For the populists, it was the loss of country. The cause of the loss of country? Immigration. To the populists, comprehensive immigration reform, which often provided a "path to citizenship" for some "illegals," would mean making the "illegals" legal; it was "amnesty"; it would institutionalize forever the populists' sense that the country had been taken away from them, both socially and politically.[21] A line had been drawn in the sand. For the establishment the solution to its existential crisis was an opening to Latinos and comprehensive immigration reform. For the populists it was an end to immigration reform and removing "illegals" from the country. This was Tea Party 3.0, when immigration was the issue that unified the movement nationally, succeeding Obamacare (Tea Party 1.0) and the "debt crises" (Tea Party 2.0). It was the version of the Tea Party whose online debates and grievances became the issues Donald Trump, immersed in these exchanges, ran on. Judson Phillips, leader of the Tea Party Nation, put the question for the populists starkly in April of 2015. (By "amnesty" here, he follows Tea Party 3.0 speak to refer to any form of immigration reform):

> For conservatives in 2016, amnesty is the *defining issue*. There is no middle ground. There cannot be any form of amnesty. We need a president who will put the interests of Americans first [emphasis added].

Americans first. Donald Trump, who mined right-wing websites for all the themes of his campaign and his presidency, would resurrect "America First" from pre–World War II infamy to serve as his political slogan. Trump's immersion in right-wing media made it clear to him that he was facing a situation where the Republican establishment and the party's populist base had become irreconcilable. This was the populist revolt Trump discovered on right-wing media and which became the touchstone of his candidacy. Each side saw its position as an existential crisis and could give no quarter. The motherlode of Republican primary voters lay with the populists, and representing their side in the most extreme manner defined the strategy Trump adopted to wrest the nomination from the Republican regulars.

And the strategy resonated. For the Tea Party, and, as it would turn out, a broader swath of the white working class and American nativists, "illegal immigrants" explained the immediate dysfunctions in American society, like unemployment and fading life chances. But something more profound was going on, a blanket sense that the country was getting away from them, that their taken-for-granted majoritarian American identity— the "real Americans"—was getting swamped by minorities from below and minorities arriving in positions of power above, both culturally and—Obama!—politically. For this existential malaise, Trump seemed like a providential delivery. As the right-wing political commentator Ann Coulter put it,

> This is not an election about who can check off the most boxes on a conservative policy list, or even about who is the best or nicest person. This is an election about saving the concept of America, an existential election like no other has ever been. Anyone who doesn't grasp this is part of the problem, not part of the solution.[22]

The Tea Party Meets Trump

Back in the 2012 election season, Tea Party blogs were in agony: an Obama reelection was nothing short of a horror and the ratification of what Tea Partiers often called tyranny, now Marxist, now Muslim.[23] Obama's tyranny was a gut feeling, a taken-for-granted tenet of everyday dialogue in the movement back in 2012. Running a "real conservative," the faithful believed, one of their own, was the Republican Party's sure path to the White House. Yet—and this created abiding resentment—the Republican National Committee, acting "like the Central Committee of the Communist Party," worked to impose Mitt Romney's, the establishment's, candidacy.[24]

In the spring of 2015 it looked as if the 2016 Republican primary season was going to be a near replay of 2012. The 2012 Republican primary battle had had a notable pattern. The field consisted mostly of an assortment of populist candidates who were chasing the establishment front-runner, Mitt Romney. One by one, the populists surged in the polls, challenging Romney. And one by one, those challenges faltered. The dynamic behind this pattern was the profound desire among the Republican populist base, concentrated in the Tea Party, to choose one of their own; to have the party nominate a candidate who spoke for the Tea Party's frustrations with the Republican establishment; to nominate a "real conservative." Not another John McCain; not another establishment choice who felt entitled, as though it was "his turn."

The succession of populist flashes-in-the-pan began with Representative Michele Bachmann of Minnesota, whose surge came after winning an August 2011 Iowa straw poll. In September, Texas governor Rick Perry's entrance into the race generated an enthusiasm that displaced Bachmann in the polls. Perry's poor showing in the September debates led to a surge in the candidacy of the pizza executive Herman Cain. Cain's candidacy faltered on reports of sexual harassment, and in November the mantle of leading opponent in the polls to Romney passed to former House Speaker Newt Gingrich. Gingrich's surge, and his "I'm going to be the nominee" confidence, elicited a negative ad campaign against him from Romney backers.[25] By the time actual primary voting began in early January 2012, the last Tea Party favorite standing was former Pennsylvania senator Rick Santorum. Santorum's candidacy benefited from being the last alternative, and he did not suspend his campaign until April 2012.

In 2016 the 2012 script was readied with Jeb Bush, the establishment's choice; and Tea Party stalwarts Ted Cruz, Mike

Huckabee, Rand Paul, the Ricks Perry and Santorum, and Bobby Jindal arrayed to take him down. But on June 16, 2015, the 2012 script went haywire. Donald Trump, until then the New York real-estate mogul and reality TV star with a passion for the look and sound of his own name, announced his candidacy for the Republican nomination. In his eponymous midtown tower, he was introduced by his daughter and surrounded by aspiring actors who had answered a casting call and were paid $50 a head to express joy at the news.[26]

The American split screen came into play immediately. Liberals and the Republican establishment routinely spoke as if Trump's candidacy were little more than an aberration, something that would swiftly dissipate. From this side of the split screen, Trump's speeches were vulgar stream-of-consciousness rambles reminiscent of barroom braggadocio, at once putting down the opposition, Republican and Democratic alike, as stupid morons, and then lionizing his own wealth, belovedness, and deal-making smarts. He invited his listeners to join in on his omnipotent fantasy solutions, be they building a Mexican-financed wall to keep out Mexicans or extinguishing the chaos in the Middle East through building a fearsome military.

But, as with the Tea Party six years earlier, it was the other side of the split screen that had the sharper bead on the political novelty that was Trump's candidacy. What the mainstream media missed in the analysis of the day was how Trump's immersion in right-wing media had loaded him up with a stockpile of Tea Party speak, complete with its resentments, conspiracy ideas, passions, and convictions. The candidate who railed "the big problem in this country is political correctness" raised political incorrectness into a winning political formula. Despite the widespread dismissive responses to his announcement, Trump shot to the top of the polls. Trump's political gift was his fluency in the populist vernacular, how readily his personal style melded with what he found on right-wing websites, television, and radio. Trump had grasped the sweet spot of the Tea Party, the Republicans' deepest well of primary voters; with unprecedented, over-the-top directness, he spoke to the movement's fiercest 2016 passion, its felt existential crisis—the immigration question.

Trump's most famous remarks in his announcement speech were a Rorschach test in split-screen America. For establishment America, both red and blue, it was appalling, beyond the pale, ridiculous, the stuff of banana republics. For right populist America, it was a stunning moment of being heard. Politically, it was having their deepest feelings weaponized. Once again, as with those earlier moments—Sarah Palin's run for the vice presidency, the early years of the Tea Party—resentment was being transformed into contempt for the elite; for their cluelessness, for their sense of propriety, for their smugness. And it was the elite newly redefined—no longer just the liberals, but with the Republican establishment rolled into it; globalists all. Trump's words were a rallying cry to which the elites were tone deaf:

> When Mexico sends its people, they're not sending their best. They're not sending you. [pointing] They're not sending you. They're sending people that have lots of problems, and they're bringing those problems with us [sic]. They're bringing drugs. They're bringing crime. They're rapists. And some, I assume, are good people.[27]

Betrayal and the Bellwether

In 2016, Garry Wills observed: "The sense of betrayal by one's own is a continuing theme in the Republican Party." In Obama's second term, this was the worm that was turning inside the Tea Party. Wills continued, "A Fox News poll in September 2015 found that 62 percent of Republicans feel 'betrayed' by their own party's officeholders."[28] This was more than the frustration of having their votes taken for granted by Republican candidates who then fail to deliver on their issues—the grievance that had dogged right-wing populists for decades. This was the sense that the Republican establishment, the Tea Party's foil, now was showing greater loyalty to the opposition, to the liberals, the Tea Party's enemy, than they were to their base. The foil was becoming one with the enemy.

Much as betrayal might have been in the Tea Party air in 2015, it was a single issue—immigration, again—that solidified the sentiment. The bellwether of this transformation had come in June 2014. An obscure young economics professor and devout Christian, David Brat, primaried the House majority leader, Representative Eric Cantor of Virginia. Cantor's advantage in campaign funding was $5.4 million to $231 thousand.[29] Cantor had won earlier primaries with as much as 79 percent of the vote. Cantor seemed on the fast track to succeed John Boehner as Speaker of the House.

Brat beat him by eleven points, 55 percent to 44 percent.

How? Brat was "the guy who turned Eric Cantor into Mr. Amnesty."[30] Cantor's sympathetic consideration of the Dream Act—creating a process for granting residency status to immigrants who arrived as minors—gave Brat this opening. In Brat's view, "[Immigration] is the most symbolic issue that captures the difference between myself and Eric Cantor in this race."[31] But Brat was also tuned in to the Tea Party's sense of betrayal, the belief that their enemy and their foil were now one. As he put it, "There is just one party up in D.C. right now."[32]

The emotional experience of feeling betrayed by the Republican establishment was accompanied by the beginning of right-wing populism's ideological migration away from free-market fundamentalism and toward nationalism. In Brat's victory, this

was a development rarely noted and, even when noted, under-
valued in the liberal world: "Was immigration an issue? Yes.
Was it the deciding factor to the tune of 11%? Not no, hell no. It's
a fairy tale."[33] Liberals and establishment Republicans were also
indifferent to crowd size and enthusiasm; this foreshadowed
the Trump campaign, when again they would discount Donald
Trump's continued boasting about his crowd sizes. But populists
took it seriously as a measure of the wind in their sails: "There
were warning signs that kept piling up—signs that [Cantor's]
supporters brushed off consistently. In April, Brat supporters
vastly outnumbered Cantor allies at local GOP meetings."[34]

One last bit of establishment incomprehension. Here is *Time*
magazine's assessment of how conventional wisdom sized up
the effects of Cantor's defeat on the Republican House leadership:

> Cantor's exit will surely create a leadership vacuum on Capi-
> tol Hill. Widely seen as the front-runner for next Speaker, his
> departure makes it even more likely that House Speaker John
> Boehner will stick around.[35]

Instead, well before the next congressional election, in September 2015, Boehner announced that he would zip-a-dee-doo-dah
his way into retirement. The Tea Party's two foremost political
tactics had decapitated Republican leadership in the House.[36]
Primarying had defeated the House majority leader. Obstructionism forced the Speaker of the House, the most powerful
Republican in Washington, to call it quits. The worm had turned.

"Hard-Hat" Populism

By late summer 2015, Trump's commanding lead over
the Republican field began to yield to a surge by black
neurosurgeon-turned-presidential-candidate Ben Carson. What

happened here was that Tea Party voters, after the first blush
of enthusiasm for Trump, began to see more of themselves in
Carson than in Trump, especially after their presentations at the
Family Research Council's Values Voters Summit in September.

And they were not mistaken in this. Despite his success in
basing his campaign irresistibly on the hottest of Tea Party populist hot buttons, Trump comes from a populist lineage distinct
from that of the Tea Party's largely exurban and evangelical
base. Rather, Trump's is a notably urban populism.[37] It is the
hard-hat populism that famously showed its face in New York
City when construction workers attacked antiwar protesters
during the Vietnam War.[38] It is a point of view that vigorously
defends police actions that liberals see as violating civil liberties. It is the conviction that would move Donald Trump in 1989
to take out an $85,000 full-page ad in the *New York Times* calling
for the death penalty for the Central Park Five; and staunchly
to refuse to reconsider after their innocence was established.[39]
It is the vein of urban resentment that was exposed as far back
as 1968 in the first presidential campaign of George Wallace. It
was the resentment mined by New York City mayoral candidate
Mario Procaccino in 1969, who popularized the term *limousine
liberal*.[40] It is the populism that urbanites identified with when
Richard Nixon relabeled them as part of the "silent majority"—a
phrase Trump resurrected; and which a few years after Nixon
was transformed into Reagan Democrats.[41]

And it is a populism Trump comes by honestly. Trump's father,
who made the family's real estate fortune building middle-class
housing in Brooklyn and Queens, taught his son the business.
This meant dealing with contractors, laborers, building superin-
tendents, and renters, and it is Trump's adoption of their Archie
Bunker–like manner and mores that marks his political style.[42]
There is long-standing cultural and political resentment—it goes
back at least to the administration of Mayor John Lindsay—that

outer-borough New Yorkers feel for the Manhattan "elites." In effect, if the Tea Party's populism is the populism of "fly-over country"—the America that feels ignored by the elites of the East and West Coasts—Trump's populism reflects the resentments of "fly-over New York."

The "real American" identity was worn more lightly among hard-hat populists than it was among Tea Partiers; it was less of a total identity. Nor did the urban populists share all the Tea Party's populist concerns. One example was the Tea Party's widespread rejection of science, like the realities of evolution or climate change. When Carson invoked the Bible as a guide to history, as in his suggestion that the Egyptian pyramids were grain silos, he endeared himself to the evangelical base in a way foreign to Trump-style populism.[43]

The hard-hat populist was nowhere as exercised over the "gay agenda" as his Tea Party brethren. Nor were Second Amendment questions as vital. The urban populist did not follow the Tea Party down some of the paths that seemed oddest, even paranoid, to American liberals, like the conviction that the Obama government planned to disarm Americans, or that U.S. military exercises, like Jade Helm, were designed to impose martial law on a red state like Texas. But in populist politics, issues and ideology are fungible while the emotional core remains abiding, and can crosscut rural-urban and other divisions. As Ralph Reed, longtime leader of the evangelical Christian right, put it:

> There is a sense for which someone who's from Queens can understand people from the South. There's this odd common bond between someone who grew up in Queens and someone who grew up in the rural or the exurban South, that for decades people have looked down their noses at them, and they're tired of it.[44]

The Donald and the *Cavaliere*

For establishment America—both left and right—the chase was on to find a model that could explain Trump as a politician. His speeches defied every expectation of an American politician. He mimicked people, including their disabilities. He mocked and insulted all of his Republican opponents. He rambled. He condoned, even encouraged, violence by his supporters at his rallies. What he stood for around immigrants seemed to fly in the face of American values. He claimed the election process was rigged against him. He treated the press as an enemy. His appearance and his personality both seemed weird.[45]

The ready-to-hand model to understand Trump was Teflon. Ronald Reagan was called the Teflon president. How Reagan could get away politically unharmed by his gaffes ("Trees cause more pollution than automobiles do"[46]) befuddled liberals, and their answer was the gaffes just slid off him, owing to some mysterious charisma. By August 2015, just two months after Trump's announcing his candidacy and settling firmly atop the polls, *Politico* called him "Teflon Don."[47] By December 2015, *The Economist* concluded that "Teflon Trump" explained how "Donald Trump's increasingly controversial comments [fail] to dent his poll ratings."[48] And so on it continued.

But Teflon was the wrong metaphor. The logic of the metaphor is that a politician—miraculously, Teflonically—manages not to be hurt in spite of relentless misstatements and embarrassments—gaffes—that *should* doom him. Instead they slide off him. With Trump, this was once again bringing a conventional-wisdom perspective to a political novelty where it did not belong. The crucial problem with Teflon to explain Trump is that in fact his gaffes not only did not, and do not, slide off him. Rather they stick to him. And they make him stronger. From a liberal and establishment perspective, Trump is not so much Teflon Man as

Magnet Man—the antihero who lumbers through a junkyard (of gaffes), where bits of junk fly up and magnetically attach themselves to him, strengthening him as the secret iron elixir behind his superpowers.

Another model to try to make sense of Trump was the figure of Silvio Berlusconi, the former prime minister of Italy who dominated Italian politics in the 1990s and 2000s. Like Trump, Berlusconi moved from real estate where he made his first fortune (he built Milano Due, a self-contained residential complex outside Milan) then switched to television (he held a monopoly position owning Italy's three major private TV networks). From those proceeds he bought the soccer team A.C. Milan and transformed it into one of the most exciting and successful teams in Europe, winning the European Champions League five times during his ownership. The reigning connection between Trump and Berlusconi is the ostentatious place of women and money in their public personas. The Trump-Berlusconi analogy has remained a constant since Trump announced his candidacy. Less than a month after the announcement, in July 2015, *New York Times* columnist Frank Bruni published "La Dolce Donald Trump."[49] In August 2019, Foreign Policy magazine published "We're All Living in Berlusconi's World Now."[50]

Berlusconi's last major star turn in American media was the 2011 scandal around his Bunga Bunga parties, which offered up aspiring women, including very young women, to Berlusconi and his cronies.[51] Berlusconi's moral code paralleled Trump's famous pussy-grabbing ethics of the *Access Hollywood* tape that threatened to bring his campaign down in October 2016.[52] Like Trump, Berlusconi had a history of shady financing of his businesses and, after skirting years of investigations and indictments (and, Trump-like, railing against "unfair judges"), Berlusconi was finally convicted of tax evasion in 2011, and had the conviction confirmed by Italy's highest court two years later.[53] Trump, who famously defied custom by refusing to reveal his income tax returns, had his and his family's decades of tax evasion exposed in a *New York Times* investigative report in October 2018.[54] Similarly, like the emoluments issues that confronted Trump as president—profiting from the politically awkward hosting of government employees, campaign events, and foreign officials in his hotels—Berlusconi's personal profit never seemed far from his government's policies.[55]

Berlusconi famously remarked, "Don't you realize that something doesn't exist—not an idea, a politician, or a product—unless it is on television?"[56] In this he articulated what might be considered Donald Trump's formula for reality testing. As president, Trump's television watching (a large portion of his daily "executive time") has been prodigious.[57] He seems symbiotic with Fox News—especially with the morning show *Fox and Friends,* and with Sean Hannity's evening show—often tweeting out on Twitter stories he sees covered there within minutes of their broadcast; these stories sometimes originate on far-right media and conspiratorial websites, which are subsequently picked up by Fox.[58] People seeking to influence Trump's thinking report making it a point to go on Fox News to talk directly to him.[59] Some Trump appointees—like Director of the National Economic Council Lawrence Kudlow or John Bolton, for five months the national security advisor in 2019—came into the administration directly off the Fox News screen.

When he first ran for office, owing to his ownership of private TV in Italy, candidate Berlusconi was able to present himself to the electorate through interviews carried out by his own employees, who were the presenters on his networks. As prime minster, he was able to add control of Italian state TV, the RAI, to his monopoly of private TV. What this offered Berlusconi was a direct 24/7 channel to the Italian public, to Italian voters, uncut by journalistic gatekeepers. The 2010 film on life in Berlusconi's

Italy coined the term *Videocracy* to describe the essential transformation Berlusconi had brought to Italy. Videocracy over time
ushered in briefer and more zealous messaging.

> Short, nuance-free, and emotionally-driven messages were
> already taking over during the era of Berlusconi's television
> stations in Italy, but they have since grown to dominate the
> entire political landscape.[60]

This trend has crowned in Trump's America. Trump's unmediated 24/7 channel to American society—to his followers; to
media; to his opposition—is Twitter: grievances, attacks, boasting, policy initiatives, now in two hundred eighty characters.
Berlusconi's Videocracy has given way to Trump's Tweetocracy.

The Tea Party's Final Agony

Toward the end of 2015, Ben Carson faltered. A combination of
his mild personality and his plain lack of knowledge of foreign
affairs, and the terror attacks of November 2015 in Paris and in
December in San Bernardino, California, seemed to take the
air out of his campaign, and his poll numbers began a steady
decline.[61] In his rise and fall, Carson resembled the Tea Party
favorites of the 2012 primary campaign. But that was 2016's last
semblance of the 2012 model. In fact, by the time voting began in
February 2016, the 2012 model had been turned on its head and
the 2016 primaries were now fully the reverse of the 2012 primaries. In 2012 the race consisted of a handful of populists chasing
the establishment front-runner. In the 2016 race it came down
to a handful of establishment candidates chasing the populist
front-runners, a pair of Tea Party favorites, Trump and Texas
senator Ted Cruz.

One after another, the establishment candidates failed. Jeb

Bush's campaigning seemed to confirm Trump's belittling of him as "low-energy." Chris Christie's tough-guy appeal proved no match for Trump's eccentric high-wire mastery of those arts. Ironically, with Jeb Bush out of the race, Marco Rubio became the establishment's great hope to beat Trump for the nomination—ironic, because Rubio had arrived in the Senate in 2010 as a Tea Party candidate. But he was never able to repair his breach with the Tea Party around his early work in the Senate, trying to collaborate on immigration reform.

Rubio was undressed by his hollow word-for-word repetition of talking points at the hands of Chris Christie in a debate preceding Super Tuesday. This was a humiliation from which Rubio never recovered, though he attempted to do so by turning from his choir-boy persona to meeting Trump at the level of the latter's gutter speech, including, finally, penis-size suggestions.

For the Republican establishment, once the primary voting began, the likelihood of a Trump nomination gathered with the chilling momentum of the Greek tragedy. The remaining establishment possibility, Ohio governor John Kasich, was never taken seriously as a winner by the Republican establishment, though with the walls closing in on them, they hoped he might win enough delegates to throw the convention into a deadlock.

Five days after the December 2015 terrorist attack in San Bernardino (and two weeks after the one in Paris), having watched his lead in the polls soften, Trump called for a "total and complete shutdown" of Muslims entering the United States until we "figure out what's going on."[62] The response to this reprised, and in many ways exceeded, the split-screen response to Trump's attack on Mexicans and his proposal to build a border wall, which began with his campaign announcement speech and continued as a staple in his campaign rallies. No Republican in a national leadership position spoke up in favor of the idea. From the Obama administration, deputy national security advisor Ben Rhodes said, "It's totally contrary to our values as Americans."[63] On the campaign trail, Democratic presidential hopeful Martin O'Malley tweeted, "He is running for President as a fascist demagogue."[64]

Yet, on the other split screen, the Republican base responded to Trump's call to halt Muslim immigration with a new round of enthusiasm.[65] Once again Tea Partiers felt as though he was channeling their thoughts.[66] Trump rose higher in national Republican polls than ever before, establishing a twenty-point cushion between himself and his nearest rival, Ted Cruz.[67] Trump maintained this lead throughout the primaries. As Trump began rolling up delegate margins, the Republican establishment provoked national conversations over the possibility of a brokered Republican convention.[68]

But short of the Republican establishment finding a way to abrogate the rules of its own primary process, the remaining alternative to Trump remained Cruz, another populist favorite. But coming up against Trump, Cruz was fatally flawed. His was the populist flavor of 2008, of 2012; of Tea Party 1.0 and 2.0. Trump's was the populist flavor of 2016; of anti-immigrant Tea Party 3.0. An extreme Tea Party free-market fundamentalist and evangelical both, Cruz's entire political career had deeply alienated the party establishment. In his run for the nomination, he based his electoral strategy in the primaries on dominating the evangelical vote. As the Greek tragedy unfolded, establishment figures began reluctantly endorsing Cruz as a means to deny Trump the nomination.[69]

Yet Trump, the thrice-married vulgarian, again confounded analysts by holding his own against Cruz, with polls showing an almost fifty-fifty split among evangelicals.[70] Some pointed to the distinctions among evangelicals in religiosity and church attendance.[71] Others suggested that a historic sense of confusion among evangelicals led them to seek a strong, if not authoritarian, leader.[72] Ben Carson endorsed Trump after dropping out of the race. So, too, did Pat Robertson and Jerry Falwell Jr.[73]

By now, the populist and free-market fundamentalist forces that had come together to form the Tea Party turned severely at odds with one another. Daily fierce debates on Tea Party websites and on talk radio raged between supporters of Cruz and supporters of Trump. Cruz supporters argued in terms of fidelity to conservative principles. He was the last gasp of the Tea Party's commitment to both free-market fundamentalist ideology and popular originalist constitutionalism. Tea Party Cruz supporters argued:

> Real conservatives have a message for the Trump campaign. We are conservatives first and then Republicans. We are Republicans because the party is allegedly the conservative party.[74]

Exasperated, Cruz supporters continued:

> Trump's deranged rantings make any sane person question what he would do when he had the power of the federal government behind him. If you insult the Donald, are you going to have the IRS knocking at your door?
>
> There is something Trump supporters need to realize. He is playing you. . . . If you are a Donald Trump supporter, he is marketing to your outrage, not to any notion of liberty, freedom, or conservatism. [75]

And the pro-Trump Tea Partiers? The populist 3.0 Tea Partiers?

> Cruz [is a] politician. . . . Smooth talking fraud . . . Donald Trump is the one that will help to bring this country back. . . . Looking at how divided this room is should frighten all of

us. . . . Hearing that Donald is going to build up the Republican Party should tell you a lot. . . . WE NEED DONALD
TRUMP. . . . He will be our Patton, Eisenhower, et cetera; he
will be strong, and he will get done what he has promised. . . .
Illegals, the wall, China, Mexico, the economy, jobs, ISIS, and
protecting our country from all evil and sharia law . . . If
you elect Cruz . . . you will be condoning everything Obama
has done while in office . . . and you're getting politics as
usual . . . [76]

This was the Tea Party in its death throes. The end came with
Trump clinching the nomination. Judson Phillips of Tea Party
Nation, a Cruz man, wrote the following obituary:

Today we have Donald Trump as the presumptive Republican
nominee. Whether you like him or don't like him, pay attention to what he is saying. He is not even giving lip service to
the idea of shrinking the government. He is not even talking
about cutting government or cutting taxes. Trump talks a lot
and says very little. He has it [sic] talking points of, "make
America great again," but he does not go into a lot of detail
about that.

Our founding fathers warned us that liberty would remain
safe in this nation only as long as the federal government was
restrained. They created a form of government and a constitution to do just that.

Today, both major candidates want to expand the size and
scope of the federal government.

Two years ago, the Tea Party was riding high. The Tea
Party had cheered the defeat of House Majority Leader Eric
Cantor. The Tea Party had brought about a Republican majority in the Senate, much as it had done for the House four years
earlier.

Yet today, we face a stunning defeat.[77]

The Imagined Other

Like the Cruz advocates in the Tea Party, what agonized the Republican establishment most profoundly was candidate Trump's rejection of the very cornerstones of modern conservative ideology: free markets, free trade, neoconservative foreign policy.[78] Trump did not share mainline American conservatism's contempt for the welfare state; he even spoke well of universal health care.[79] He was an unabashed fan of government use of eminent domain. His unrelenting use of lawsuits in both business and politics made a mockery of establishment Republicans' long-held animus toward "the trial lawyers."

In foreign affairs, although he was for a no-holds-barred approach to ISIS (e.g., waterboarding and more; going after terrorists' families), he was contemptuous of neoconservatism's signature endeavor: the invasion of Iraq.[80] He even breached the taboo about criticizing George Bush for allowing the 9/11 attacks on his watch.[81] Trump's criticism of free-trade agreements was a drumbeat throughout his electoral campaign. The economic dispossession of the white working class was a forty-year wave that, in politics, finally broke in the 2016 electoral cycle. A widely publicized study published in December 2015 showed that epidemic rates of suicide and substance abuse—alcohol, heroin, and prescription opioids—combined to increase the mortality rate for whites between the ages of forty-five and fifty-four, with high-school education or less, in a manner paralleled "only [by] HIV/AIDS in contemporary times."[82]

But the redoubling of support for Trump when he added Muslims to Mexicans, as those he would use exceptional measures to keep outside the country's borders, confirms that the populist-establishment existential standoff over immigration remained the significant through-line of the Republican nominating race. The emotional, identity-driven impetus behind populist support of Trump was a more deeply rooted motivator than the material issues that confronted rural and rust-belt America. In an extraordinary study published in 2016, Jonathan T. Rothwell and Pablo Diego-Rosell demonstrated that the best predictor for Trump support was geographic: living in areas with little or scant exposure to immigrants:

> The analysis provides clear evidence that those who view Trump favorably are disproportionately living in racially and culturally isolated zip codes and commuting zones. Holding other factors constant, support for Trump is highly elevated in areas with few college graduates and in neighborhoods that standout within the larger commuting zone for being white, segregated enclaves, with little exposure to blacks, Asians, and Hispanics.[83]

This is an important conclusion that seems almost counter-intuitive at first: Distaste for immigrants—willingness to buy into Trump's relentless disparaging of them as criminals and subhuman—does not correlate with having immigrants in one's midst. Quite the contrary. It correlates with immigrants at a remove. It correlates with one's knowledge of immigrants being second-hand, being something one gets told about rather than something one sees, hears, or otherwise directly experiences. It is a sentiment based not on a concrete experience, but on an abstract image, an effigy.

In his seminal study of nationalism, Benedict Anderson called the fellow-feeling nationalism engenders among millions who will "never know most of their fellow members, meet them, or even hear of them" an "imagined community."[84] It is a relationship to something abstract, but felt with passion. And it gives one identity. What the Rothwell study illustrates is the inverse of Anderson's imagined communities. Both are acts of imagination. But instead of Anderson's imaginary object, which is about "us," the members of the imagined community, the imaginary object among Trump supporters is about "them," the Other. What Rothwell is telling us is that among Trump voters, the most compelling Other, the scariest, most depraved Other is the Imagined Other. Anderson's imagined community confers identity through the feeling of positive bonds toward one's fellows. But in Trump's community, identity emerges through othering; defining "us" follows as a negation of defining the odious "them." Othering is the alternative route to identity formation. And it is a route to establishing identity that, as pointed out earlier, operates through opposition to and vilification of this Other.

When the Other is imaginary, it is a blank screen. The attributes assigned to it are the products of the imagination of the observer. They are projections. Over the course of his presidency, Obama would become the nonpareil object of Tea Party projection. Projected theories of his birth abounded; as well his plans to Muslimize America, or his own covert Muslim faith; or an agenda inculcated in him by a Communist or his anti-colonial father. This projection reached a height at the Republican Convention of 2012. The actor Clint Eastwood gave a speech with the conceit of Obama "sitting" in an empty chair by his side. This was projection in pure form. On a handful of occasions in his speech, Eastwood conveyed that Obama had responded to the questions he asked of him. Those responses were either "Shut up" or "Go fuck yourself" (which Eastwood conveyed obliquely). For weeks thereafter, populist activists across the country placed empty chairs on their porches, or posted photos pointing at empty chairs in their living rooms, an activity they called "Eastwooding."[85]

Arguably, the mother text of American right-wing studies is Richard Hofstadter's 1964 essay, "The Paranoid Style of American Politics." For Hofstadter, the condition of irreconcilability is crucial to the emergence of paranoid politics. He wrote:

Perhaps the central situation conducive to the diffusion of
the paranoid tendency is a confrontation of opposed interests
which are (or are felt to be) totally irreconcilable, and thus
by nature not susceptible to the normal political processes of
bargain and compromise.[86]

As we have argued here, 2016's irreconcilability on the American right—the two competing irreconcilable existential crises,
that of the populists and that of the Republican establishment—
was the cornerstone condition that created both the populists'
final repudiation of the Republican establishment and their
migration to Trumpian nationalism. Projection (or projective
identification in this case) is fundamental to paranoid thinking,
in individuals and in political movements. In the case of projection on to the figure of Obama, what ended with the pure form
of Eastwooding began with Trump's initial foray into politics,
birtherism. In between, and closely related to birtherism was
distrust of Obama's Christianity and the belief that he was a
secret Muslim. Polls in Alabama and Mississippi in advance of
their primary elections in 2012 found that only an astounding 12
and 14 percent of Republicans respectively believed Obama to
be a Christian.[87] As late as September 2015, 43 percent of Republicans nationally believed Obama was a secret Muslim according to a CNN/ORC survey.[88]

Like the conspiracy thinking that ran through received Tea
Party conceptions of liberals down through the decades, projection depends on unfalsifiability—the ability for the person or
group projecting to be able to tell off their antagonists, finally:
"You can't prove I'm wrong."[89] This is the endgame of paranoid
thinking, the logical end of all paranoid argumentation. It is
the point at which counter evidence can no longer touch a fixed
and immovable idea. An example: In October 2009, Rush Limbaugh was caught out having fallen for a hoax. This hoax was an

alleged Obama college thesis that had been posted online, and which seemed to attack the Constitution. After the hoax was revealed, logically Limbaugh had to face his error. Instead, he believed that the fact that the thesis was a fake was immaterial. He managed to hang this projection on Obama, saying, "I know Obama thinks it."[90]

Try disproving that.

The conspiracy theories that animated the Tea Party for seven-plus years migrated in 2016 to reside under the Trumpian umbrella of a world "rigged" by the "globalists."

4

Othering Nationalism

The (Bookend) Revolution of 2016

"We need a political revolution:" The line was a standard in Bernie Sanders's speeches during his campaign for the Democratic nomination for president in 2016.[1]

While Bernie may have talked revolution, it was the election's eventual and improbable winner, Donald Trump, who ushered one in.[2] Trump, whose perspective was more egotistical than global, was not himself much of a revolutionary. Rather, he was the vehicle for revolution. His election was the second such startling development among the established Western democracies in 2016. That June, in the Brexit referendum, the United Kingdom voted to remove itself from the European Union, of which it had been a member for over forty years. The global dimension of this zeitgeist—a challenge to the international arrangements and Western democratic norms that had been in place since the end of World War II—had been apparent for years. Anti-immigrant parties had been making headway in Western Europe since before the refugee crisis of 2015; since then they had burgeoned and become forces in national parliaments and in the European parliament. Already, such parties had come to power beyond the West, in the former Soviet bloc, in Turkey and India, in the Philippines. But now, shockingly, they had won winner-take-all national elections in the two oldest democracies, in the very citadels of the Western liberal tradition.

In the U.S. election, the most conspicuous of the revolutionary voices was that of Stephen Bannon.[3] Bannon served as Trump's final campaign strategist and senior White House advisor in the first months of the new administration. Recalling the role of Karl Rove, in whose chair he sat in his brief tenure in the administration, Bannon was frequently referred to as Trump's "brain."[4] Barely a week into the new administration, Bannon outraged the political world by telling the *New York Times* to shut up.

> The media should be embarrassed and humiliated and keep its mouth shut and just listen for a while," Mr. Bannon said in an interview on Wednesday.
>
> "I want you to quote this," Mr. Bannon added. "The media here is the opposition party. They don't understand this country. They still do not understand why Donald Trump is the president of the United States.[5]

What Bannon was talking about was incompatible worldviews. For him, the media, what the British call the "chattering classes," were stuck in a conventional-wisdom worldview that had been superseded by a new order.[6] In the conventional view, politics is seen as a closed bipolar game: liberals versus conservatives; Democrats versus Republicans; right versus left. This conventional thinking could even accommodate the extremes on this spectrum, Bernie Sanders's democratic socialists on the left and the Obama-era Tea Party insurgency on the right. But it could not, Bannon was saying, grasp his insurgency, the Trump insurgency.

For Bannon both the standard bipolar view of the political order, as well as its very protagonists, the Republican and Democratic Parties, were tired, weak, and worn out. They were no match for his vital new movement, the political revolution for which he spoke and which had prevailed in the Trump election. The established political forces' very resistance to Bannon's new message diminished the old order and nurtured the new. At his most Hegelian, Bannon wrote in an email to the *Washington Post*:

> What we are witnessing now is the birth of a new political order, and the more frantic a handful of media elites become, the more powerful that new political order becomes itself.[7]

Bannon's telling the *Times* to shut up bore an eerie and ironic resemblance to an earlier admonition at a time of cultural revolution in the United States. In the words of the 2016 Nobel laureate:

> *Come writers and critics . . .*
> *Come senators, congressmen . . .*
> *Come mothers and fathers*
> *Throughout the land*
> **And don't criticize**
> **What you can't understand . . .**
> *For the times they are a-changin' [emphasis added]*[8]

The F Word

For seventy years after the end of World War II, "fascism" was an epithet. It was a word thrown by one side, right or left, at the other (or sometimes within a side) when argumentation failed, when it ended in frustration and anger. It was to label the opponent with what was, ironically, the calumny both left and right agreed upon to indicate that what the opponent was saying or represented was beyond the pale. It was to tar the other with the most odious word in the collective political vocabulary. In recent years, as political argumentation has mushroomed across the internet, it has become a cliché that sooner or later arguments will likely dead end in someone calling someone else Hitler.[9]

And there was good reason for fascism to be considered the ultimate epithet. The enduring odium of fascism lay in its having been forged in war. By its scale and by its trauma, war is unsurpassed in its capacity to produce lasting images and memories and categories that bedevil the worldviews of individuals and nations. The unprecedented level of death and dislocation in World War II would by itself have been sufficient to condemn the enemy, fascism, in the minds of its adversaries, well after the conflict was over. Unlike World War I, the hostilities and the horrors of the second war in Europe were not confined to the distant front. The Nazis' early sweep across the face of the continent, according to plan, ensured that the distinction between civilian and combatant would dissolve. Cities quickly became accepted targets for bombardment. Nazi diplomacy and its occupation forces respected no local authority or custom. Occupied countries were administered to serve the interests of the Reich—they were sources of loot and labor. Who was to serve what purpose was determined by rigid racial criteria. Whole populations were uprooted and transported to be used as slave labor.

The operative principle of this regime was terror. Such atrocities were unknown to contemporary European populations. Never mind that similar systems had been imposed on African and Asian peoples by the governments of several of the countries the Nazis conquered. That was imperialism. Its tactics of domination were distant and shielded from its citizens.[10] From the point of view of the vast majority of Europeans, what was happening to them was unheard of. But the Nazis went even further than in Africa and Asia. Some populations were selected simply to be exterminated. War's end would reveal that the familiar means of mass production had been harnessed for the sole purpose of genocide. In short, not only would fascism come to be associated with atrocities previously unseen on the planet;

not only would it be associated with having visited unknown brutalities on conquered populations; fascism had also produced the greatest mass mobilization of sadism in history. It had done the unspeakable.

But fascism as purely an epithet ended in 2015 in the United States. And it ended at the level of presidential politics. For the first time since World War II, Donald Trump's 2016 presidential campaign provoked a serious discussion of the threat of fascism in America. Above all, it was Trump's scapegoating of immigrants that gave rise to this conversation. Scapegoating arguments are simple, if barefaced. In the first place, they require identifying, and exaggerating, the dysfunctions of American life—what Trump would call "carnage" in his inaugural address:

> But for too many of our citizens, a different reality exists: Mothers and children trapped in poverty in our inner cities; rusted-out factories scattered like tombstones across the landscape of our nation; an education system, flush with cash, but which leaves our young and beautiful students deprived of knowledge; and the crime and gangs and drugs that have stolen too many lives and robbed our country of so much unrealized potential.[11]

The second step in scapegoating is vehemently to assign blame for the dysfunctions. This blaming was the political and emotional heart of Trump's campaign: the scapegoats were the immigrants. They were criminals. They were vermin.[12] To the ears of liberal America, to the ears as well of much of this country's traditional right, this scapegoating evoked Nazism. It evoked the political movement that came to power scapegoating the Jews. That called them less than human. That, in power, engaged in genocide.

The concern that Trump evoked over fascism spanned both

the liberal Democratic world and establishment Republicans. Martin O'Malley twice called Trump a fascist from the stage of the Democratic Party's primary debates. The last orthodox Republican to stay in the primary race against Trump, Ohio governor John Kasich, ran a campaign ad that aped German Protestant pastor Martin Niemöller's famous admonition ("First they came for the socialists . . . ") against apathy in the face of the rise of Nazism.[13] Conservative *New York Times* columnist Ross Douthat began considering the question of Trump and fascism as early as December 2015, months before the first votes were cast in the Republican presidential primaries.[14] In the spring of 2016, neoconservative éminence grise Robert Kagan saw in Trump's campaign "how fascism comes to America."[15] *The Washington Post* published a scorecard grading Trump's fascist "attributes."[16] Umberto Eco's 1995 article in which he offered a list of features that are typical of what he called Ur-Fascism, or Eternal Fascism, became an internet sensation, informing dozens and dozens of writers who took up the charge of transforming fascist from a scattershot word of opprobrium in American political discourse to a pressing analytical concern.[17]

Since the inauguration, observers' fears of fascism expanded to include the Trump administration's wholesale subversion of democratic norms and its affinity with the illiberal, or authoritarian, international zeitgeist. The conservative writer David Frum both anticipated and documented these developments.[18] Historian Timothy Snyder published his alarm, *On Tyranny*, within a month of the inauguration.[19] Jason Stanley's *How Fascism Works* and Levitsky and Ziblatt's *How Democracies Die* mapped the use of fascism's tactics and strategy on to the world's current illiberal regimes, including the Trump government in the United States.[20] In 2018, former secretary of state Madeleine Albright addressed how democracies move in authoritarian directions in a volume she called *Fascism: A Warning*.[21]

With their frank white nationalism, the most ideologically extreme of Trump's supporters, what came to be called the alt-right, radicalized and racialized the sentiment of dispossession they shared with Trump's populist base. Their infamous Charlottesville chant, "You will not replace us," was at once a cry of defiance to the multicultural trends of American society and an angry promise to restore the white nationalists' gauzy-eyed image of an earlier age of white domination, when, in their imaginations, people in this country knew their proper places. Trump's faint criticism of Charlottesville, his conviction that there were "good people" in the alt-right's torch-lit march, evoked a notable frisson among those who feared the resurrection of fascist power.

The Donald and the Duce

Fascism is of Italian invention. The pre–March on Rome movement and the post–March on Rome state were the first historical entities to label themselves fascist. The term "fascism" is an anglicization of the Italian *fascismo*. The adoption of the Italian term was a universal linguistic transformation in the international political vocabulary of the twentieth century. Fascism in Italy was a product of the immediate post–World War I period, founded at a sparsely attended meeting in Piazza San Sepolcro in Milan. Three-and-a-half years later, on October 30, 1922, the king of Italy asked the movement's leader, Benito Mussolini, to form a government after thousands of his supporters had marched on Rome. With Mussolini's accession, the liberal parliamentary regime that had come into existence in 1860, the product of the Italian Risorgimento, the Italian unification, was doomed. By early 1926, the new regime had consolidated its power to the point where opposition parties were illegal, their leaders for the most part in exile or in prisons; civil liberties, including freedom of the press, suppressed; organized labor crushed; and the process begun of formally merging the organs of government with the structure of the Fascist Party. Justification for the regime's policies and general brutality was to be found in a mystified vision merging the interests of the nation with Fascism, and in the elevation of the movement's leader, the Duce, into a figure of nonrational and unquestioned authority.

The most striking parallel between Trump and Mussolini as each was aspiring to power was the ideological goulash that each represented. From the heights of the conservative establishment came the lament that Trump was no conservative.[22] Cruz supporters called him a liberal. But liberals were appalled at Trump's views on everything from tax policy to policing to immigration to civil rights. So too, Mussolini utterly frustrated contemporary stabs at fitting him into established boxes. The very name of his movement stood out from every other contemporary political party—liberals, socialists—in embracing no political principle. His was the ism of the *fascio*—emphasizing a random collection, originally a handful of straw. The ideology we associate with fascism came later.

Like Mussolini, who had been a radical socialist for many years, Trump made a transit from the left—he is a former Democrat—to the hard right. Each man rose in a political environment conventional wisdom viewed as bipolar. And each conflated the two opposing parties of that bipolarity. Trump managed to attach the intense feeling of betrayal the populists of the Republican right felt toward that party's establishment to their long-standing resentment toward the Democratic "liberal elite." He presented himself as the outsider crusading against a single corrupt establishment, the "globalists." Mussolini used the opposition both conventional poles of Italian politics—liberals and socialists—mounted against Italy's entering World War I to conflate them as "neutralists" or "defeatists."

As he would write looking back after a decade in power: "Fascism was not given out to the wet nurse of a doctrine elaborated beforehand round a table. . . . in its first two years it was a movement against all parties."[23]

On style points, Trump, as candidate and as president, has given Mussolini a run for his money. Each was dismissed as a clown (*pagliacccio!*[24]). Their rallies offered ritualized back-and-forth exchanges between the leader and his supporters.[25] Each was famous for exaggerated comic-opera gestures as well as facial contortions. Each introduced a level of vulgarity into political discourse, gutter talk and insults, the likes of which had never been heard before.[26] Each had been a notable success in media—Mussolini as a newspaper editor, Trump as a reality TV star. A favored expression in Mussolini's movement was "*Me ne frego*," politely translated as "I don't give a damn." The motto of Steve Bannon, who unleashed Trump to be Trump when he came on as the "CEO" of Trump's campaign, is "Honey badger don't give a shit." Mussolini and Trump both disliked shaking hands.[27]

Significantly, Trump evokes what scholars of fascism call the leadership principle, one of fascism's most breathtaking departures from democracy's caucusing, coalition-seeking political culture. Like Hitler, the Führer, Mussolini, the Duce, was regarded as the vessel of the national will, a providential deliverance to the nation. Ann Coulter summarized what his followers have felt about Trump: "Thank God for raising up Donald Trump and giving us a chance to save the country."[28] Trump would meet this adulation with such remarks as "I am the chosen one"; "I am the only one who matters."

Like Mussolini, who conjured up the glories of the ancient Roman empire, Trump captivates audiences feeling downtrodden by conjuring up a return to a golden age, when America was "great." "I am your voice," Trump told his convention audience. As to the state of the country: "I alone can fix it." One is reminded of a favored slogan of Italian Fascism, one that would be immortalized in framed sayings in classrooms across the country during Mussolini's twenty years in power: *"Mussolini ha sempre ragione."* (Mussolini is always right.)

Like Trump, Mussolini struck his profoundest chord with a class of people suffering from a profound feeling of dispossession. His earliest followers were returning war veterans whose experiences in the trenches of World War I rendered them no longer fit for the traditional village life that awaited them as it had generations of their forbearers.[29] The settlement of the war at Versailles, which rejected many of Italy's war claims, left them also feeling dispossessed of the heroic victory they felt they had earned in battle. Trump's followers' strongest sentiment across the board—from the populists to the alt-right—is that of feeling dispossessed of the America they have known. Trump's candidacy represented a last hope of turning around the direction of a demographically changing country.

La Rivoluzione Mancata

Italian political commentators during the rise of Fascism were dealing with an unknown, an historical novelty. Like current American observers and politicians, they looked for models in contemporary political thinking in seeking to understand the new political permutation that had thrust itself on the country. One such model was what the Italians called *la rivoluzione mancata*. Translated, it means "the failed revolution" or "the would-be revolution." As failed revolution, *la rivoluzione mancata* emerged as an explanation for the shortcomings of the Italian Risorgimento, the 1860–70 unification of the country that among other dysfunctions left a yawning and enduring economic and cultural gap between north and south.[30]

But it was as would-be revolution that *la rivoluzione mancata* was invoked by political commentators in 1921 and 1922 who observed the unprecedented tactics, and success, of Mussolini's Fascist movement. Previously, 1919 and 1920 were the *biennio rosso*, the "red two years," in Italy. The *biennio rosso* saw a remarkable series of workers' triumphs outside parliament. In the major agricultural zones of Italy, the Po Valley and Apulia, vast numbers of rural day laborers were organized into peasant leagues, establishing a socialist infrastructure that controlled municipal governments and the hiring and wages of farmworkers. In the northern industrial cities labor reached unprecedented power, taking over local administrations and, as in the countryside, transforming the conduct of business, public services, and everyday life and culture. Trade unions won unprecedented contracts in the industrial centers of the north. The Factory Council movement, modeled on Russian soviets, established workers' control over production. The first national elections after the war returned the Italian Socialist Party as the strongest political party in parliament. Russia had turned into the Soviet Union. Revolution was threatening in Germany. In Italy, the expectation was widespread that the Socialist Party would shortly come to power and that socialist revolution, building on workers' victories in the factories and in the fields, was imminent.

The tide turned when the April 1920 occupation of the FIAT factory in Turin ended in a lockout and the workers' capitulation to the company's intransigence. It was at that point that Fascism found its historical calling. The Fascists would halt the Socialists' momentum with violence. With truncheons and castor oil, they turned back the accomplishments of the *biennio rosso*. Fascist squads—its members were known as *squadristi* or Blackshirts—would wreck offices of Socialists and government administrations the Socialists controlled. These attacks were called *spedizioni punitive*, punitive expeditions.[31] It was a politics of terror, but a terror that was at one with the electoral party; they were part and parcel of the same political organization. The Fascist Party ran candidates at local and national levels, while the squads were unleashed against their political opposition. Fascist leaders, including Mussolini, sat in parliament and spoke openly of a carrot-and-stick policy—insisting they would get their way legally and in line with parliamentary procedure (the carrot) or through violence outside parliament (the stick.)[32]

This was something utterly new in a parliamentary regime, in an electoral democracy, and invoking the *rivoluzione mancata*, the would-be revolution, was an explanation that looked to the *biennio rosso* for an answer. The Socialists had been making a promise they failed to keep—the would-be socialist revolution. The collapse of the *biennio rosso* created a political vacuum. Another revolution, a counter-revolution, the fascists, filled the vacuum.

The transition from Obama to Trump follows the would-be *rivoluzione mancata* model. With the widespread talk of a "transformative" administration on its way, of the coming new New Deal, the Obama government-elect was burdened with great expectations. *Time* magazine published a cover of Obama as Roosevelt behind the wheel of a 1930s car, smiling a toothy FDR smile, wearing a Rooseveltian hat and glasses with a cigarette in a long holder clamped between his teeth.[33] Equally widespread was the subsequent sense that Obama backed off the revolutionary promise once in office.[34] In this view, much is made of Obama's moderation and his dependence on a veteran economic team bound to the Democrats' neoliberalism of the Bill Clinton years. Here is a recent opinion piece that is exemplary of this view of Obama:

If he'd been in the mood to press the case, Obama might have found widespread public appetite for the sort of aggressive, interventionist restructuring of the American economy that Franklin D. Roosevelt conjured with the New Deal. . . . [When] Obama took office . . . rather than try for a Rooseveltian home run, he bunted: Instead of pushing for an aggressive stimulus to rapidly expand employment and long-term structural reforms in how the economy worked, Obama and his team responded to the recession with a set of smaller emergency measures designed to fix the immediate collapse of financial markets.[35]

There have been arguments that disappointment in Obama may have played a part in the coming of Donald Trump, a point of view with particular weight among supporters of the energized left wing that began vying for clout in the Democratic Party as it approached the presidential election of 2020.

Incrementalism during the Obama years was small steps to nowhere, ones that far from cementing a new progressive majority actually helped open the door to the populist right.[36]

Obama's election created a right-wing populist backlash that was institutionalized in the Tea Party. The idea of the *rivoluzione mancata* raises the counterfactual question of what direction those populists might have taken if the would-be revolution had materialized. Free-market fundamentalist ideology was held only epidermically by the Tea Party populists. It was relinquished to follow Donald Trump's nationalism. Might a robust transformative agenda realized under Obama have moved them in a different ideological direction? The meaning of the *rivoluzione mancata* of 2009–2016 was a fundamental question that confronted the Democratic Party in anticipation of the 2020 election. As Eli Zaretsky noted:

> Obama's articulation of the need for what he called a "new mindset," not just a new policy, was in good part responsible for his charisma in 2008 (much greater than Trump's). Obama's switch from charismatic leader to pragmatic manager once he took office left a void into which Trump stepped eight years later. It is impossible to understand Trump's historic role without seeing that he is fulfilling, however perversely, the promise of a new beginning that Obama made in 2008.[37]

Othering Nationalism

All that said, we are not in a moment stalked by a real fascist movement. Fascism's novel political invention was the marriage of an electoral party with a private militia.[38] Without the looming threat of violence that lies at the heart of terrorism, without punitive expeditions, without uniforms or black, brown, or other color shirts, we may have politics that share fascism's rejection of democratic norms, or even of democracy itself; but we do not have fascism. True, candidate Donald Trump made repeated invitations at his rallies to resort to violence. But this merely produced a few sporadic events. No systematic organized vigilante force, uniformed, shirted, or otherwise, developed around the Trump campaign. Nor did it develop after the inauguration. Fascism's signature feature—the private militia married to the electoral party—is absent.[39]

The more accurate historical analogy to the current moment is not the rise of fascism in the wake of World War I. It is instead the rise of a new nationalism, above all in Europe, around the turn of the twentieth century and in the two decades before the war. What arose then was a novel and aggressive nationalism, different from its nationalist predecessors in its thought, appeal, and goals. Earlier nationalisms stemmed from two related motivations. One was a sense of communal destiny, a conviction that atomized states that shared a common language and culture belonged together, represented a higher moral and political unity: a nation. German unification, the 1871 pulling together of dozens of political entities under the leadership of Prussia, is illustrative of this national destiny impulse. On the Italian peninsula, this sense of national destiny was accompanied by the second motivation: to be rid of rule—Austrian, Bourbon—by those not of the nation. This motivation, similar to what would come to animate movements of national liberation in the second half of the twentieth century, had had an earlier and revolutionary expression in the 1823 Greek War of Independence against the Ottomans.

These were inward-looking nationalisms, focused on bringing political and geographical reality in line with a cultural imperative. When the new turn-of-the-century nationalism looked inward, it was with a novel, quarrelsome, and often confrontational attitude: those living inside the nation, but not judged part of the nation—culturally, linguistically or, eventually, racially—came to be seen as injuries to the very feeling of the national community. Tolerance for the presence of "Others" became a perishing value among the new nationalists. Intolerance could be expressed in assertions of superiority or in scapegoating—the "Other" responsible for the dysfunctions of the emerging modern world. Intolerance was finally an expulsive itch—the desire for what would come to be called "ethnic cleansing" a century later. At an extreme, the "Other" could come to be regarded as "the enemy within." After World War I, most of these nationalist movements became absorbed by their countries' fascist movements.

Nationalism can be an elusive concept. How, for example,

does it differ from patriotism, the feeling of identity and pride in one's country? Certainly, nationalism is an exaggeration of patriotic feeling. But it is more than that. It is a statement about how the world works. It is a theory of history. Or better, a theory of history with a master concept, an ideological key—the nation. The most radical of the new nationalists at the turn of the twentieth century regarded themselves as revolutionaries. Often—and not without irony—the nationalists would transpose revolutionary socialist thinking into their image of what their revolution would look like.

Marx's well-known theory of history (and theory of revolution) is driven by a master concept, class. In Marx's familiar drama, a rising capitalist class, the bourgeoisie, overthrew feudalism. And the bourgeoisie would get its comeuppance at the hands of a rising class that they themselves had spawned, the proletariat. The "motor force" of history is class conflict. As a first approximation, this new nationalism resembled the Marxist theory of history where the concept of class is simply replaced by the concept of nation. And history is the story of struggle for dominance among nations. For example, the Italian Nationalist Association, founded in 1910, called Italy a "proletarian nation." Marx's dialectics remained intact, but "nation" was slipped into the theoretical slot "class" had formerly occupied. With nation as its master concept, the motor force of history was no longer "class struggle" but the rise and fall of nations. For the nationalists, the nation provided the basis for both a theory of revolution and a theory of history. When class struggle morphs into the struggle between nations, revolution in this worldview occurs through war.

The new nationalism swept across borders, taking root largely among young men, often artists, who felt profoundly alienated from the unheroic possibilities they saw on offer in their societies. The new nationalism was vital. It engaged the fierce us/them group emotions—loyalty inwards, aggression outwards—that characterize human relations at simpler sociological levels like the family or the tribe. What was new at the turn of the twentieth century, and has been resurrected in recent years, was attaching these passions to the nation. This experiment of the early 1900s demanded that what had traditionally been feelings directed toward discrete groups, usually no bigger than a city, now moved to something more abstract. A new, and often mystical, symbolism was required to encompass the new object, the nation, within the sphere of human passion, human worship. Yuri Slezkine, a historian who specializes in understanding the place of outgroups in the face of Eastern European nationalism, writes:

> The worship of the new state as an old tribe (commonly known as nationalism) became the new opium of the people. Total strangers became kinsmen on the basis of common languages, origins, ancestors, and rituals duly standardized and disseminated for the purpose. The nation was family writ large: ascriptive and blood-bound but stretched well beyond human memory or face recognition, as only a metaphor could be.[40]

In his exceptional study *Fin-de-Siècle Vienna*, Carl Schorske called this "politics in a new key." Why? Because in both style and substance the new nationalists acted outside the bounds of what was known across the left-right spectrum in conventional politics—just as Donald Trump has comported himself from day one in his presidential campaign, throughout the Republican and presidential debates, in his rallies, and into his administration, defining an American version of politics in a new key. In Vienna, the left were the Social Democrats; the right were the liberals. Schorske observes:

> Though one might reject a socialist's position, one could argue with him in the same language. To the liberal mind, the Social Democrat was unreasonable, but not irrational.[41]

In 1994, the English-American historian of modern Europe, Tony Judt, looked at the rise of nationalism in the former Soviet bloc in the wake of the end of the Cold War. What he saw was the beginning of the movements that have now taken center stage across Europe, Asia, and the United States. Judt called the phenomenon "the new old nationalism." He wrote:

> The nature of this nationalism is to seek out the Other inside the body politic. From Estonia to Romania, no sooner are small countries back on the map than their first order of business is to set up language tests to determine who is and is not a "real" Latvian, Ukrainian, etc.[42]

In Trump's worldview, that of a familial rather than a corporate businessman, the nationalist theory of history as the struggle among nations remains intact, but the struggle has been transposed to international trade. Now, the key to reversing the fortunes of the American working class lay in renegotiated trade deals. This is the guiding principle of the nationalist America-First ideology in Donald Trump's politics. The likes of China and Mexico are not trading partners, but economic enemies. Wilbur Ross is Trump's secretary of commerce. Peter Navarro is the director of the White House National Trade Council Trump initiated, modeled on the National Security Council.[43] Together Ross and Navarro wrote the 2016 Trump campaign's economic plan. In it they challenged their critics as follows:

Those who suggest that Trump trade policies will ignite a trade war ignore the fact that we are already engaged in a trade war.[44]

In May 2019, in a *Washington Post* op-ed, Steve Bannon made clear the Manichaean policy implications under this world-view: "We're in an economic war with China. It's futile to compromise."[45]

The Nationalist International

In 2014, a year before Trump announced his run for the presidency, Viktor Orbán, the prime minister of Hungary and arguably the world's foremost advocate and practitioner of illiberal democracy—regimes that retain and claim legitimacy through elections, but systematically curtail civil liberties and institutional checks and balances—offered his view that illiberalism was the uniquely viable capitalist path forward after the world financial crisis of 2008 and the subsequent Great Recession. Orbán argued that "the great global race . . . is underway to create the most competitive state." In his view countries operating under the rules of international organizations, like the European Union, or ones that tolerate the functioning of international nongovernmental organizations (NGOs) in their societies, would not advance themselves in the current version of the struggle among nations that is the motor force of history in the nationalist perspective.

> Societies that are built on the state organization principle of liberal democracy will probably be incapable of maintaining their global competitiveness in the upcoming decades and will instead probably be scaled down unless they are capable of change.[46]

Orbán argued that there were "three great changes in the global regime during the 20th century:" one each at the end of the two world wars, 1918 and 1945; and one at the end of the Cold War, 1989. After 1989, the reigning global regime, à la Fukuyama, became liberal democracy. But that changed, according to Orbán, after the global financial crisis of 2008. In his view, though it was more subtle, the aftermath of the financial crisis was of the same world-historical moment as the end of the twentieth-century wars. Liberal democracy was (and is) being overtaken.

In 1848, Karl Marx and Friedrich Engels wrote *The Communist Manifesto*. Their view was that as capitalism had overtaken feudalism, what Europe was then living through was the process of capitalism being overtaken by its dialectical successor. Thus, they began the manifesto with their famous opening sentence: "A specter is haunting Europe—the specter of Communism."

It is not so much a specter as an oxymoron that is now haunting Europe. And the Americas. And points beyond. That oxymoron is the Nationalist International.

At the international level, too, the current synthesis of ideological nationalism and anti-immigrant populism of which Trumpism is a part differs from twentieth-century fascism. Unlike Communism which developed a Communist International, and unlike Socialism which developed a Socialist International, there was never a viable Fascist International. There are several reasons for this, but one reason, given the nature of identity formation, stands out from the others. Nationalism based purely on the nation-state breeds identities that necessarily come into conflict with similarly defined nationalisms. This is especially true when those nationalisms are bellicose and assert the superiority of one's own nation.

It is hard, in short, to have comradely relations when one

nation calls itself the master race and another the Mediterranean Superman.

But today's version of populist nationalism has overcome this
problem. How? The nationalists in country after country share
a Common Other. And through their "othering," the Nationalist
International has forged a Common Identity. This is the crucial
difference in identity formation that distinguishes current populist nationalism from the fascist nationalisms of the interwar
years of the twentieth century. With a Common Other you get a
Common Identity. With a Common Identity you have the mak-
ings of a Nationalist International.

The shared Other of the Nationalist International are immigrants and refugees. Almost always dark skinned. Often of different religions. And largely hailing from places like the Middle
East and Africa. The USA has an othering specialization in
refugees and immigrants from Latin America. The Nationalist
International's political opposition are the "politically correct"
multiculturalists and feminists, whom the nationalists often call
Cultural Marxists, or the global liberal elite, or simply the globalists, whose power and international organizations—like the
European Union—are in the nationalists' crosshairs.

The shared identity of the Nationalist International, what its
various branches see themselves standing for, goes by many
names. Sometimes they are the defenders of Western civilization. Or of Western culture.[47] Or European civilization. One
American alt-right group called itself Identity Europa. In
Europe, as well as in the United States, some simply call themselves Identitarians. Or Generation Identity.

In the same vein, branches of the Nationalist International
see themselves as the defenders of Christian civilization. Or the
defenders of traditional values. These are the movements that
breed a special animus for gays and feminists. In Poland, the

ruling party, Law and Justice, grounds its populist nationalism in its Catholic culture. At its party's convention in March 2019, the party's leader, Jarosław Kaczyński, declared war on the "gay threat":

> It comes down to, as we know today, sexualization of children from the earliest childhood. We need to fight this. We need to defend the Polish family. We need to defend it furiously because it's a threat to civilization, not just for Poland but for the entire Europe, for the entire civilization that is based on Christianity.[48]

At the top of this food chain is Putin's Russia. More than any other populist leader in Europe, Putin is operating with a geopolitical strategy in mind. He loosely follows the theories of his "brain," the eccentric political philosopher Alexander Dugin, who is something of a cross between Steve Bannon and Rasputin.[49] Dugin's strategy calls for controlling the Eurasian land mass and North Africa, and is based on the 1904 paper "The Geographical Pivot of History" by the British father of geopolitics, Halford Mackinder, who called this, the largest landmass on the planet, the "world island." Mackinder's most famous pronouncement was:

> Who rules East Europe commands the Heartland; Who rules the Heartland commands the World-Island; Who rules the World-Island commands the World.[50]

Dugin's is the thinking behind Putin's projects like the takeover of Crimea and the war of attrition in eastern Ukraine. The goal here is to expand Russian control as far as possible back into the footprint of the former Soviet Union. The complementary strategy has been to undermine the power and solidarity of Russia's neighbors to the west.[51] As Michael McFaul, Stanford political scientist and, between 2012 and 2014, the U.S. ambassador to Russia, argues, this means subverting the alliances that hold the liberal world together:

> The end of the liberal international order . . . that's what he's aiming to do. The breakup of states as you have in the UK, the breakup of alliances and NATO, the breakup of the European Union, those are all things that Putin thinks are in his national interest. Tragically, he had some wins lately.

McFaul sees this vision as inextricably tied to an "ideological affinity" Trump shares with Putin: "[They're] both kind of a self-styled conservative, self-styled nationalist, anti-multilateralist, kind of 'nation-state should come first.'"[52]

At the far end of the Trump coalition, at the white-supremacist alt-right end, Putin is revered. Those who focus on opposing feminism and multiculturalism often call themselves defenders of "tradition." In 2016, Matthew Heimbach, who then headed the alt-right Traditional Workers Party, called Putin "the leader of the free world," and "Russia . . . kind of the axis for nationalists."[53] In the same way that the border between the alt-right and the alt-lite blurs in the USA, as indeed in the Trump coalition itself, what is called traditionalism elides into white nationalism. A report on the neo-Nazi Andrew Anglin observed:

> He developed an almost religious infatuation with Vladimir Putin, or "Czar Putin I, defender of human civilization," as Anglin called him. For Anglin, Putin was a great white savior, a "being of immense power."[54]

Alt-right "founder" Richard Spencer called Russia "the sole white power in the world."[55] America's most well-known KKK figure, David Duke, viewed Russia as holding the "key to white survival."[56] Sam Dickson, a white supremacist and former Ku Klux Klan lawyer who frequently speaks at alt-right gatherings, summarized the view of Putin's Russia as the improbable lodestar of white nationalists:

> I've always seen Russia as the guardian at the gate, as the easternmost outpost of our people. . . . They are our barrier to the Oriental invasion of our homeland and the great protector of Christendom. I admire the Russian people. They are the strongest white people on earth."[57]

Whiteness is the most virulent category of identity in the Nationalist International. The gulf in toxicity between German Nazism and Italian Fascism derived from Nazism's definition of the Other, the Jew, in racial terms. For the Nationalist International, whiteness is, in a perverse manner, the logical final category of identity, where the definition of "us" versus the Other becomes essentialized and its most capacious. Focusing on current dark-skinned immigrants and refugees has neutralized older, sometimes ancient, national antagonisms.[58] It was only in 2018 that Matteo Salvini's League in Italy changed its name from the Northern League, which had been its name since it was established in 1991 as an alliance of six regionalist parties, the most prominent being the Lombard League. Its entry onto the national stage in the wake of the end of the Cold War had a devastating effect on the Communist Party in the industrial north of Italy, where it lustily ate into its vote. The Other of the Northern League was southern Italians; the Northern League argued for northern Italy to separate as the state of Padania from the south of

Italy, which they ruthlessly characterized as a backward country full of thieves and worse. Now—behold populism's ideological fungibility—as the League, southern Italians are in the League's fold.[59] This follows the pattern in the United States where white immigrants—the Irish, the Italians—have moved over time from despised newcomers to within the white sphere. It is a story exemplified in Noel Ignatiev's 1995 study, *How the Irish Became White*.[60]

The sense of solidarity within the Nationalist International is robust. They meet with regularity and appear to love being photographed together. Steve Bannon, whose grasp of contemporary nationalism was key in putting Donald Trump in the White House, has traveled in Europe and Latin America acting as nothing short of an evangelist for the Nationalist International, or what he calls "the Movement."[61] But above all, these groups are networked. The Nationalist International, like much of contemporary commerce of all kinds, is a creature of the age of the internet and social media.

This has resulted in cross-fertilization of ideas across the Atlantic. The chant in Charlottesville that so chillingly exposed the core of America's alt-right movement was "You will not replace us." Replacement theory is an import from right-wing thinkers in France, who began talking about *Le Grand Remplacement* decades ago and now talk about the French having been "invaded," suffering "reverse colonization," or even ethnic "genocide." In Spain, the Vox party entered Parliament for the first time in April 2019 with the imported-from-America slogan "Make Spain Great Again."[62] Meanwhile in countries like Italy, Poland, and Ukraine, there are now activists marching and organizing in the name of whiteness.[63] Culturally and politically this was inconceivable in these and other European countries in years past, but white nationalism and white identity are this era's baleful imports from the USA.

The Fascistogenic Moment
and the Bookends of the Industrial Age

At the turn of the twentieth century, the industrial system was restructuring societies wholesale. It was creating the material circumstances we in the advanced societies take for granted: electrification, modern sanitation and medicine, automobiles, airplanes, radio, mass circulation, newspapers, cinema, and much else.

But it did not come easily. Populations were displaced on a massive scale. Life patterns that had been stable for generations were disrupted as factories demanded labor. Cities grew as people migrated from the countryside and struggled to adjust to rigid clock-based schedules. Life was raw in the new urban settings. Emerging cities not only fed the factories' manpower needs, but also introduced new problems of civil order, novel forms of delinquency, and often ghastly public health problems. Scapegoating seemed to provide an answer to these ills. The very presence of the Other explained lives that were bleak and grim. The new nationalism came into being.

In the 1960s and 1970s writers like Barrington Moore, Nicos Poulantzas, and A.F.K. Organski analyzed the conditions that made societies ripe for successful fascist movements.[64] Fundamental to these theories was citing a national economic structure that had a great disparity in terms of modernization. Post–World War I Italy and Germany both had systems of agricultural land holdings (*latifondisti* and *Junkers*) largely unchanged since feudalism. This was in contrast to highly developed economic sectors like the automotive sector and aeronautics. These were countries that held within them populations profoundly differing in the very stages of economic development they experienced. One stage was the modern, with its severe growing pains. The other was traditional society, largely rural, which was suffering not simply economically but from a sense of disruption and displacement on a historical scale. In these theories, the co-existence of such mismatched sectors in a single country, sectors manifestly at different stages of economic development, created a fascistogenic potential: the mismatched stages offered the most fertile ground for successful fascist movements.

Structurally, something similar is happening in the twenty-first-century United States and much of the West. Industrial systems that offered livable wages and self-respect have degenerated into rust belts. Manufacturing itself has become robotized. The thriving parts of national economies have migrated to financial and information sectors. In the United States, it is as though the dramatis personae of the modern world that was built between the turn of the twentieth century and the early 1970s have parted company—the largely coastal and metropolitan professional, educated classes have moved on to the post-industrial information economy; the laboring classes have not only not moved on, they have fallen backwards, out of the modern industrial system, with no ready replacement. It is the economic-stage disparity, the fascistogenic formula, the likes of Moore and Poulantzas were talking about.

These eras of mismatched economic stages are the bookends of the industrial age, present at the age's coming and going. In each case, the age has been characterized politically by the rise of nationalist movements "in a new key"—othering nationalism. At the end of the industrial age, as at its beginning, aggressive nationalist scapegoating has found a fertile audience. In the United States it was Donald Trump who gave voice to the scapegoating: Foreign countries are stealing our jobs. Illegal Mexican immigrants are not only wrecking the labor market or living off the dole, "they're bringing drugs; they're bringing crime; they're rapists."[65] Muslims are infiltrating the country, bringing sharia law and threatening national security. As Americans watched the election returns that gave Trump the presidency, his eked-out margins in the very heart of blue-collar America—Ohio, Pennsylvania, Wisconsin, Michigan (the home of the United Auto Workers, the very symbol of working-class prosperity and advancement!)—we were watching the industrial age come full circle. The conditions that gave rise to aggressive and othering nationalism at the dawn of the industrial age were again revolutionizing a shaky liberal order.

At this point in America and the West, it makes sense to look back and ask what brought about the transition from a fascistogenic moment into fascism proper. The answer to this is quite straightforward. What transpired in the passage from the early-twentieth-century blossoming of othering nationalism to the rise of fascism was war. It was a mere four months after the armistice that ended World War I that Fascism was born in the meeting in Milan's Piazza San Sepolcro. The March on Rome, Fascism's coming to power, came three-and-a-half years later— less than the duration of one presidential term in the United States. The nationalist thinking that had engaged the handful of activists before the war schooled the young men by the millions in the trenches. When dissatisfaction and a yawning sense of displacement overtook the boys who returned to civilian life, the enemy was now on the home front and the way to defeat them that came ready to hand was as a militia.

One of Donald Trump's many occasions for clarification during the campaign was in reference to his remarking "I love war."[66] Commentators have speculated that, like other authoritarians, he might try to cure sagging popularity or divert attention from scandal by going to war.[67] If Americans' anxieties about the dangers of fascism are to amount to a real emergency, war is the likely intervening variable to make it happen.

5

The Road to the Tiki Torches

The Blurry Convergence of Alienation and White Nationalism

Donald Trump's illiberal movement, his campaign, and his government, are distinguished from fascist movements by the absence of an organized militia.

But that absence was not for a want of trying.

The serious white nationalist and neo-Nazi elements of Trump's coalition, the alt-right, believed the time had come to go to the next level, to create a militia the thrust of whose politics would be street fighting. That was the meaning of Charlottesville. The goal of the August 2017 Unite the Right rallies they organized at the home of the University of Virginia was to create a unified right militia. The planners hoped to coalesce their militants into a single militia—this was the image they prefigured on their tiki-torch-lit march the evening before the major violence took place.

Earlier, in April 2017, the alt-right had engaged in street fighting in Berkeley, the home of the University of California. Among the alt-right leadership and rank and file, this became known as the Battle of Berkeley, and it was a watershed.[1] After the Battle of Berkeley, Richard Spencer, the alt-right's most well-known leader, often regarded as the founder of the alt-right, exalted in the violence. "We have entered a new world," he declared on his website. "We have entered a world of political violence. And I don't think anything is going to be the same. We are back in the 1930s."[2]

Spencer was certain American politics had now reached

what he summarized as "Weimar"—the German parliamentary democracy that emerged post World War I, after the fall of the Kaiser, and which dead-ended in Nazism in 1933 when, in a post-election environment, German president Paul von Hindenburg appointed Adolph Hitler chancellor. The specific element of "Weimar" Spencer was referring to was street fighting. The Nazis, following the model of the Fascists in Italy, created paramilitary squads—Brown Shirts—who often battled members of Germany's Communist Party on the streets.[3]

The alt-right fully racializes the acid sense of *dispossession*—loss of a seat at the table—that distinguishes right populist identity movements from "traditional" identity movements, whose motivations are based in *deprivation*—never having had a seat at the table. The movement is explicit about its white identity and its conviction that whites in the USA have no choice but either to retreat to a pure white ethnostate or to organize as white people to claw back their lost status.[4] In Spencer's words:

> White dispossession is so real, it's so obvious, it's just something that one can't ignore, that a reaction had to occur and it was only a question of when or how; it wasn't a question of whether.

The alt-right felt their historical moment had arrived with the coming of Donald Trump's presidential campaign. The alt-right does not see Trump as one of them, but as a vehicle to carry white identity politics into the mainstream, and their support for him has been unflagging. In July 2019, Trump attacked four Democratic congresswomen of minority backgrounds. He tweeted:

> So interesting to see "Progressive" Democrat Congresswomen, who originally came from countries whose governments

are a complete and total catastrophe, the worst, most corrupt and inept anywhere in the world now loudly and viciously telling the people of the United States, the greatest and most powerful Nation on earth, how our government is to be run.

Why don't they go back and help fix the totally broken and crime infested places from which they came. Then come back and show us how it is done.[5]

Andrew Anglin of the *Daily Stormer*, though he saw it as an election ploy, could not contain his elation at this. As David Neiwert reported:

Anglin had posted several laudatory pieces about Trump: "This is the kind of WHITE NATIONALISM we elected him for. And we're obviously seeing it only because there's another election coming up. But I'll tell you, even knowing that, it still feels so good," he wrote.

Noting that among the people Trump attacked was an African American congresswoman, Ayanna Pressley, who was born and raised in Chicago, Anglin said, "This is not some half-assed anti-immigrant white nationalism. Trump is literally telling American blacks to go back to Africa." He later added, "All Trump is doing is once again expressing our collective anger. . . . This is what elected Trump and this is what will always be the best way for him to gain support."[6]

On his website after the Battle of Berkeley, Richard Spencer said he had not expected to see the politics of street fighting—"Weimar," as he called it—arrive in the United States in his lifetime. But he nevertheless had clear thoughts about how it arrived and how it would play out. In Spencer's view what he called the "fragmentation" of American politics had moved into "extreme polarization." There were now two different camps that saw each other as existential foes, who would fight for space on the ground and for "ideological space"—"for who's going to control society and culture going forward." The "new normal" is going to be a politics of occupying space, with violence at its core; and people will be forced to choose one or the other side.[7] This was the mindset that drove the planning of the demonstration at Charlottesville. As Spencer wrote on his website:

> The Alt-Right is finished debating, negotiating, surrendering. We're ready to close ranks and fight for what is ours. . . . We stand poised to conquer the continent.[8]

The MO of the Fascist squads of the 1920s and 1930s was what the movement called punitive expeditions, which involved direct violence perpetrated against their political opponents and against the functioning of government they disliked.[9] Before the Battle of Berkeley, direct violence was not much of a factor in the alt-right's support of Donald Trump.[10] The violence instead was virtual. It took place online. This took the form mostly of trolling and doxxing: trolling, or attempting to foment discord on "enemy" websites; doxxing, or creating dangerous conditions for the opposition by publicizing names, addresses, telephone numbers, and the like.[11] On their own websites the alt-right published a nonstop and ever-evolving suite of virulent and volatile memes. With far far too many of these memes to sketch out here, we will offer two paradigmatic examples. One is the use of triple parentheses ((( ))) to surround Jewish names, especially those of journalists. A second is the use of gas chamber imagery. A victim is trapped in a cell with a small window through which his or her face is visible. Outside the cell stands a Nazi, next to wall-mounted buttons. In the animated GIF versions of this meme, the Nazi presses the green button and gas fills the cell from above until the victim is no longer visible through the fumes. As the alt-right's support for Donald Trump solidified, the character at the button became Donald Trump, smiling broadly, dressed in Nazi uniform, pressing the button with Hillary Clinton the prisoner inside the cell.[12]

With the coming of "Weimar," Spencer and his fellow alt-right leadership decided the time was ripe for moving punitive expeditions from the internet to the streets. In this they were attempting to fulfill the still-absent signature feature of a fascist movement, the organized militia. To move from the virtual violence of cyberspace to the real violence of spaces on the ground was to grasp the alt-right's aspirational fascist heritage; it was the heritage Spencer embraced when he celebrated Donald Trump's electoral victory in his November 2016 address to an alt-right gathering in Washington where he led his followers in chants of "Hail Trump, Hail Victory" and they responded with Nazi salutes.[13]

After Charlottesville

But the plan came a cropper.

At the level of public opinion, Charlottesville was a disaster.[14] Any notion that the alt-right were merely pranksters who were infatuated with Donald Trump melted away. PayPal immediately cut off accounts of "more than three dozen hate groups and other extremist organizations," for fear of their role in raising money for the groups.[15] Other online venues of alt-right financial support, like the Amazon Affiliate program, followed suit. Comity among various alt-right groups dissolved as leaders and activists faced charges for the Charlottesville violence. Some demonstrators have been convicted and jailed for their actions at Charlottesville, including the life sentence for James Alex Fields, who ran down and killed Heather Heyer with his automobile.[16] On behalf of Charlottesville citizens, the case *Sines v. Kessler* was brought in federal court against fifteen individuals and groups.[17] Kessler's attempt to stage a second "Charlottesville" in Washington on its one-year anniversary fizzled.[18] Without a unified goal—like the Trump campaign or the planning of the first Unite the Right march—alt-right activists and their organizations were atomized and lacked direction.

A lawsuit filed in a Virginia state court explicitly took up the militia goals of the Charlottesville organizers. Lawyers from Georgetown University's Institute for Constitutional Advocacy and Protection argued that "these paramilitary organizations and their leaders [the Alt-Right Defendants] wielded their weapons on Aug. 12 not 'as individuals' exercising their Second Amendment rights to self-defense, but 'as members of a fighting force.'" Acting as a private militia, the complaint contended, violated Article I, Section 13 of the Virginia State Constitution, which states, "In all cases, the military should be under strict subordination to, and governed, by the civil power."[19] All defendants settled in the case, agreeing not to return in groups of two or more armed protesters at any future demonstration or event in the city.[20]

But the alt-right's dream of an armed militia—and its inheriting the mantle of a true fascist movement—will not die easily. The Nazi Party in Germany came to power in 1933. Ten years earlier Hitler staged his Beer Hall Putsch, an armed attempt to take over municipal power in Munich, which he planned to use as a base to orchestrate a march on Berlin, emulating Mussolini's seizure of state power by the March on Rome the year earlier in Italy. Instead, the putsch was thwarted by Munich-based German army forces and Hitler was jailed. But the putsch was sacralized by the Nazis, who, once in power, held a yearly commemoration of it in Munich, marching from the beer hall to the spot where the army intervened and produced "martyrs" to the Nazi movement. In short, the Beer Hall Putsch came to be seen among the Nazis as the movement's consecration in blood, the event that foreshadowed the ultimate victory. A parallel sentiment about Charlottesville is not without its adherents among the alt-right. As the neo-Nazi Andrew Anglin put it simply, "This was our Beer Hall Putsch."[21]

Finally, much of the motivation of the vanguards of Italian Fascism and German Nazism was rooted in a Nietzschean attitude of rejection based on aesthetic considerations or on the celebration of instincts and heroism, of military and war. What was rejected was what liberal society—bourgeois society—had on offer for young men. What was on offer was, above all, boring. It left the spirit wanting. Nothing seemed more soul-destroying than to spend a man's adult life bringing up a family and running a grocery store. Many of these Nietzscheans had already been activists in the othering nationalist movements of the turn of the twentieth century. For example, along with Charles Maurras, Maurice Barrès was one of the central thinkers and artists in the turn-of-the-century nationalism in France that was supercharged by the Dreyfus affair.

> Maurice Barres, who called himself a "National Socialist," . . .
> feared for the effect of liberal individualism and materialism
> on France, lamenting that on the tomb of bourgeois "man"
> should be engraved the epitaph, "Born a Man. Died a Gro-
> cer."[22]

The Italian Futurist movement is remembered today, a hundred years after its heyday, alongside cubism as having revolutionized art, pushing it into the modern age. The movement's founder, F.T. Marinetti, was deeply involved in the successful agitation, known as the Interventionist Movement, to involve Italy in World War I. It was this issue that occasioned Mussolini's break with the Italian Socialist Party (PSI) and put him on the path to his postwar founding of Fascism. The Fascist movement first participated in an electoral campaign in November 1919. The election did not go well for the Fascists. Mussolini headed a Fascist slate in Milan that received 4,796 votes to 170,315 for the PSI. Marinetti was one of the nineteen candidates on the Fascist slate.[23] In the *Futurist Manifesto*, which Marinetti authored in 1908, he prefigured not only the Nietzschean nihilism still broadly to be found in the alt-right, but as well the misogyny that in particular has most animated the alt-lite. Here are four of the eleven points of the Futurist Manifesto:

1. We want to sing the love of danger, the habit of energy and rashness.

2. The essential elements of our poetry will be courage, audacity and revolt. . . .

9. We want to glorify war—the only cure for the world— militarism, patriotism, the destructive gesture of the anarchists, the beautiful ideas which kill, and contempt for woman.

10. We want to demolish museums and libraries, fight morality, feminism and all opportunist and utilitarian cowardice.[24]

In light of the failure of Charlottesville to have birthed a unified alt-right militia, it is fair to conclude that Richard Spencer had certainly misjudged the American public. But more than that, he misjudged the historical moment. It was not Weimar in the USA. Or, not yet Weimar. But Spencer and his ilk, both in the United States and abroad, will be at the ready for their moment, not alone for their animating ideological malevolence for multiculturalism, but as well for the Nietzschean predispositions they share with their forbearers from a century ago. In Spencer's words:

American society today is so just fundamentally bourgeois. . . .
It's just so, pardon my French . . . it's so fucking middle-class
in its values. There is no value higher than having a pension
and dying in bed. I find that profoundly pathetic. So, yeah,
I think we might need a little more chaos in our politics, we
might need a bit of that fascist spirit in our politics.[25]

The Double Game

In an interview with Sarah Posner at the 2016 Republican nominating convention, Steve Bannon famously boasted that the
online daily he headed, Breitbart News, was "the platform of the
alt-right."[26] Plainly, the defining characteristic of the alt-right is
its white identity politics.[27] Yet Bannon denies the white nationalist element of his ideology and insists that what he stands for
goes by the name either "populist nationalism" or "economic
populism"—the scourge solely of the globalists who would level
national cultures. At a CPAC (Conservative Political Action Conference) appearance in February 2017, while he was still a senior
advisor in the Trump administration, Bannon made explicit his
plans to gut globalist power on the home front by undermining
what he called the administrative state, the professional bureaucracy that manages federal agencies and programs.[28] Trump
effectively institutionalized the alt-right when he made Bannon
his campaign's "CEO" in August 2016 and then installed him in
the administration.

This duality between an economic populist argument on the
one hand, and an othering nationalist argument (that turns
white nationalist for alt-right-ers) on the other hand is a profound
yet functional dissonance that threads through the whole of the
Trump phenomenon in the USA and illiberalism abroad. Populist nationalism is presented as an economic solution for a "left
behind" working class as a country's elites, both left and right,

have hewed more and more to a globalist agenda; nationalism is globalism's very opposite, and its remedy. But this is not the argument that these movements rely on to win over voters. That argument is the scapegoating argument. It is the red meat of these movements. It is the argument that puts the blame for economic and social "carnage" (in Trump's terminology) on the shoulders of immigrants. In theory, Trump's populist national-ism argument is about curing economic conditions. But selling his populism is about fear. Electorally and as president, Trump as a campaigner is not running on the economic arguments. He is running on the fear.

This dual face is a fundamental component of Trump's suc-cess. Talk to a Trump supporter and you will hear talk of jobs moving overseas and immigrants on the welfare rolls. But go to a Trump rally and that supporter will cheer him as he thunders about invading caravans and reciting "The Snake," describing immigrants as criminals and lowlifes and threats to national security. Tales of the lethal danger Americans face at the hands of immigrants regularly make it into the most august adminis-tration's statements—like Trump's inaugural speech or his State of the Union speeches.[29]

The presence of these two components—economic populism and scapegoating—is a novelty in contemporary American politics. It breaks down the clear distinction between left and right populist movements—the left based on resentment toward financial elites, and the right based on resentment toward cul-tural elites.[30] The hybrid political movement it introduces is at the heart of Steve Bannon's political vision. Bannon's project for American politics is that the Trump coalition, which in his view blends the working class with traditional right-wing populists, will establish itself as an enduring movement, and its role will be the successor to the Tea Party. Using the Tea Party tactics of primarying and obstruction, Bannon sees the Trump movement adopting a kingmaker role in the Republican Party, enforcing its ideology on national and state candidates alike.[31]

In theory this moves the Trump Republican Party toward the model exemplified by European right populist parties for decades. Conservatism in the United States has for so long been married to free-market economics that it often comes as a surprise to Americans to learn that much of the European right does not argue against their notably more generous welfare states than that which exists in the United States, and that right populist parties and their constituencies are welfare-state champions. But in practice, the Trump administration has retained the support of the Republican Party by largely cleaving to Republican orthodoxy—as exemplified in its Federalist Society nominations not only to the Supreme Court but throughout the federal judiciary—and in its singular legislative achievement, the 2017 tax cut.[32]

Where the Trump administration continues to rub up against Republican orthodoxy, on immigration and on tariff policy, highlights the two faces of Trump's hybrid populism. One is about red-meat scapegoating, invoking continuously the Imagined Other; the other is about economic theory that contradicts free-trade principles. Each face is associated with senior figures who are notable for their longevity in an administration where turnover at the top is unprecedented.[33] Stephen Miller guides the administration's immigration policies. He has been the architect of a number of initiatives that critics often view as extreme and cruel. These include, among others, the travel ban on Muslims; the zero-tolerance policy at the border, which takes children away from their parents; and the no public charges policy, which attempts to screen any immigrants "likely" to seek public assistance.[34] Trump's tariff policies are in the hands of Peter Navarro. Like Miller, Navarro got to put into practice at the highest level ideas that he had long held as an economist whose views were in sharp contrast to Republican orthodoxy. For Navarro, who focuses his criticism of trade policy on the U.S. trade deficit, the issue has been China. Navarro has argued for years that China has embarked on the ambition to supplant the United States as the greatest global power and that American trade policy has abetted China's ambition, and that only war, tariff war, can turn back that tide. In Navarro's analysis, while the United States offset around 55 percent of its 2017 trade deficit with Europe through higher value-added exports, with China, whose economic strategy is to try to dominate the supply chain of high value-added industries, only 15 percent of low-value imports were offset in the same year.[35]

Networking the White Nationalist Right

For eighty years what today is the alt-right was the fringe of American politics—outside the mainstream, without a role in national politics, and largely regarded as a sort of leftover from an earlier and politically uglier age. Before Donald Trump's candidacy, the last time the Ku Klux Klan and pro-Nazi organizations had purchase in national politics was in the 1920s and 1930s.[36] But their politics did not disappear. Instead, small, atomized groups continued to exist in corners—in the Midwest, in the South, over time in the West.

The internet cured their atomization. As Kathleen Belew shows in her book *Bring the War Home: The White Power Movement and Paramilitary America*, white supremacists were early adopters of networking technology:

> [Louis] Beam created a series of code-word-accessed message boards that linked the white power movement around the country and beyond. Liberty Net, implemented in 1983, fea-

tured recruitment materials; personal ads and pen pal match programs . . . and messaging about targets to sabotage and assassination. It enabled the forging and maintenance off the social connections that sustained white power activism and violence.[37]

Social media supercharged the ability of white supremacists to network and set the stage for the rise of the alt-right. In the early days of the internet, the prefix "alt" arose as a shorthand for "alternative." It was widely used as the basis for forming online affinity groups that understood themselves as rejecting the standard version of a genre of almost any sort, in favor of, say, alt-folk-music. When Richard Spencer started his website in 2010 he was distinguishing himself from paleoconservatism: while agreeing with the paleos' rejection of interventionist foreign policy, their advocacy of restricted immigration and rejection of free trade, Spencer raised their contempt for multiculturalism into explicit white nationalism.[38]

But after so many decades in the wilderness, what really established white nationalism as a force in American politics was Donald Trump's presidential candidacy. Suddenly, at the level of presidential politics, someone was talking the white nationalists' language. It was electrifying, like a siren call from a thoroughly unexpected and almost unbelievably elevated province. The long political experience of being marginalized, of being the fringe, turned on a dime. The alt-right mobilized and became a participant in the election of 2016 in a way that white nationalist ideological warriors had not participated in American elections since the 1920s and 1930s. Kathleen Blee, a sociologist who has studied the far right for three decades, said, "Until Trump ran for office, nobody I talked to was ever interested in electoral politics."[39] America's most famous Ku Klux Klanner,

David Duke, summed up his experience: "I'm overjoyed to see Donald Trump and most Americans embrace most of the issues that I've championed for years."[40]

When Steve Bannon left the administration he went back to Breitbart, which he fondly called his "killing machine."[41] Breitbart News had played a crucial role in the mobilization of the alt-right during Trump's presidential campaign, a role it, and others, have continued throughout Trump's presidency. Breitbart was not simply the platform for the alt-right, it was its publicist. Breitbart functioned as a hinge, becoming the leading conduit for moving material from alt-right sites into the mainstream media, including hard white-nationalist and white-supremacist sites like Stormfront (as well as often foreign-based fake news sites). This was the errand Bannon discovered for himself when his research arm, the Government Accountability Institute (GAI), underwrote Peter Schweizer's 2015 book *Clinton Cash* and watched its indictment of Hillary and Bill Clinton's financial dealings turn into a story in the *New York Times*. No longer would the charges and themes that arose in far right and alt-right media be siloed there forever. Instead these charges would be weaponized by appearing in the mainstream press.

> A damaging story published on the front page of the *New York Times* has infinitely more political utility for conservative partisans than the same story appearing on Breitbart.com.[42]

Bannon's attempts to become an international leader of the illiberal movement did not go well.[43] Robert Mercer and his daughter Rebekah, who had underwritten much of Bannon's media empire, including Breitbart News, Cambridge Analytica, and the GAI, dropped him from their patronage. But what he fostered, the movement of the alt-right into the political mainstream, is not going to go away; there is no putting the genie back in the bottle. No matter the fate of Trump and his administration, the Nationalist International still has the wind at its back, and its cross-fertilization with the American alt-right will continue. The alt-right still has committed financial backing. But the alt-right will maintain its role in U.S. politics above all for having established the movement's media presence. The alt-right is the spawn of social media in much the same way as Fox News was the spawn of cable television. As of September 2019, eight of the fifteen most popular news websites on the internet were either of the alt-right or deeply sympathetic to it. Post-Bannon, Breitbart was number two.[44]

From RINOs to Globalists to Cuckservatives

I often ask, "What do you want to work at? If you have the chance. When you get out of school, college, the service, etc.". . .

The usual answer, perhaps the normal answer, is "I don't know," meaning, "I'm looking; I haven't found the right thing; it's discouraging but not hopeless.

But the terrible answer is, "Nothing." The young man doesn't want to do anything.

—Paul Goodman, *Growing Up Absurd*[45]

The problem of alienated young men is not a new one. In today's idiom, these are the young men who "fail to launch." Typically housebound historically, the alienated young man's outstanding characteristic has been his extreme isolation: he is relegated to "Counting Flowers on the Wall."[46] The last thing one would associate with this population was collective action. It was a world of loneliness, but also, as Paul Goodman pointed out, a breeding ground for nihilism. Poet and essayist Garret Keizer offers the lineaments for understanding twenty-first-century American nihilists:

> I would define nihilism as a combination of three basic elements: a refusal to hope for anything except the ulti-mate vindication of hopelessness; a rejection of all values, especially values widely regarded as sacrosanct (equality, posterity, and legality); and a glorification of destruction, including self-destruction—or as Walter Benjamin put it, "self-alienation" so extreme that humanity "can experience its own destruction as an aesthetic pleasure." Nihilism is less passive and more perverse than simple despair. "Nihilism is not only despair and negation," according to Albert Camus, "but, above all, the desire to despair and to negate."[47]

Even more so than the neo-Nazis and KKKers who became the alt-right, the internet has revolutionized the fortunes of America's alienated young men.[48] It prepared them to develop into the alt-lite. The internet overcame their isolation and atomi-zation. For the first time, shut-ins had a means of being in touch with one another. And it was not simply one-on-one contact. Affinity groups and later social media created the unprecedent-ed capacity for individuals to participate in collective discus-sion and play with one another. If ever there were a revolution among the lonely shut-ins, this was it. They created their own online subculture. It was a subculture whose outstanding char-acteristic was its nihilism, their collective agreement that every-one out there was, as Holden Caulfield used to put it, a phony.

Collectively, however, the subculture would turn darker than Holden could ever have managed on his own.

The subculture was edgy and often playful. It was a subculture drawing aesthetically on the precedents of anime and cyberpunk.[49] Visually, the images that proliferated in this subculture drew upon the exaggerated head size and pop-eyed figures of anime, like the Pokémon character Pikachu.[50] Among the many figures and memes that arose, perhaps the most well-known example, the one that was the virtual mascot of the subculture, its talisman, was Pepe the Frog; or, better, the green-faced, broad red-lipped, pop-eyed, half-human/half frog. The subculture's narrative content was immersed in cyberpunk—the dystopian sci-fi future genre emphasizing both high-tech innovation, including altering human biology, and antiheroes whose adventures unfolded, often violently, in the mean underbelly of worlds dominated by distant and powerful authoritarian rulers and corporations. A classic of the genre is the 1982 film *Blade Runner*, based on the Philip K. Dick novel *Do Androids Dream of Electric Sheep? as* well as William Gibson's novel *Neuromancer*.[51] Cyberpunk told stories of a particular kind of antihero, men with clear resonance with the alienated young men:

> Classic cyberpunk characters were marginalized, alienated loners who lived on the edge of society in generally dystopic futures where daily life was impacted by rapid technological change, an ubiquitous datasphere of computerized information, and invasive modification of the human body.[52]

The subculture's gaming followed its cyberpunk style. And it followed it in a big way. The subculture moved in droves to MMOs—massively multiplayer online games.[53] These games can accommodate thousands of players at the same time, and their draw among stay-at-home young men was overwhelming. One unsympathetic observer described the cyberpunk subculture—the alienated young men networked!—as:

> A place full of young guys with no social lives, no sex lives and no hope of ever moving out of their mothers' basements. . . . They're total wankers and losers who indulge in Messianic fantasies about someday getting even with the world through almost-magical computer skills.[54]

One acute observer of this propensity was Steve Bannon. According to Joshua Green,

> Back in 2007, when he'd taken over Internet Gaming Entertainment, the Hong Kong company that systemized gold farming in *World of Warcraft* and other massively multiplayer online games, Bannon had become fascinated by the size and agency of the audiences . . . [55]

It was an observation that would stay with Bannon through his Breitbart days and into the Trump campaign. In 2016, "He wanted to attract the online legions of mostly young men he'd run up against several years earlier, believing that internet masses could be harnessed to strike a political revolution."[56] He would find a way to leverage the subculture into the alt-lite.

The prequel to the transformation of the alienated into the alt-lite was Gamergate. With Gamergate the subculture morphed, turning into the kind of identity group that has come to the fore with the right-wing populism of the Tea Party and Trump eras. Unlike identity groups like women or gays, which organized on the basis of deprivation (of justice, equality, etc.), this was an identity group organized on the more acid basis of dispossession, of the feeling of having had something taken away. Identity followed from the furious sense of what was taken away. Unlike the alt-right, whose identity was based on whiteness, for this subculture the identity was based on maleness. For the alt-right the Other were immigrants and people of color. For the alienated young men, the Other was women. This is the identity, and the Other, that would follow them into becoming the alt-lite.

The Gamergate spark was a boyfriend spurned. The ex-girlfriend was a game developer who came out with a game called *Depression Quest* that dealt with the psychological condition of depression. This aroused displeasure in the subculture; gaming was supposed to be about simulated violence and *Depression Quest* seemed to introduce a strain of political correctness into a hostile environment. Gamergate broke when the ex-boyfriend reacted to a gaming reporter's mention of *Depression Quest* and this reporter subsequently became the developer's new boyfriend. The incensed ex published a 9,500-word screed about their breakup; his inclusion of her emails, texts, and other communications foreshadowed the tsunami of trolling and doxxing that made Gamergate infamous and frightening.[57] Above all the ex accused her of sleeping with the reporter to obtain a good review of the game. The scale and the viciousness of Gamergate was astonishing. Not merely the developer, but female journalists who covered the case, were subject not only to months of trolling and doxxing, but to rape and death threats. Beyond simply having to alter or abandon their online identities, in some cases these women, whose addresses were made public, were forced out of their homes.[58]

For Steve Bannon, Gamergate was a confirmation of his ideas about the political potential of alienated young men. Gamergate could be a gateway drug to political mobilization. He realized, as he put it, "You can activate that army. They come in through Gamergate or whatever and then get turned onto politics and

Trump."[59] Bannon went about this by bringing Milo Yiannopoulos into Breitbart.[60]

In effect, Bannon created a division of labor inside Breitbart. The division of labor corresponded with the two pillars of Donald Trump's persistent attack on "political correctness" that resonated throughout his right-wing populist base. One pillar of political correctness was multiculturalism. That was addressed through the populist nationalism and its cultivation of white nationalism that was Bannon's trademark. The other pillar was feminism. That was Yiannopoulos's remit. He was a specialist.

Yiannopoulos in practice met the playful side, the Pepe the Frog side, of the gamer subculture. He was fun, in his writing and in his national bus tour of college campuses. Yiannopoulos was good at outraging the "normies," uninhibited like a Sacha Baron Cohen of the right. His weird pedigree disoriented his critics: Greek, British, gay, entitled, and a touch Jewish. Yiannopoulos loved nothing better than to expound on his extended metaphor, "Feminism is Cancer."

> No matter how you look at it, Feminism is Cancer. Some of you might call me radiation therapy. But the analogy is bad. Radiation therapy damages normal tissue in a desperate attempt to kill cancer.
>
> But my humor, facts, and charming personality are harmless to normal people. Only feminists, their Muslim buddies and black lives matter suffer from post traumatic stress disorder when I speak.[61]

With the alt-lite, Yiannopoulos was following the formula for mobilizing the arc of right-wing populism, from the "real Americans" of the Tea Party to the Identitarians of the alt-right: he spoke to the intense resentment that they were being dispossessed, and worked at turning the resentment of the Other into contempt for it. Amanda Marcotte observes:

> [Yiannopoulos] told his readers that they were justified in their feeling that women had, by striving for equality, stolen something from them. He offered them an anti-feminism stripped of any pretense towards chivalry, instead giving them permission to embrace a politics composed of nothing but resentment and destructive urges.[62]

Inevitably, the line between alt-lite and alt-right became blurry.

> So, if a young white man can be convinced that gaming "belongs" to him and that it is on the verge of being taken away, he might be more easily persuaded to accept similarly structured arguments about, say, the dangers of nonwhite immigrants to take over the country from under the noses of "real" Americans.[63]

But since 2015, there has been a unifying factor for the alt-lite and the alt-right, for the gamers and the white nationalists, for the alienated and the anti-Semites alike. That unifying factor is Donald Trump. Where the Daily Stormer could put Trump in a Nazi uniform, gassing Hillary Clinton, the alt-lite turned him into Pepe-Trump. And where Trump could refer to the "good people" marching with tiki torches in Charlottesville, he also retweeted images of himself as Pepe.[64]

In the alt-lite subculture, when someone's interests turned from gaming to politics—whether explicitly anti-feminist or simply pro-Trump—they called themselves red-pilled. Getting red-pilled is the gamer's version of the conversion experience. Those left behind, the normies, flipped from being objects of resentment to objects of contempt. The red pill meme was based on the film *The Matrix*, where popping the red pill took one out of the mundane and into an empowered "reality." Like the alt-right, the politicized alt-lite, in the form of the "manosphere," developed virulent extremes. This has essentially taken two forms. One is focused on sexual frustration, feeling both entitled to sex and victimized by women for denying it to them. These sites range from pick-up-artist tip-swapping to incel (involuntary celibates) and other male supremacist sites.[65] A second tendency is toward celebration of antediluvian hyper-Nietzschean evocations of men's power, before women and elites cowed them into submission. A startling example of this is *Bronze Age Mindset*, a self-published mix of youthful slang, mythological and classic references, and relentless bombast, which moved to the top 150 titles on Amazon shortly after its June 2018 appearance.[66]

Along with the right-wing populists who migrated his way, and the Republican regulars who overwhelmingly came around, the alt-right and the alt-lite rounded out Donald Trump's electoral constituency. What the alts had in common with the populists was not merely their rejection of the Republican establishment, but their conflation of the Republican establishment with liberals and Democrats. Tea Party RINOs became globalists, from the populists' new nationalist perspective. From the alt-lite subculture emerged the portmanteau "cuckservative," redolent of the subculture's edginess and sexualized finger-pointing. The portmanteau (cuckold plus conservative) was readily picked up by the alt-right, for whom it came to mean Republicans who refused to make white identity the center of their politics; (so-called) conservatives, weaklings who would collaborate with liberals on issues like immigration reform.[67] It was for both alts an expression of the utmost contempt.

Across the board of Trump's populist and alt constituencies, their support was tied to Trump having run against both the Republican and the Democratic establishments; or better,

Trump's having conflated the two so that it was just the elites *tout court* he was running against. For the alt-lite, nothing was closer to their nihilist heart than this—being against all the powerful. This new elite was a hybrid; it spanned the conventional left-right political dichotomy, and in so doing it defined a new oppositional identity, a new hybrid populist movement, one that similarly unwound the left-right divisions of conventional politics. This reshuffling of the bipolarity of conventional politics was the centerpiece of Steve Bannon's vision of the future of U.S. and Western politics.

In his evangelizing in Europe, no movement excited Bannon as much as the Five Star movement in Italy. Five Star was a purely internet-based movement, founded by a comedian, Beppe Grillo, and which from the outset defined itself as an opposition to politicians of all parties. What was particularly exciting for Bannon was that the greatest migration to Five Star came from the major center-left party in Italy, the Democratic Party; and that the movement's politics were both anti-immigrant and anti–European Union. Five Star came close to being Bannon's ideal. By the national elections of 2018, Five Star had become the strongest party in Italy, winning 32.7 percent of the vote and 227 seats, the most of any party, in the Chamber of Deputies.

Before formally declaring Five Star a movement in 2009, it existed more or less as Grillo's blog. While the blog was growing in its following every year, what established its place in Italian politics was Grillo's first VDay in 2007. The *V* stands for *"vanffanculo." Vaffanculo* translates best in English as "Go fuck yourself." VDay in 2007 filled the enormous Piazza Maggiore in Bologna. Grillo named politicians, read out accusations of corruption, and led the crowd in roaring *vaffanculo* at them. Three hundred fifty thousand people across the country signed Grillo's petitions in the span of a couple of days.

Many have observed that more than his political promises

what drew voters to Donald Trump was the opportunity to give the finger to politicians across the political spectrum in America. Nowhere among his supporters was this more powerful than for the nihilists of the alt-lite. Both Bannon and Trump understood this about the populists and the alt-ists who migrated to the Trump movement. What Grillo offers his followers in explicit terms—the chance to say *vaffanculo* to the political class—Trump offers his followers in his only slightly coded language.

6

(Grayed-Out) Illiberalism
The Road Taken

For Blue America—liberal, Democratic America—election night and the Trump transition evoked dread. Blue America had lived with a generation and a half of conservative ascendency. But this was different. To the liberal eye, the course of the past three-and-a-half decades of the Republican populist right resembled the successive generations of William Faulkner's Yoknapatawpha County, offering up politicians who acted more and more inbred over time. Their thinking seemed stunted, frequently only making sense within their own circles; their words and actions could not only be incomprehensible to outsiders, but they often seemed unprecedented and outrageous, beyond the bounds of known political practice and etiquette.

Still Trump was different. He was disconcerting at a level that had not yet been touched by earlier populist right proximity to power. He was not so much an extension as a leap. He was not the next Yoknapatawpha County generation. He was from a county apart. That earlier succession went from Reagan, through Gingrich, who impeached a president over a sex scandal; DeLay, who attempted to create a permanent Republican majority in the House of Representatives through the K Street Project and unprecedented redistricting tactics; and Bush-Cheney, who declared the Geneva Conventions "outdated" when it came to pursuing their wars. From the ashes of the manifest failures of Bush-Cheney rose the Tea Party movement, the 2010 generation of Republican populist radicalism that spoke of defaulting on the national debt and could not let go of fantasies about Barack Obama, which ranged from alleging his foreign birth, to alleging his Muslim faith, to alleging his planning to round up the political opposition into concentration camps.

But still Trump was different. There was every other president-elect and then there was this one. For Blue America, no one else had made racist dog whistles so explicit and raised them to the center of his campaign, made it his brand. No one else suggested he might not accept election results. No one led his rallies, even his convention, in chanting "Lock her up" about his Democratic presidential opponent. For Blue America this was a uniquely repulsive personality in politics. No one looked and acted as weird as Trump: orange-hued tan with whites under his eyes; hair an oddly colored parody of a comb-over; a singularly disjointed debate and rally style, rich in name-calling mockery and made-up anecdotes like stories of Arab Americans dancing in the streets on 9/11. No one flaunted expectations, like refusing to reveal his tax returns with blatantly bogus reasons. No one celebrated pussy grabbing.

Still, it was hard in Blue America to put your finger on exactly what Trump dread was about. The dread did not reside simply at the level of odious politics and electoral flimflam. It went deeper than that, and that was what was novel and so profoundly disconcerting about Trump. He put into question something that felt as if it was the foundation of politics, below the level of platform and rah-rah. It was about what was taken for granted in American politics, what previously even the worst insults Blue America felt it had endured from conservative and populist America had not put into question. Trump dread was about what Blue Americans never had to think about before; it felt more like a deep malaise than something you could easily name. And it felt like something that, once it had momentum, could be irrevocable. It was what put more people than any previous demonstration in American history in the streets in Washington, across the country, and around the world for the Women's March the day after Trump was inaugurated.[1] It was what put thousands of demonstrators spontaneously into American airports the following week when the Trump administration issued an executive order banning travel from Muslim-majority countries.[2] It was what led progressive Americans to organize into thousands of Indivisible groups (based on the model of the Tea Party) within weeks of the new administration taking power.[3] It was what gave rise to voices in Blue America calling themselves the Resistance.

Liberal Democracy

The dread Trump evoked took the form of malaise—more feeling than articulation—in large part because Blue America had not yet parsed the meaning of liberal democracy. In America we are used to equating democracy with voting. It is our typical common-sense answer to what democracy means. Journalism in America can seem addicted to horse-race coverage of elections, and academic political science to voting and polling data. When the Democrats finally decided to pursue impeachment against Donald Trump, it was not for judicial interference, not for depriving people of their rights at the border, not for emoluments, not for obstruction of justice around the FBI and Mueller investigations, not for perjury, but for messing with elections—in this case Trump attempting to use his office to suborn a foreign power to undermine Joe Biden's 2020 presidential candidacy. This was something, the Democratic leadership felt, that could be widely understood and supported. It was the kind of assault on democracy—on voting—that resonated most readily with how democracy is perceived in America.

By his second inaugural, in 2005, George W. Bush was

justifying his invasion of Iraq as part of his "freedom agenda," the aim of which, following the neoconservative thinking that guided pre-Trump Republican foreign policy, was to bring democracy to all benighted nations on the planet. The first post–Saddam Hussein election was held in Iraq in January 2005. Bush and the Republican Party celebrated what they portrayed as having successfully brought democracy to Iraq by ostentatiously dipping their fingers in purple ink, as Iraqis who voted had done.[4] But this celebration ignored the fact that Iraqis were still being blown up wholesale at markets and were settling old scores by denouncing neighbors to the American authorities. It was as ghastly a premature claim of "democracy accomplished" as Bush's May 2003 misbegotten aircraft-carrier claim of military "mission accomplished," two months into an invasion that would keep Americans at war for another eight years.[5]

Democracy proved to be a more complicated confection than simply holding elections. Democracy required institutional and cultural foundations that would accomplish two overarching purposes: (1) to prevent unitary power in an individual, a political party, or government institution. This is accomplished by the rule of law and by institutions that act as checks and balances on the accumulation of unitary power; among these institutions are an independent judiciary, a free press, freedom to assemble, and freedom of speech in civil society;[6] (2) to prevent majorities in power from undermining the rights and civil liberties of other individuals or groups. The exercise of political power does not authorize deprivation of individual freedoms or the scapegoating and persecution of any group in a society's pluralist makeup; indeed, vigilance of those rights is the obligation of those entrusted with power.[7]

This substructural scaffolding fills out the picture of what liberal democracy consists of. Pre-Trump, they are the values and protections that Blue America had taken for granted—they

had not had to think about them. True, these values and protections could be and often were violated in the breach. Liberals in
America had a long history of criticizing and organizing against
government activity that ran afoul of these principles. Donald
Trump's novelty was that he raised the violations into a set of
countervalues. He raised them into his presentation of self as a
politician. That the Republican Party and 63 million voters supported his accession to the presidency had turned Trump from
a punch line into a scalding, surreal Blue America nightmare.
What had been taken for granted in the foundation of American democracy—what was unnecessary to think about until it
seemed in jeopardy of being lost—was the object of Blue America's malaise.

Illiberal Democracy

As we have seen with the case of Viktor Orbán, illiberal democracy proceeds by undermining the foundation of democracy
while keeping voting intact.

Undermining democracy's foundation is the theme of books,
like Madeleine Albright's *Fascism: A Warning*, that emerged in
the wake of Trump's candidacy; the books that were part of the
country's unprecedentedly serious conversation about fascism.
One of these books, Yascha Mounk's *The People Vs. Democracy*,
is particularly trenchant in Mounk's systematic parsing of the
meanings of "liberalism" and "democracy." This gives his writing a profound insight into the nature of contemporary right-
wing populism, and allows him to develop a comprehensive
fourfold typology of forms, democratic and undemocratic, liberal and illiberal, that are in power around the globe.[8]

Fascism provides a compelling heuristic for measuring the
breadth of illiberal erosion of democratic foundations. Each of
the two historic fascist regimes, Italian Fascism and German

Nazism, had versions of what the Nazis called their Enabling Act. Passed after the Reichstag Fire (likely set by the Nazis), the Enabling Act allowed the government to enact any laws without the consent of the German Parliament. (This act stayed in force throughout the Nazi era; the Weimar constitution stayed in place, too, but was rendered moot.) In Italy, a year into Mussolini's government, parliament passed the Acerbo Act, which gave the party winning the greatest number of votes two-thirds of all seats in parliament. These laws not only effectively ended all permitted opposition to the ruling party, they provided as well the legal basis for the unfolding of the totalitarian regimes that followed.[9]

Illiberal democracies lie across a continuum of how much the foundation of democracy has been vitiated. Fascism lies at the extreme of this continuum, the foundation annihilated. In both Italy and Germany, fascism came to power through legal democratic means. The changes these regimes effected provide a yardstick to judge the effectiveness of illiberal transformations of current democratic polities. As Primo Levi observed:

> There are many ways of reaching [fascism], not just through the terror of police intimidation, but by denying and distorting information, by undermining systems of justice, by paralyzing the education system, and by spreading in a myriad subtle ways nostalgia for a world where order reigned.[10]

Unlike in George W. Bush's Iraq, where the institutional foundation of democracy was never established, illiberalism around the globe today—in India, Turkey, Poland, Brazil, and others—proceeds by undermining institutions already established. What this means for America is significant. The wall of liberal institutions in the USA is over two centuries in the making. The contrast to recently established democracies, like

Poland and Hungary, is stark. Illiberalism has much more to overcome in the United States than almost anywhere else. But this relative insulation also makes Trumpism's assault on liberal democracy stand out all the more in American culture.

Fascism has an unbridgeable gulf from illiberalism, which resides not in the foundation of democracy but in the electoral superstructure, in voting, in the capacity of suffrage itself to legitimize the state or the regime. Illiberal regimes across the globe, while fecund in introducing measures to cripple the political opposition and jeopardize civil liberties, still mount elections and assert their legitimacy on that basis, on the basis of being electorally democratic. This allows the illiberal regimes that now dominate Poland and Hungary still to maintain their troubled memberships in the European Union, which famously barred Spain, Portugal, and Greece from joining the EU until democratic regimes replaced dictatorships in those countries.[11] In contrast, Italian Fascism was explicit on the matter of electoral democracy: Fascism rejected it. In a famous interview given to the *New York Times* in 1928, Mussolini said, "Democracy is beautiful in theory; in practice it is a fallacy. You in America will see that some day."[12] As for voting, Mussolini wrote in the 1932 "Doctrine of Fascism":

> Fascism denies that numbers, as such, can be the determining factor in human society; it denies the right of numbers to govern by means of periodical consultations; it asserts the irremediable and fertile and beneficent inequality of men who cannot be leveled by any such mechanical and extrinsic device as universal suffrage.[13]

Undermining the foundation of democracy begins at the cultural level. Political culture in the United States, as elsewhere, relies on unwritten norms. Norms are the sure but informal guides to behavior found in all societies and groups. In the USA, shaking hands when people are introduced is a norm. So is tipping your waiter. Norms are proscriptive as well as prescriptive—what not to do, like using insulting racial or ethnic terms for individuals or groups, or picking one's nose. It is precisely because norms are agreed upon at a deep cultural level, and socialized into individuals who grow up in those societies, that they have their taken-for-granted quality; things taken for granted become conscious when they are violated. It was with norm-breaking bombast that Donald Trump introduced himself as a political candidate. As one observer put it, Trump "turn[ed] dignified debate formats into a political version of the Jerry Springer show."[14]

As president, Trump's norm breaking became legion.[15] In the eyes of Blue America it sometimes seemed as though Trump was someone who simply had never learned what was appropriate behavior in social situations. To take a couple of paradigmatic examples among a wealth of others: his pushing aside the prime minister of Montenegro to get to the front row in a 2017 NATO picture taking;[16] his grinning and thumbs-up pose in an August 2019 photo, standing next to his grinning wife who was holding an infant orphaned by a mass shooting in El Paso, Texas.[17] At other times, Trump appeared to Blue America to resemble a petty Mafia don. Paradigmatic examples here include his calling his former lawyer, Michael Cohen, a "rat" for his testimony to federal investigators, contrasting him to "stand-up guy" former campaign manager Paul Manafort, who did not "break";[18] Trump's "shakedown" of the Ukrainian president, which led to his impeachment inquiry, in which he made urgent military aid and a White House meeting contingent on Ukraine's publicly opening investigation into potential 2020 presidential opponent Joe Biden.[19]

But norm breaking is only the opening act of how illiberal

regimes establish themselves. In the most entrenched of the illiberal democracies, successive steps have followed something of a blueprint, a blueprint that the Trump administration mirrors only as a kind of grayed-out shadow of possible future directions. The blueprint begins with election to control the national executive. Then, by increments—salami tactics—the executive moves to control all branches of government and to monopolize the institutions of civil society. The executive comes to control most mass media. The courts are stacked. The country's electoral system is weighted to reduce to a minimum any chance of being voted out of office. Public campaigns of ethnic nationalism, isolating "enemies of the people," are mounted. In the most effective of illiberal states, like Viktor Orbán's Hungary, the national constitution is rewritten.[20]

A Nation of Epistemologists

Corey Lewandowski, Donald Trump's original 2016 campaign manager, offered a corrective to the mainstream press shortly after Donald Trump's election to the presidency: "This is the problem with the media: You guys took everything Donald Trump did so literally. And the problem with that is the American people didn't."[21] Lewandowski had a point. Literalism is how we grope our way in an unfamiliar culture; literalism is the shaky tool we use to ascribe meanings to words and phrases when we are at sea in a foreign environment—meanings that unfortunately are often humorously (or disastrously) off the mark. Donald Trump is fluent in the culture of right-wing populism that thrived online and on Fox News. "The media" Lewandowski refers to, the mainstream media, Blue America's media, is not. Ideas that seem wildly off-kilter to liberals and Democrats make sense to Lewandowski, and to Trump and to his right populist followers, the way that local customs make sense to the native born. For Blue America, having little other recourse than to take right populism literally meant sharing a mismatched national discourse and came to feel like it was operating in a "post-truth" political culture.

Trump's preparation for his presidential run, which consisted of his immersion in right-wing media, brought him face-to-face with unreal ideas that were rampant among the populists who convened there. Among much else, a couple of paradigmatic examples include the multiplicity of Obama birther stories and the certainty that Obama's elections had been stolen. With Trump, this kind of counterfactual reality landed on fertile, even kindred, ground. This was, after all, the man who (again to take a couple of paradigmatic examples from a great universe of possibilities) had mounted framed pictures of himself on a false *Time* magazine cover in his golf clubs around the world and in his own office, which was housed in an eponymous building whose height he inflated by ten stories.[22] Falsehood was Trump's métier. For Trump, falsehood created a conduit to his base that did not register with Blue America. It recapitulated in words and slapstick gesture, like a stand-up routine, the made-up drama and thrills of professional wrestling, where Trump learned to play to a live audience, a live crowd; where the idea that the spectacle was a contest, was actually competitive, somehow survived the knowledge that the contest was scripted, was rigged. This would only bother the literalists. (See note 25 in chapter 4.)

Hannah Arendt is the theorist par excellence on the relationship between lying and politics. As of October 14, 2019, the *Washington Post* counted 13,435 "false or misleading claims" during Trump's term in office.[23] Arendt argues that lying has the effect of distorting reality, reducing what is real and factual into an epistemological soup where it becomes indistinguishable from what is false. Her insight into the question bears a profound resonance with the American experience of Donald Trump as president.

> The result of a consistent and total substitution of lies for factual truth is not that the lie will now be accepted as truth and truth be defamed as a lie, but that the sense by which we take our bearings in the real world—and the category of truth versus falsehood is among the mental means to this end—is being destroyed.[24]

Within two days of Trump's inauguration, his administration introduced the reality-challenging phrase "alternative facts" into the American political lexicon.[25] Trump's press secretary was obliged to deny contrasting photos of Trump's and Obama's inaugurations and claim a greater crowd for Trump that the photos plainly belied.[26] Trump's having the inaugural-crowd photos edited to bolster this fabrication anticipated such enterprises as "Sharpiegate" over thirty months later, when Trump extended by hand the map of Hurricane Dorian to encompass the state of Alabama, which Trump insisted was in the path of the storm.[27] By then, the administration's insults to scientific fact had become a routine event, undermining social policy and turning public discourse into an enervating daily test of what was real.

Trump transformed the meaning of the phrase "fake news." The term emerged as a characterization of false stories, inventions planted for political gain especially in online media. Trump seized on the term with metronomic frequency to characterize press reporting he found critical of him and his administration, utterly transforming its meaning. The daily challenge to distinguish "real" fake news—the planted fabrications—from Trump's "fake" fake news—his and his political supporters' term for any coverage that rubbed them the wrong way—sunk Americans into an epistemological crisis that turned living in Trump's America into a collective experience of the mind-numbing miasma Trump had cultivated as his salesman's advantage throughout his business and show-business life.

Karl Rove was credited with calling liberal America and the mainstream media the "reality-based community" during his run as the chief strategist throughout the presidency of George W. Bush.[28] For Rove, the reality-based community were fusty empiricists, rendered history's bystanders and viewers, left in the dust by the doers, like the Bush administration, who forged ahead with actions based on their gut-derived vision. Ron Suskind narrated his experience of Karl Rove revealing the term:

> [Rove] said that guys like me were "in what we call the reality-based community," which he defined as people who "believe that solutions emerge from your judicious study of discernible reality." I nodded and murmured something about enlightenment principles and empiricism. He cut me off. "That's not the way the world really works anymore," he continued. "We're an empire now, and when we act, we create our own reality. And while you're studying that reality—judiciously, as you will—we'll act again, creating other new realities, which you can study too, and that's how things will sort out. We're history's actors . . . and you, all of you, will be left to just study what we do."[29]

Trump rendered Rove's dichotomy a mere warm-up act. Under Trump, the reality-based community were no longer simply bystanders, they became the Other. Its minions in the press became "the enemy of the people." In the cult of personality mounted by totalitarian regimes, the leader was the voice of the nation's interests, a providential deliverance to the nation. In contrast, with Trump the leader's personal and political interests became conflated with the nation's interests. Treason was redefined as disloyalty toward him. The Tea Party movement had made liberal politics the criterion of treason; the Tea Party Nation routinely called the Democrats the "party of treason" based on its approach to domestic policy. Trump called out treason against both the author and the *New York Times*, when "Anonymous," a senior member of his administration, published "I Am Part of the Resistance Inside the Trump Administration" in the paper.[30] So, too, did he label as a traitor the whistleblower whose report led to the House impeachment investigation; later leaders of the investigation, Nancy Pelosi and Adam Schiff, became accused of treason.[31] Earlier, participants in the investigation of pro-Trump Russian interference in the 2016 election were the alleged traitors.[32] The conspiracy thinking that so dominated the Tea Party populists' fabrications about the Obama administration's intentions and actions transferred under Trump into the core conviction Trump shares with his supporters (and much of the Republican Party) of a "deep state" conspiracy to undermine his presidency.[33] In America's split-screen reality, every development in mainstream-press or congressional investigations into scandals involving Russia or Ukraine, was paralleled by elaborations in right populist media (and among congressional Republicans) that projected the mainstream findings onto treasonous "enemies" of the president.

Trump's turning hot and cold on personnel in his administration was head-spinning. A paradigmatic example: When he announced his nomination of Rex Tillerson as his first secretary of state, Trump said, "I can think of no one more prepared, and no one more dedicated, to serve as Secretary of State at this critical time in our history."[34] Two and a half years later, Trump said, "Rex Tillerson [is] a man who is 'dumb as a rock' and totally ill prepared and ill equipped to be Secretary of State."[35] Similar head-spinning occurred on policy matters, including issues of critical importance. In Trump's estimation, Kim Jong-un of North Korea went from being "Little Rocket Man . . . a madman with nuclear weapons" who was opening his country to "fire and fury like the world has never seen" to "a great personality and very smart . . . a great leader," with whom Trump now enjoyed "a great chemistry" and with whom he had "fallen in love."[36] In June 2019, having approved air strikes against Iran for shooting down an unmanned American drone, Trump recalled the planes already in the air on their way to targets in Iran.[37]

Fake fake news, deep-state conspiracy allegations, the constant lying, vulgarity and ridicule, and head-spinning personnel and policy shifts—all that and more contributed to the collective miasma which, in some ways, approximated a psychiatric condition, a kind of epistemological insanity.[38] Commentators on the Trump era introduced "gaslighting" into America's political vocabulary. Based on a 1944 George Cukor movie, starring Ingrid Bergman, gaslighting refers to psychological manipulation that results in the victim doubting her or his own reality and, eventually, own sanity. Finally, this was Trump's signal achievement in reality shape-shifting: surpassing Karl Rove's designation and dismissal of the "reality-based community," Trump got into the community's heads, disorienting them on both political and psychological levels, making the community's reality something that required unprecedented, daily energy simply to maintain. As Jonathan Rauch put it:

> The ultimate power of the gaslighter is to make it impossible for his targets to imagine a reality different from the one he imposes. While Trump is far too weak to pull this off on a massive scale, as a successful fascist dictator might, he has already done significant damage and may do much more. With the media's unwitting complicity, he may be strong

enough to prevent a coherent shared alternative vision from emerging.[39]

The Tweetocracy

From his official declaration of candidacy in June 2015 through the first two-and-a-half years of his presidency, [Trump] tweeted over 17,000 times. Since early in his presidency, his tweets have been considered official statements by the president of the United States.[40]

As president, Donald Trump was in continuous campaign mode. He thrived on rallies where he gave clear voice ("Knock the crap out of him") to undermining the foundations of American democracy.[41] As though the 2016 election was not quite resolved in his mind, he never tired of attacking both Barack Obama and Hillary Clinton in press conferences, be those conferences in formal settings, with foreign leaders in the White House, or beside the roaring blades of his helicopter.[42]

Of all Trump's engines to manipulate the contents of what was in the public debate and on the public's minds, his use of Twitter was his foremost tool. Trump's tweeting must be understood in context: Monitoring the media on television was the outstanding daily preoccupation of his White House routine, at times taking up to eight hours of his day; his tweets more often than not were his speaking out—or acting out—after a provocation encountered in the media.

[Trump] seems driven by . . . watching the watchers. In a 24-hour-news version of burying oneself in press clippings, Trump spends hours a day parsing political coverage about

him and reacting in an endless and agitated feedback loop. . . .
His tweets and public comments suggest he spends hours a
day watching shows, even on the networks he dubs "fake
news" (mainly, CNN).[43]

Fox News had a special place in Trump's TV routine. He would
bring people into his administration, including in senior positions, who had been talking heads he admired on Fox News.[44]
He would make impromptu appearances on his favorite show,
Fox and Friends, in the morning.[45] His favorite commentator,
Sean Hannity, "basically ha[d] a desk at [the] White House."[46]
On the rare occasion he did not like what was on Fox he would
accuse them of betrayal.[47] When Fox acted as a hinge raising up
false and conspiratorial stories from the online world of right
populist media, Trump was ready to bite.[48] More than any other
source, Trump's tweeting was heavily influenced by what was
on Fox News; often his tweets followed directly from what had
just been broadcast.

> Many of the president's most vicious tweets, which often
> baffle observers because they seem to come out of nowhere,
> make more sense when you realize that they are actually his
> responses to Fox's programming.[49]

Twitter gave Trump—both as candidate and as president—
an unmediated avenue to the public—both pro and con. In a
somewhat improbable way, as head of state, Twitter also gave
Trump his most profound resemblance to Benito Mussolini as
head of state. Like Trump on Twitter, Mussolini had his own
unmediated connection to the public, his newspaper, called (in
the most populist manner) *Il Popolo d'Italia* (*The People of Italy*),
which he founded upon his break from the Socialist Party in

1914. Except for a few brief tenures as a teacher in his early twenties, journalism had been the consistent occupation of his adult life. Always, he was a journalist in the sense of editorialist—or propagandist—rather than reporter. And always, his opinions were bellicose and provocative. Mussolini continued to publish *Il Popolo d'Italia* until his ouster from power in 1943. Here is the British historian F.W. Deakin's description of Mussolini as head of state. Note the rather astonishing overlap between the place of parsing the news in Mussolini's and Trump's everyday routines:

> The reading of the Italian and foreign press occupied a central position in [Mussolini's] activity, and the daily directives to the Ministry of Popular Culture were the essence and revelation of the personal direction of the Duce. A study of these directives would give a detailed picture at any given moment of the shifts and trends of Italian policy. A change in headlines or pagination in the totally-controlled Press would indicate imminent and future developments and recent decisions.
>
> This was Mussolini's real world, and the measure of his genius lay essentially in the manipulation of the masses by the written and spoken word. . . . In a sense Mussolini governed Italy as if he were running a personal newspaper single-handed, setting the type, writing the leaders, interviewing everybody, chasing the reporters, paying the informers, sacking staff incessantly, defining the policy to be adopted and the causes to be defended.[50]

In this behavior, both Trump and Mussolini violated liberalism's notions of the relationship between the press and political power. Murray Kempton pointed out the central role Mussolini's skills as a journalist had in his political career, and the top-heavy representation of journalists among the *gerarchi*, the fascist

leadership—so much so that Kempton called this a fundamental
reversal of the rational arrangements of the liberal state:

> In democratic societies journalism is often a branch of govern-
> ment; but in Mussolini's, government was a branch of journal-
> ism . . . [a] curious reversal of the normal arrangements of
> nature and reason.[51]

The difference between Trump's and Mussolini's violations of
the place of journalism in liberalism is that Fascism institutionalized it. Fascism in Italy created the "corporate state." Under
the corporate state the citizen as a participant in political life
was defined not geographically (as in voting in the location one
lives in) but in terms of the sector of the economy one worked
in, each of which was called a corporation, and the relations
among corporations were mediated by the state. In the Fascist
state, "*giornalista*," or journalist, was enshrined as a corporation.
There were three categories of journalists officially recognized
in the corporation: One was simply called journalist, defined by
working for the press in much the way the liberal world would
define journalist. The second was "*giornalista praticante*," appren-
tice journalist. The third? "*Pubblicista*." *Pubblicista* roughly translates as publicist but is best understood as eliding the difference
between the publicist and the journalist. The Fascist constitution, as it were, officially recognized publicity as a sub-category
of journalism; it muddied the distinctions between journalism
and advertising, publicity and public relations. This has been
the effect of Trump's political ascendency on American culture;
it is an informal effect, not yet reaching into the country's legal
structure, but at large in the miasma that Trump has introduced
into the country's political culture.

In the 1980s, Trump used a telephone pseudonym, John Barron, to assert fictitious estimates of his net worth.[52] As a politician, hiding behind a fiction like John Barron has been scuttled. Instead Trump's self-aggrandizement has constantly been out in the open—in his speeches, in his off-the-cuff remarks (calling himself a "stable genius") and in tweets noting such qualities as his "great and unmatched wisdom." Unlike illiberal leaders abroad, like Viktor Orbán in Hungary, Trump has not been able to institutionalize a transformation of journalism à la Mussolini in the USA. He has simply been able on an individual basis—but in the country's most powerful political position—to act like a *pubblicista*-style journalist.[53] This reflects both the strength of liberal institutions in the USA, and Trump's limitations as a politician, owing to both personality and his ignorance of history and political philosophy.

Trump's Tweetocracy has not yet transformed into a robust illiberal democracy, like Hungary, Poland, or Russia. Instead, what he has wrought is rather like a grayed-out version of illiberalism: grayed-out in the way that websites gray-out options that are not yet available. The options are there, but as potentials, upcoming options when prerequisites are all in place; possibilities just over the horizon. The conditions to move an option from grayed-out to live have not yet fully been realized. So it is with Donald Trump's Tweetocracy: The potentials for institutionalized illiberalism are present as never before in American public life. As yet they remain grayed-out.

The New New Nationalism

This liberal idea has become obsolete. It has come into conflict with the interests of the overwhelming majority of the population. . . . This liberal idea presupposes that . . .

*migrants can kill, plunder and rape with impunity because
their rights as migrants have to be protected.*

—Vladimir Putin[54]

American nationalists were quick to applaud Putin's post-
mortem for liberal democracy. Pat Buchanan saw Putin as a leader who correctly understood liberalism's "failure to deal with the
crisis of the age: mass and unchecked illegal migration." Buchanan added approvingly, "Putin also sees the social excesses of
multiculturalism and secularism in the West as representing a
failure of liberalism." Buchanan pointed out how Putinism might
have been a bulwark against the "politically correct" offense he
observed the week he was writing his column—"a week where
huge crowds celebrated the 50th anniversary of the Stonewall
'uprising' in Greenwich Village, as it is now called . . . "[55]

Buchanan was the most well-known figure of the paleoconservative movement that most significantly prefigured the
nationalism that came to power under Donald Trump. Paleoconservatism had more serious intellectuals than Buchanan,
like Sam Francis, whose writings in the 1990s envisioned the
rise of white nationalism a generation later; and Paul Gottfried,
Richard Spencer's teacher, who coined the term paleoconservatism.[56] Sam Francis went over the line in making explicit the
place of whiteness in his nationalism, losing his position as a columnist for the *Washington Times* in 1995. But by and large paleoconservatism was able to play the double game Steve Bannon
so successfully played at Breitbart and in the Trump campaign,
denying a racist orientation but relentlessly alleging the injuries
and crime minority populations were inflicting on American
society. The 1990s also saw the rise of explicitly anti-immigrant
organizations like VDARE, founded by Peter Brimelow, whose

racist politics could no longer be tolerated at William F. Buckley's *National Review*, where he had been an editor.[57] The largest such group was NumbersUSA, founded by Roy Beck, who published *The Case Against Immigration* in 1996.[58] At the level of national political leaders, the outstanding figure in the movement was former Alabama senator Jeff Sessions, who joined the Trump administration as attorney general, and whose chief of staff, Stephen Miller, has been the mastermind in the administration behind its anti-immigrant policies.[59]

At its heart, paleoconservative and anti-immigrant nationalism dissented from the liberal point of view in seeing the underpinning of democracy as traditional, rather than as propositional. It was not the words that were contained in America's founding documents that defined the nature of American democracy; but it was the culture, religion, and ethnicity of the authors of those words that formed the enduring and immutable basis of that democracy.[60] Propositional national feeling in this view is spiritually unsatisfying and leaves the body politic vulnerable to political correctness.[61] Trumpism represents a radicalization of this point of view: It suggests not merely that liberalism has misunderstood and distorted the essential premise of the American nation, but that in its globalist hegemony since 1945, encompassing both Democratic and orthodox Republican thinking and policy—and in particular with its current multiculturalism, gay and feminist political correctness, and, above all, its openness to immigration—liberalism has brought the country to the point of an existential crisis.

During the presidential campaign the outstanding expression of this point of view came in the September 2016 publication of "The Flight 93 Election," which explicitly analogized the jeopardy America faced in a Hillary Clinton presidency with the dilemma of the passengers in the plane hijacked on

September 11 that was brought down over Pennsylvania by the action of its passengers:

> 2016 is the Flight 93 election: charge the cockpit or you die. You may die anyway. You—or the leader of your party—may make it into the cockpit and not know how to fly or land the plane. There are no guarantees.
>
>   Except one: if you don't try death is certain.[62]

The article's byline was "Publius Decius Mus." PDM turned out to be Michael Anton, who would become the deputy assistant to the president for strategic communications, a senior posting in the National Security Council; it was a position he would hold until April 2018, when he resigned rather than serve with the incoming national security advisor, John Bolton, whose career had been as a grandee, if a rather bellicose one, of Republican foreign policy orthodoxy.

Anton was part of the southern California–based Claremont Institute, publisher of the *Claremont Review of Books*; the institute would emerge not only as having the ear of the administration, but as the locus for elaborating the meaning of Trumpian nationalism in the years since Trump's inauguration as president.[63] It is interesting that the intellectual heartbeat of Trumpian thought is located in California. In its voting behavior California confirms the implication of the "imagined Other" (see chapter 3), that if support for Trump varied inversely to the presence of immigrants in a voter's near environment, then the presence of immigrants, the reality of immigrants, would mean relative inoculation against Trumpian fear-mongering of immigrants as criminal. Already majority minority, California voters preferred Clinton over Trump by 4.25 million votes (or 62 percent to 32 percent).[64] But the story reverses for right intellectuals and ideologues. The minority and immigrant footprint in California is precisely the political and social nightmare that haunted the proto-Trumpian intellectuals.[65] Not only is Claremont the center of Trumpian nationalist theory in the United States, but the state has provided some of the most important ideological players in the administration: these include Steve Bannon, Stephen Miller, Peter Navarro, Anton, and others.

In July 2019, Daniel Luban attended the National Conservatism Conference in Washington and observed:

> Usually, intellectual movements precede the rise of political ones, but in this case, Trump's camp followers are reverse-engineering an intellectual doctrine to match Trump's basic instincts.[66]

The outstanding figure in this ideological endeavor is the Israeli scholar Yoram Hazony. The author of *The Virtue of Nationalism*, Hazony defines a conservative as "someone who strives to defend and build up the political and intellectual traditions of his or her own tribe or nation."[67] Accordingly, conservativism in America must hew to "the conservative tradition of English-speaking countries," or *"Anglo-American conservatism,"* which derives not from "rationalist-liberal axioms," but above all from the "Hebrew Bible." National Conservatism stands in contrast to the liberal "mythology" of America as a "creedal nation" (or a "propositional nation"), defined solely by certain abstractions found in the American Declaration of Independence or the Gettysburg Address. Important though these documents are, they cannot substitute for the Anglo-American political tradition as a whole—with its roots in scripture and the English common law—which alone offers a complete picture of the English and American legal inheritance.[68]

Hazony sees the period of "liberal democracy" in the West as an historical anomaly deriving from "the trauma of World War II." It is this anomalous ideological dependence "on a closed system of Enlightenment-rationalist principles—liberalism—as the sole foundation for public life" that has resulted in the U.S. and other Western nations "hurtling toward [the] abyss," as Michael Anton described in "The Flight 93 Election."[69]

If Western post–World War II liberalism is an anomaly, Hazony's national conservatism represents a return to (historical) normalcy. The route to that return is to reimagine fundamentally the current conventional-wisdom (post-Fukuyaman) view of what constitutes the defining political bipolarity of the age, namely the antithesis of liberalism and nationalism. Hazony obliges by proposing that the real bipolarity of the age is nationalism versus imperialism. In this view, the liberalism shared by the Western powers constitutes the contemporary version of imperialism, which squashes national cultures in favor of international culture, and makes achieving true conservatism, national conservatism, impossible. The perception that globalism is shared by both Republican and Democratic elites is America's transgression in this regard; and here Donald Trump achieves his highest national-conservative marks for making his attack on globalism the heart of his presidential campaign. Internationally, the most significant offender of national conservatism is the European Union.

> Hazony criticizes the neoconservative dream of global American hegemony, which he depicts as one manifestation of this imperial mindset. But the main target of his ire is the European Union, "a universal state . . . whose reach will be limited only by the power that this empire can bring to bear"—the most insidious of empires because it looks [the] least like one.[70]

The Grayed-Out Illiberal State Going Forward

In the end, Trump's government has participated more in the spirit of illiberalism than in illiberalism's concrete restructuring of liberal society. While American institutions are indeed a formidable barrier to structural change, so too liberalism in America has benefited from the considerable political limitations of Donald Trump. Benito Mussolini was not the first post–World War I political leader to stake out the role of the Duce. The poet and war hero Gabriele D'Annunzio had already done so in his year-long seizure of the city of Fiume in Yugoslavia. Mussolini, named for the hero of the left, the indigenous Mexican president Benito Juarez, had grown up in politics since he was a boy in Emilia-Romagna, had been an activist all his life, and had read the important political writers of the day. This put him in the position to eclipse D'Annunzio as leader of the revolt against both the liberal order of the day and its socialist opposition. Will there be a successor to Donald Trump who can sweep up and mobilize right-wing populism in the United States? And if so, will that successor be a more able political actor than Trump?

Under Trump, illiberal structural changes have remained largely potential—like the grayed-out options on a web screen. But there has been an exception, where harsh illiberal policy has been in place, and where it provides a model of how that might be made to spread to other spheres of national life. The exception has been the treatment of refugees on the country's southern border. Giorgio Agamben has taken the notion of the "state of exception" from the Nazi-era political German philosopher Carl Schmitt. A state of exception occurs when one element of government, typically the executive, takes on powers above the law that allow that actor (whom Schmitt calls "the Sovereign") to impose arbitrary rule over some part or the whole of a population.[71] In practice this means that the population in question is deprived of its rights or redefined as noncitizens or nonpersons who are without rights altogether. Agamben argues vigorously that the government of George W. Bush imposed a state of exception in its treatment of prisoners of wars in Iraq and Afghanistan, who were declared outside the rules—outside the very definitions of personhood, in this case "prisoners of war"— of the Geneva Convention. The Bush administration's doctrine of the unitary executive acted as an approximation of the state of exception and allowed the administration to take captured prisoners to Guantánamo Bay and where they were held without trial.

According to the anonymous author of *A Warning*, "Donald Trump proposed designating all migrants entering the US without permission as 'enemy combatants' and shipping them to Guantánamo Bay."[72] The Trump administration's treatment of detainees at the border "would violate the Geneva Conventions," according to Lauren Suken.[73] The legal means the administration used to enforce its border policy was to declare a state of emergency at the border.[74] Julian De Medeiros argues that Trump's very idea of a wall at the border "prefigures a state of exception rather than a state of emergency."[75] In general, how the state of exception under illiberalism is expressed is by showing no respect for minority rights. At an extreme this means defining groups as nonpersons.

In more politically competent hands, Trump's use of declaring a state of emergency to advance predetermined policy goals, especially those that single out groups for less than full citizen rights, could serve as a model for an unencumbered executive operating under the conditions of a state of exception. The technologies that have helped Trump create epistemological chaos are sure to advance in the coming years. Already the capacity to create "deepfakes" is becoming available. These are videos where individuals, like public figures or political opponents, can be made to appear to be saying whatever the videographer wishes; it is a technology that conjures up the movie *Face Off*, where two individuals swapped faces and could operate seamlessly in one another's lives. Deepfakes will make current versions of (real) fake news look as prehistoric as silent movies; it will make Sharpiegate look pre-Gutenberg.[76]

Today the buttons of illiberal power remain largely grayed out on U.S. screens. With a more able populist leader, armed with technologies enabling fabrication of unimpeachable political fables, those buttons could begin lighting up like corn in a popper.

Blue America in 2020

By 2020 Blue America had found their voice. The threats to the foundations of democracy they intuited in their opening exposure to Trumpism four years earlier had become explicit. As Adam Schiff, the lead House Manager in Trump's Senate impeachment trial, put it in January 2020:

> We may be remembered . . . for a single decision . . . affecting the course of our country. I believe this may be one of those moments. A moment we never thought we would see. A moment when our democracy was gravely threatened and not from without but from within.[77]

The impeachment came after Blue America felt it had endured not merely Trump's daily assault on the canons of public discourse, but his skirting criminal behavior. The Mueller Report had adduced ten occasions that merited investigation for obstruction of justice.[78] Michael Cohen went to jail for carrying out Trump's orders![79] The impeachment trial itself was crippled by the administration's refusal to part with documents and the

Republican Senate's refusal to call witnesses. Attempts to hold Trump accountable were met with a two-step hair-trigger: deny the accusation, then mirror the charge, projecting it back on the accusers. Back in 2016, when Donald Trump was first introducing himself as a political candidate to a Blue America at once aghast and amused, the two-step seemed like Trump's personal tic.[80] By 2020, it had morphed into the operative principle of the William Barr's Justice Department, Fox News, and the whole of the Republican Party.[81]

For Blue America, the political business of 2020 was unseating Trump in the November elections. After the impeachment, Blue electoral chances looked fairly straightforwardly good—negative partisanship seemed to rule national elections.[82] In 2016 Democrats were unenthusiastic about Hillary Clinton, but Republicans despised her and turned out in droves. In the 2018 midterms, after enduring two years of Trump, Democrats turned out massively. They had the numbers, and revulsion at Trump had not diminished. Without a fatal self-inflicted error, things looked promising for Blue America. Democratic primary voters rallied around Joe Biden when it looked as though Bernie Sanders might take the nomination—safeguarding against alienating moderates, independents, and Republicans repulsed by Trump. There was a gnawing doubt about what might be happening out of sight and beyond the polls. Trump named Brad Parscale, who had orchestrated his 2016 web strategy, as campaign manager, pushing his campaign chips out on the mastery of cutting-edge and massive microtargeting on Facebook and the like.[83] Still, there was cause for optimism.

But the coronavirus pandemic introduced an unprecedented element into the 2020 electoral calculus. On the one hand, reality—people dying in heightening numbers—made short work of Trumpian dismissals of "hoax." From the perspective of Blue America, could the mortal nature of the pandemic finally break the hold Trump had maintained on his legions throughout four years of nonstop outrage and error? But on the other hand, the pandemic gave a fresh impetus to populist organizing. Trump fanned the flames of a new anti-sheltering movement that put protesters in the street and resembled, even self-consciously, nothing so much as the early Tea Party.[84] Tea Party constitutionalism reappeared in the populists' insistence on their superior grasp of the meanings of tyranny and liberty; indeed this thinking was now accompanied by what could only be called populist epidemiology.[85] Abroad, in the name of coronavirus emergency, illiberalism's leading light, Hungary's Viktor Orbán, effectively used the pandemic to give himself an enabling act, the power to rule by decree.[86] Trump's assertion of *his* "total" powers in the face of the pandemic echoed the impulse behind this development.[87] Blue America's route to restoring democracy's status quo ante Trump had unprecedented shoals to navigate.[88]

ACKNOWLEDGMENTS

I want to thank the University of California at Berkeley. In 2009, the university agreed to house a research unit dedicated to academic study of right-wing movements, history, and ideology. The Berkeley Center for Right-Wing Studies, of which I am the founding director, remains a unique institution, and it has fostered the emergence of a robust field of study both in the United States and abroad. The Center survives entirely on private donations, and I wish to offer the most profound thanks to the many individuals who have contributed to our work. As the saying goes, you know who you are.

For ten years Christine Trost was the key person designing the Center's programs and making the enterprise succeed. Beyond that, Christine is an intellectual force, and my own thinking developed in ongoing collaboration with her. Dozens of visiting scholars, symposium presenters, and graduate students have been though the Center over the years, and they have been an unending source of stimulation and intellectual challenge. My thanks to all of them.

My closest intellectual relationships over the past years have been with Troy Duster, Harry Levine, and Yiannis Gabriel. My work on this book and otherwise has drawn on what have been inexhaustibly fruitful conversations with each of them. Harry and Troy read and commented on this book throughout its writing, for which I have been intensely grateful. Arlie Hochschild read the full manuscript, offering acute observations. I also benefited from comments on portions of the work read by Eliah Bures and Emily Bruce.

This project never would have got off the ground without the work and encouragement of my literary agent, Andy Ross. Thank you, Andy. At The New Press my thanks go to Carl Bromley, who believed in the book from the outset, and championed it despite its sometimes all too slow progress. Thanks, too, to Emily Albarillo, who brought the project home.

I've written *Empire of Resentment* at a time of global and domestic political upheaval, which the book addresses head on. For as long as I can remember in the United States, both left and right have more caricatured one another than seriously tried to understand the other's thinking and actions. These days, this incomprehension is increasingly resolving into a combustible gulf between liberal democracy and nationalism—a gulf that, ominously, is often labeled tribal. For the left, thinking on the right appears more baffling and impenetrable than ever before in our lifetimes. An overriding goal of my work has always been to make sense of right-wing thought to those outside it. *Empire of Resentment* is the attempt to accomplish that goal in this fraught historical moment.

NOTES

1. The Ideological Migration of 2016

1. See Gabriel Sherman, "Inside Operation Trump, the Most Unortho-
dox Campaign in Political History," *New York Magazine*, April 3, 2016, nymag
.com/daily/intelligencer/2016/04/inside-the-donald-trump-presidential
-campaign.html. See also Charlie Warzel and Lam Thuy Vo, "Here's Where
Donald Trump Gets His News," *BuzzFeed*, Dec. 3, 2016, buzzfeednews
.com/article/charliewarzel/trumps-information-universe#.cfdD4Wolo.
From Warzel and Vo:

> During campaign season Trump shared more *Breitbart* links to his
> more than 15 million followers than any other news organization. . . .
> While Trump also shares links from mainstream sites—his second
> most shared site during the time period analyzed was the *Washington
> Post*—Trump's preferred content seems to be right-leaning, hyper-
> partisan sites and opinion blogs including *Newsmax* (18), the *Gateway
> Pundit* (14 links), the *Conservative Treehouse* (11), the *Political Insider*
> (1), *Conservative Tribune* (1), *Infowars* (1), newsninja2012.com (5), and
> westernjournalism.com (1). Trump's Twitter account also shares links
> from a number of obscure personal blogs, like agent54nsa.blogspot
> .com, which hosted a joke post about a fake game show about Monica
> Lewinsky hosted by a character named "Stink Fartinmale."

2. "Populism Revealed as the Word of the Year by Cambridge University Press," Nov. 30, 2017, www.cam.ac.uk/news/populism-revealed-as
-2017-word-of-the-year-by-cambridge-university-press.

The global rise of populism, especially of right-wing populism, has
sparked a considerable outpouring of both academic and journalistic

studies of populism in the past few years. Some of the most important works include:

- Cas Mudde and Cristóbal Rovira Kaltwasser, *Populism: A Very Short Introduction* (Oxford, 2017).
- John Judis, *The Populist Explosion* (Columbia Global Reports, 2016).
- Mabel Berezin, *Illiberal Politics in Neoliberal Times* (Cambridge University Press, 2009).
- Donatella della Porta, Manuela Caiani, and Claudius Wagemann, *Mobilizing on the Extreme Right: Germany, Italy, and the United States* (Oxford University Press, 2012).
- Ruth Wodak, *The Politics of Fear: What Right-Wing Populist Discourses Mean* (Sage, 2015).
- Cynthia Miller-Idriss, *The Extreme Gone Mainstream: Commercialization and Far Right Youth Culture in Germany* (Princeton University Press, 2018).
- Chantal Mouffe, "The Affects of Democracy," *Eurozine*, Nov. 23, 2018, www.eurozine.com/the-affects-of-democracy.

Recent work draws upon older treatments of populism. Among the most important include:

- Margaret Canovan, *Populism* (Houghton, Mifflin, Harcourt, 1981); and *The People* (Polity Press, 2005). (Also see her articles, Margaret Canovan, "Patriotism Is Not Enough," *British Journal of Political Science* 30, no. 3 (Jul. 2000): 413–32; and "Populism for Political Theorists?," *Journal of Political Ideologies* 9, no. 3: 241–52.)
- Ernesto Leclau, *On Populist Reason* (Verso, 2005).
- Michael Kazin, *The Populist Persuasion: An American History* (Basic Books, 1995; revised, Cornell University Press, 2017).

In addition, see the contrasting views of the relationship between populism and the Tea Party in Lawrence Rosenthal and Christine Trost (eds.), *Steep: The Precipitous Rise of the Tea Party* (University of California Press, 2012); Charles Postel, "The Tea Party in Historical Perspective: A Conservative Response to a Crisis of Political Economy (Chapter 1, pp. 25–46); and

Chip Berlet, "Reframing Populist Resentments in the Tea Party Movement (Chapter 2, pp. 47–66).

3. See, for example, Ileana Johnson, "Liberals and Progressives, Telling Other People How to Live Their Lives," ileanajohnson.com/2014/04 /liberals-and-progressives-telling-other-people-how-to-live-their-lives.

4. Pierre Bourdieu, *Distinction* (Routledge, 1984). See especially chapters 1 and 3, pp. 1–54 and 165–206.

5. The ad may be seen at www.youtube.com/watch?v=K4-vEwD_7Hk. The ad was the touchstone for Geoffrey Nunberg's 2006 analysis of the dominance of conservatism's narrative in American politics and the heavily populist content of that narrative. See his *Talking Right: How Conservatives Turned Liberalism into a Tax-Raising, Latte-Drinking, Sushi-Eating, Volvo-Driving, New York Times-Reading, Body-Piercing, Hollywood-Loving, Left-Wing Freak Show* (PublicAffairs).

6. Michael Gerson, "The Last Temptation," *The Atlantic*, April 2018, www.theatlantic.com/magazine/archive/2018/04/the-last-temptation /554066.

7. See Harry G. Levine, "The Birth of American Alcohol Control: Prohibition, the Power Elite and the Problem of Lawlessness," *Contemporary Drug Problems* (Spring 1985): 63–115.

8. See Edward J. Larson, *Summer for the Gods: The Scopes Trial and America's Continuing Debate Over Science and Religion* (Harvard University Press, 1998).

9. See www.imdb.com/title/tt0815241.

10. Gerson, "The Last Temptation."

11. In his *Rule and Ruin: The Downfall of Moderation and the Destruction of the Republican Party from Eisenhower to the Tea Party* (Oxford University Press, 2012), Geoffrey Kabaservice offers a wider view of the development of radicalism in the Republican Party. He dates it from the 1960 end of the Eisenhower presidency—four years before the Republicans nominated Barry ("Extremism in defense of liberty is no vice") Goldwater for president. This prehistory of the Tea Party is also covered in the Rick Perlstein trilogy, beginning in the run-up to Goldwater through the election of Ronald Reagan. See *Before the Storm: Barry Goldwater and the Unmaking of the American Consensus* (Nation Books, 2001); *Nixonland: The Rise of a President and the Fracturing of America* (Scribner, 2008); and *The Invisible Bridge: The*

Fall of Nixon and the Rise of Reagan (Simon and Schuster, 2014). E.J. Dionne also covers this ground in *Why the Right Went Wrong: Conservatism—From Goldwater to the Tea Party and Beyond* (Simon and Schuster, 2016).

12. Arlie Russell Hochschild, *Strangers in Their Own Land: Anger and Mourning on the American Right* (The New Press, 2016).

13. Katherine J. Cramer, *The Politics of Resentment: Rural Consciousness in Wisconsin and the Rise of Scott Walker* (University of Chicago Press, 2016). See also Robert Wuthnow, *The Left Behind: Decline and Rage in Rural America* (Princeton University Press, 2018).

14. J.D. Vance, *Hillbilly Elegy: A Memoir of Family and Culture in Crisis* (HarperCollins, 2016). For an historical approach to the "hillbilly" question, see Nancy Isenberg, *White Trash: The 400-Year Untold History of Class in America* (Viking, 2016), especially pp. 269–309.

There were a few Democrats who foresaw Trump's upset, based on an understanding of the issues raised by Hochschild, Kramer, and Vance. Perhaps foremost among them was the film-maker Michael Moore. See Michael Moore, "5 Reasons Why Trump Will Win," michaelmoore.com, Jul. 21, 2016.

15. See, for example, Michael Savage, *Liberalism Is a Mental Disorder* (Nelson Current, 2005).

16. Charles Krauthammer, "No-Respect Politics," *Washington Post*, Jul. 26, 2002. The mirror image to Krauthammer in this is a classic statement from John Stuart Mill in parliamentary debate, 1866: "I did not mean that Conservatives are generally stupid; I meant, that stupid persons are generally Conservative. I believe that to be so obvious and undeniable a fact that I hardly think any hon. Gentleman will question it." This is quoted widely, and can be found at en.wikiquote.org/wiki/John_Stuart_Mill.

17. See Saheli Roy Choudhury, "President Trump Cites China's Respect for His 'Very, Very Large Brain,'" Sep. 27, 2018, www.cnbc.com/2018/09 /27/president-trump-cites-chinas-respect-for-his-very-very-large-brain .html.

18. See www.thedailybeast.com/trump-im-like-really-smart-a-very-sta ble-genius?ref=home. Trump's assertions of how much smarter he is than others are legion. Here is a tweet from May 13, 2018: "Sorry losers and haters, but my I.Q. is one of the highest -and you all know it! Please don't feel stupid or insecure, it's not your fault."

19. See *Missouri Biographical Dictionary*, 3rd ed., vol. 1, (Somerset, 2001), 50.

20. Quoted in Elaine Ganley, "France's Far-Right Soars in Vote, Joins Mainstream Parties," *Washington Post*, Dec. 7, 2015.

21. Bess Levin, "Trump Wants His Supporters Called the 'Super-Elite' Because 'We Got More Money' and 'Nicer Boats,'" *Vanity Fair*, Jun. 28, 2018, www.vanityfair.com/news/2018/06/trump-wants-his-supporters-called -the-super-elite.

22. See George Joyce and Larrey Anderson, "Anti-Birthers Are Beginning to Worry," *American Thinker*, Aug. 2, 2009, www.americanthinker.com /blog/2009/08/antibirthers_are_beginning_to.html.

23. See Ed Pilkington, "Obama Angers Midwest Voters with Guns and Religion Remark," *The Guardian*, Apr. 14, 2008, www.theguardian.com /world/2008/apr/14/barackobama.uselections2008.

In terms of offering a ripe target for mobilizing around resentment, Obama's clinging remark was the functional equivalent to Hillary Clinton's "deplorables" remark made at a New York City fundraiser in her 2016 presidential campaign.

> You know, to just be grossly generalistic, you could put half of Trump's supporters into what I call the basket of deplorables. Right?" Clinton said. "The racist, sexist, homophobic, xenophobic, Islamaphobic—you name it. And unfortunately there are people like that. And he has lifted them up."

Kate Reilly, "Read Hillary Clinton's 'Basket of Deplorables' Remarks About Donald Trump Supporters," *Time*, Sep. 10, 2016, time.com/4486502/hillary -clinton-basket-of-deplorables-transcript.

24. Alan Rappeport and Maggie Haberman, "Sarah Palin Endorses Donald Trump, Which Could Bolster Him in Iowa," *New York Times*, Jan. 19, 2016.

25. See the *New York Post*'s coverage, nypost.com/video/sarah-palin -rambles-on-possibly-endorses-trump.

26. An excellent account of this "Fusionism" can be found in Jerome Himmelstein, *To the Right: The Transformation of American Conservatism* (University of California Press, 1990), especially chapter 2, pp. 28–62.

27. James Taranto, "Social Issues and the Santorum Surge," *Wall Street*

Journal, Feb. 18, 2012. The book Taranto references is Jeffrey Bell, *The Case for Polarized Politics: Why America Needs Social Conservatism* (Encounter Books, 2012).

28. See, for example, "Warning to Democrats: Most Americans Against U.S. Getting More Politically Correct," *All Things Considered,* Dec. 19, 2018, www.npr.org/2018/12/19/677346260/warning-to-democrats-most-ameri cans-against-u-s-getting-more-politically-correct.

29. Carol Mason, "An American Conflict: Representing the 1974 Kanawha County Textbook Controversy," *Appalachian Journal* 32, no. 3 (Spring 2005), 352–78.

30. See Kevin DeYoung, "Republican Party Platforms on Abortion," *The Gospel Coalition,* Sep. 4, 2012, www.thegospelcoalition.org/blogs/kevin -deyoung/republican-party-platforms-on-abortion.

31. John Sides et al., *Identity Crisis: The 2016 Presidential Campaign and the Battle for the Meaning of America* (Princeton University Press, 2018), 77.

32. See Steve Benen, "A Trip Down Memory Lane with Newt Gingrich," *Washington Monthly,* Jan. 11, 2011, washingtonmonthly.com/2011/01 /11/a-trip-down-memory-lane-with-newt-gingrich. See also Frank Rich, "Journal: Gingrich Family Values," *New York Times,* May 14, 1995, www .nytimes.com/1995/05/14/opinion/journal-gingrich-family-values.html.

On the right, this tendency to blame, in an ideologically shotgun manner, specific horrible events on cultural tendencies they disapprove of has remained an enduring staple. Famously, the biggest names in Christian TV evangelism, Jerry Falwell and Pat Robertson, blamed the September 11, 2001, attacks on the "secularizers": the ACLU, abortionists, pagans, feminists, gays, lesbians, People for the American Way: www.youtube.com /watch?v=kMkBgA9_oQ4.

More recently, an Ohio state representative blamed the August 3, 2019, weekend mass shootings (in El Paso and Dayton) as follows:

Keller, in the post, placed the blame for mass shootings on "the breakdown of the traditional American family (thank you, transgender, homosexual marriage, and drag queen advocates); fatherlessness, a subject no one discusses or believes is relevant; the ignoring of violent video games; the relaxing of laws against criminals (open borders); the acceptance of recreational marijuana; failed school policies (hello, parents who defend misbehaving students): disrespect to law enforcement (thank you, Obama)."

Scott Wartman and Jessie Balmert, "Southwest Ohio Politician Blames Shootings on 'Drag Queen Advocates' and Open Borders," *Cincinnati Enquirer,* Aug. 4, 2019, www.cincinnati.com/story/news/politics/2019/08 /04/ohio-shooting-state-rep-blames-shootings-drag-queen-advocates-and -open-borders/1918106001.

33. The government shutdown was also motivated by the attempt to bring down the Patient Protection and Affordable Care Act, or Obamacare.

34. See Chuck Jones, "Trump's Twin Deficits Are Exploding," *Forbes,* Mar. 9, 2019, www.forbes.com/sites/chuckjones/2019/03/09/trumps-twin -deficits-are-exploding/#46ee56897ffa.

In July 2019, Rush Limbaugh had the following exchange on his daily radio program (www.rushlimbaugh.com/daily/2019/07/16/caller-wants-to -nominate-a-normal-republican):

CALLER: (unintelligible) . . . Trump Derangement Syndrome, and that will allow any normal Republican to get elected in 2020. Republicans can nominate a young, potentially two-term president, one that believes in fiscal conservatism. We're gonna have . . . In 2019, there's gonna be a $1 trillion deficit. Trump doesn't really care about that. He's not really a fiscal conservative. We have to acknowledge that Trump has been cruelly used.

RUSH: Nobody is a fiscal conservative anymore. All this talk about concern for the deficit and the budget has been bogus for as long as it's been around.

35. A writer with day-to-day experience on a right-wing website observed: "Even in the early days of the campaign, cultural conservatives, fiscal conservatives, the weirdos who talked only about chemtrails—they all had one thing in common. They wanted a president who would stick it to the liberals. *They didn't care that supporting him would mean changing their positions on any number of issues* [emphasis added]." Adam Sokol, "The Life of a Comment Moderator for a Right-Wing Website," *New York Times,* Mar. 2, 2019.

36. "A Survey of Italy: The Triumph of Populism," *Economist*, Jul. 7, 2001, www.economist.com/special-report/2001/07/07/the-triumph-of-populism.

37. Lawrence Rosenthal, "Italy's Election Reflects Forces That Gave Us President Trump," *San Francisco Chronicle*, Mar. 16, 2018. For election results, see *The Local It*, May 27, 2019, www.thelocal.it/20190527/winners -losers-italy-eu-election-results.

38. The Haas Institute for a Fair and Inclusive Society has explored Othering and Belonging in the form of journals and conferences. See haas institute.berkeley.edu.

39. Yiannis Gabriel, *Organizing Words: A Critical Thesaurus for Social and Organizational Studies* (Oxford University Press, 2008), 213.

40. Karl Mannheim, *Ideology and Utopia: An Introduction to the Sociology of Knowledge* (Routledge, 2000), 107.

41. In *Ideology and Utopia*, p. 110, Mannheim writes:

> Historical conservatism is characterized by the fact that it is aware of that irrational realm in the life of the state which cannot be managed by administration. It recognizes that there is an unorganized and incalculable realm which is the proper sphere of politics. It focuses its attention almost exclusively on the impulsive, irrational factors . . . entirely beyond human comprehension and infers that . . . human reason is impotent to understand or control them.

The seminal statement of this point of view, of this awakening to conservative identity, was Edmund Burke's *Reflections on the Revolution in France* (1790)—a direct response to the liberal and democratic aspirations of the French Revolution. In the U.S., the seminal attempt to ground American conservatism in the Burkean tradition was Russell Kirk's 1953 *The Conservative Mind*, which, via William F. Buckley's *National Review*, became integrated into the worldview of the New Right that came to power in the Reagan election of 1980.

42. Ashley Jardina, *White Identity Politics* (Cambridge University Press, 2019), 36.

43. "Who We Are," *The American Conservative*, www.theamericancon servative.com/who-we-are. Last accessed June 2016.

Thomas Chatterton Williams cites what is perhaps Carl Schmitt's most fundamental work, "The Concept of the Political," where

> he posed the question that still defines the right-wing mind-set: Who is a people's friend, and who is an enemy? For Schmitt, to identify one's enemies was to identify one's inner self. In another essay, he wrote, "Tell me who your enemy is, and I'll tell you who you are."

Thomas Chatterton Williams, "The French Origins of 'You Will Not Replace Us,'" *The New Yorker*, Nov. 27, 2017.

Schmitt was the Nazi philosopher whose thinking was influential for Leo Strauss, who played the role of intellectual éminence grise for much of American neoconservatism; Schmitt later became influential on the left, in the 1990s, among Andrew Arato's *Telos* group and the Italian thinker Giorgio Agamben, who would apply one of Schmitt's fundamental concepts, "the state of exception," to analyzing the policy directions of George W. Bush's administration in the USA (see chapter 6).

44. Todd Gitlin, "The Left, Lost in the Politics of Identity," *Harper's Magazine*, Sep. 1993.

45. See Susan Davis, *Wall Street Journal*, Oct. 17, 2008.

46. Scott Eric Kaufman, "Majority of Likely GOP Primary Voters Could Believe Operation Jade Helm 15 Is Probably a Federal Invasion of Texas," *Salon*, May 14, 2014.

47. See takingourcountryback.net/about-us. Last accessed June 2016.

48. Niccolò Machiavelli, *The Prince*, trans. W.K. Marriott (Project Gutenberg, 2006), www.gutenberg.org/files/1232/1232-h/1232-h.htm.

49. Sides et al., *Identity Crisis*. See also Jardina, *White Identity Politics*, pp. 116–17.

2. The Tea Party: Right Populism with a Koch-Brothers Mask

1. Jesse Byrnes, "Trump Clinches GOP Nomination," *The Hill*, May 26, 2016, thehill.com/blogs/blog-briefing-room/281350-ap-trump-clinches-gop-nomination.

2. See twitchy.com/gregp-3534/2015/06/17/clown-runs-for-prez-ny-daily-news-taunts-donald-trump-with-brutal-cover.

3. "Truthiness" was Merriam-Webster's word of the year in 2006. A dictionary definition reads: "the quality of seeming to be true according to one's intuition, opinion, or perception without regard to logic, factual evidence or the like." From Dictionary.com, May 12, 2018, www.dictionary .com/e/word-of-the-day/truthiness-2018-05-12.

4. Todd Beamon, "Michael Reagan: Trump Saying What All of Us Are Thinking," *Newsmax*, Aug. 26, 2015, www.newsmax.com/Newsmax-Tv /Michael-Reagan-Roger-Stone-Trump-tapping/2015/08/26/id/672096.

5. Quoted in Ellen Barry, "Boris Johnson Says Immigrants to U.K. Should Be Forced to Learn English," *New York Times*, Jul. 7, 2019.

6. Libertarians have been left out of this description of the makeup of the Tea Party. It is true that on issues of political economy Libertarians overlap with free-market fundamentalists—and indeed often surpass them in the Ayn-Randian objectivist, self-interest-is-the-unique-moral-virtue direction. Some Libertarians, like Rand Paul and Justin Amash, ran as Tea Partiers at the outset of the movement. They, like some commentators and academics, were quick to call the Tea Party a movement based on libertarian principles and tended to dismiss the movement's association with populism as either irrelevant or attempts coming from the left to discredit the movement. Much, including the movement's ideological fluidity, has demonstrated the wishful thinking of this point of view.

Examples of this thinking include:

- David Kirby and Emily Ekins, *Libertarian Roots of the Tea Party*, Cato Institute, Aug. 6, 2012, object.cato.org/sites/cato .org/files/pubs/pdf/PA705.pdf.
- Elizabeth Price Foley, *The Tea Party: Three Principles* (Cambridge University Press, 2012).

7. For an investigative examination of the extent of the Koch brothers' prodigious use of their money in politics, see Jane Meyer, *Dark Money: The Hidden History of the Billionaires Behind the Rise of the Radical Right* (Anchor Books, 2016). For the rise of the Koch brothers as a business empire, see Christopher Leonard, *Kochland: The Secret History of Koch Industries and Corporate Power in America* (Simon and Schuster, 2019).

8. See Matthew Belvedere, "Freedom Caucus Member: Obamacare Replacement Bill Is Largest Welfare Program in GOP History," CNBC,

March 24, 2017, www.cnbc.com/2017/03/24/freedom-caucus-member-oba
macare-replacement-bill-largest-welfare-program-in-gop-history.html.

See also this excerpt from Mo Brooks's speech using traditional free-
market rhetoric to oppose disaster aid to Puerto Rico after Hurricane
Maria:

> Puerto Rico, like America, suffers from a bloated central government,
> welfare programs that undermine the work ethic, decades of finan-
> cial mismanagement by elected leaders. . . . Only 40 percent of Puerto
> Ricans are employed or looking for work. Why bother to get a job
> when American tax-payers pay Puerto Ricans to not work by doling
> out free food, free health care and other welfare . . .
>
> *Congressional Record,* April 20, 2016.

The Freedom Caucus maintained their free-market fundamentalist ideology well into the Trump administration. See, for example, Juliegrace Brufke,
"Freedom Caucus Formally Opposes Trump's Budget Deal," *The Hill,* Jul.
23, 2019 (thehill.com/homenews/house/454439-freedom-caucus-formally
-opposes-trumps-budget-deal):

> The House Freedom Caucus took an official position Tuesday not to
> back President Trump's spending deal and agreement to lift the debt
> ceiling, citing concerns with its impact on the national debt.

This, despite bending toward Trump in most other matters. Mick Mulvaney, a founding member of the Freedom Caucus, became Trump's director of the Office of Management and Budget, acting director of the Con-
sumer Protection Bureau, and acting White House chief of staff.

9. Sam Tanenhaus, *The Death of Conservatism* (Random House, 2009).

10. See www.cnn.com/videos/politics/2016/02/15/donald-trump-jeb-bu
sh-george-w-bush-911-attacks.cnn.

11. On the debt: "With no fanfare and little notice, the national debt
has grown by more than $4 trillion during George W. Bush's presidency.
It's the biggest increase under any president in U.S history." Mark Knoller,
"Bush Administration Adds $4 Trillion to National Debt," CBSNews.com,
www.cbsnews.com/8301-500803_162-4486228-500803.html, Sep. 29, 2008.

On job creation: "The Bush administration created about three million jobs (net) over its eight years, a fraction of the 23 million jobs created under President Bill Clinton's administration and only slightly better than President George H.W. Bush did in his four years in office. . . . The current President Bush, once taking account how long he's been in office, shows the worst track record for job creation since the government began keeping records 1939." Sudeep Reddy, "Bush on Jobs: The Worst Track Record on Record," *Wall Street Journal Real Time Economics* (blog), Jan. 9, 2009, blogs.wsj.com/economics/2009/01/09/bush-on-jobs-the-worst-track-record -onrecord.

12. See Clarence Y.H. Lo, "Astroturf Versus Grass Roots: Scenes from Early Tea Party Mobilization," in Lawrence Rosenthal and Christine Trost, *Steep: The Precipitous Rise of the Tea Party* (University of California Press, 2012).

This question gets at the two-headed nature of the movement, as described earlier, free-market fundamentalism and populism, and asks, essentially, was the populist, or grass-roots quality, of the movement a genuine uprising, or was it somehow a front for the powerful and established interests of free-market absolutism. In the USA, this debate is framed as: was the Tea Party a grassroots movement or an Astroturf movement? (Astroturf is synthetic grass that was developed in the 1960s for indoor baseball stadiums in the USA.)

The answer is, the movement was both. While the "Astroturf" wing established right-wing institutions, and helped form and guide the movement toward focusing on free-market fundamentalism, they soon discovered that the groups that formed in other American cities and small towns would act with considerable autonomy.

Focused as they were on extreme free-market policies, the "Astroturf" Tea Party very much wanted to separate the Tea Party from the social issues: that collection of moral and, often, religious, issues that are central to the traditionalists of the right wing—issues like opposition to abortion, and opposition to the separation of church and state. The "Astroturf" wing often claimed that focusing on the place of the social issues in dealing with the Tea Party was a reflection of liberal media bias—attempting to show the Tea Party in a negative light, as "wingnuts." But at the grassroots level, there was no question about the weight and importance of the social issues. In one Pennsylvania Tea Party group, a fierce debate broke out about whether the social issues should be part of the agenda. Here's how one activist put it: "God did not wake me up for four months at a time at four in the morning to say . . . 'we've got a tax issue.' . . . He woke me up because he said, 'my country doesn't love me like it used to love me.'"

13. In "The Tea Party and the Remaking of Republican Conservatism," Vanessa Williamson and her fellow researchers identify "deservingness" as the Tea Partiers' key discriminator between themselves and those they oppose.

Vanessa Williamson, Theda Skocpol, and John Coggin, "The Tea Party and the Remaking of Republican Conservatism," *Perspectives on Politics*, vol. 9 (2011): 25–43. See also Theda Skocpol and Vanessa Williamson, *The Tea Party and the Remaking of American Conservatism* (Oxford University Press, 2012).

14. Jonathan Capehart, "Republicans Had It In for Obama Before Day 1," *Washington Post*, Aug. 10, 2012, www.washingtonpost.com/blogs/post -partisan/post/republicans-had-it-in-for-obama-before-day-1/2012/08/10 /0c96c7c8-e31f-11e1-ae7f-d2a13e249eb2_blog.html.

15. Jonathan Weisman and Ashley Parker, "Republicans Back Down, Ending Crisis Over Shutdown and Debt Limit, *New York Times*, Oct. 16, 2013:

> The result of the impasse that threatened the nation's credit rating was a near total defeat for Republican conservatives, who had engineered the budget impasse as a way to strip the new health care law of funding even as registration for benefits opened Oct. 1 or, failing that, to win delays in putting the program into place.

16. Ewen MacAskill, "US Debt Crisis Threatens Global Markets as Congress Is Locked in Blame Game," *The Guardian*, Jul. 24, 2011.

17. See the letter the Kochs sent to all U.S. senators in 2013 arguing in favor of the goals of the Tea Partiers, but refusing to endorse the tactic of government shutdown. They write:

> Koch believes that Obamacare will increase deficits, lead to an overall lowering of the standard of healthcare in America, and raise taxes. However, Koch has not taken a position on the legislative tactic of

tying the continuing resolution to defunding Obamacare nor have we lobbied on legislative provisions defunding Obamacare.

cdn.theatlantic.com/assets/media/img/posts/Letter%20to%20Capitol%20 Hill%20100913.pdf.

18. Lawrence Rosenthal, "Tea Party Tuesday in Tampa," *Huffington Post*, Aug. 30, 2012, www.huffpost.com/entry/tea-party-tuesday-in -tamp_b_1843756.

19. "Just as surely as the Nazis during World War Two and the Soviet communists during the Cold War, the enemy we face today is bent on our destruction. As in other times, we are in a war we did not start, and have no choice but to win."—Vice President Dick Cheney, speech at Republican National Convention, 2004.

20. Chip Berlet, "Reframing Populist Resentments in the Tea Party Movement," in Rosenthal and Trost, *Steep*, 57.

21. Vanessa Williamson, Theda Skocpol, and John Coggin, "The Tea Party and the Remaking of Republican Conservatism," *Perspective on Politics* 9, no. 1 (Mar. 2011): 25–43, scholar.harvard.edu/files/williamson/files /tea_party_pop.pdf.

22. The Commerce Clause is Article I, Section 8, Clause 3 of the Constitution. It reads:

United States Congress shall have power to . . . regulate Commerce with foreign Nations, and among the several States, and with the Indian Tribes.

Before Franklin Roosevelt's 1932 election to the presidency in the Great Depression, the Commerce Clause had been invoked to create the Interstate Commerce Commission in 1887 (largely to attack monopolistic practices in the railroad industry) and the major anti-trust acts of the Progressive Era (Sherman Act, 1890, Clayton Act, 1914, Federal Trade Commission Act, 1914). But in FDR's first term, New Deal legislation, especially the National Recovery Act, was nullified as unconstitutional by a series of 5–4 votes in the Supreme Court. However, after FDR's landslide reelection in 1936 (523 electoral votes to Republican Alf Landon's 8; 61 percent of the popular vote), one Supreme Court Justice, Owen Roberts, switched sides and New Deal legislation proceeded apace and the Commerce Clause was established as settled law supporting the federal government's initiatives in the national economy. Roberts's changing sides was the so-called "Switch in Time That Saved Nine" as it pre-empted Roosevelt's designs on expanding the number of Supreme Court justices to the end of successfully enacting the New Deal.

23. Randy Barnett, "We Lost on Healthcare. But the Constitution Won," *Washington Post*, Jun. 29, 2012.

24. At a Tea Party rally in the spring of 2009, Texas governor Rick Perry suggested secession as a possible remedy for an overreaching federal government. W. Gardner Selby and Jason Embry, "Perry Stands by Secession Idea, Says He Won't Push It," *Austin American-Statesman*, Apr. 17, 2009.

25. Randy Barnett and William J. Howell, "The Case for a Repeal Amendment," Cato Institute, Sep. 16, 2010, www.cato.org/publications/commentary/case-repeal-amendment.

26. Skousen was a Mormon (Beck converted to Mormonism in 1999, and attributed his success in life to his new faith) who sympathized with the conviction of the John Birch Society (JBS) founder, Robert Welch, that Dwight Eisenhower was a committed member of the International Communist conspiracy. This was the view that led the New Right, spearheaded by William F. Buckley, to essentially read the JBS out of the conservative movement for its extremism. Only during the Tea Party era was the JBS again to be seen in attendance at such national conservative events as the annual CPAC convention. Skousen's most famous book, *The Five Thousand Year Leap: Twenty-Eight Great Ideas That Are Changing the World* (National Center for Constitutional Studies, 1981), argued for the Biblical origins of the U.S. Constitution. Beck's promotion of the book led to sustained interest in it and unprecedented sales in 2009–2010.

27. Beck would regularly promote Tea Party events on his program. His direct organizing included his 9-12 Project, and culminated in his Restoring Honor Rally, held at the Lincoln Memorial in Washington, DC, on August 28, 2010, coinciding with the anniversary of Martin Luther King's "I Have a Dream" speech, which took place at the same location. Estimates run from 300,000 to 650,000 attendees. See content.time.com/time/photogallery/0,29307,2016058_2185996,00.html.

28. Randy Barnett appeared on Beck's program on April 9, 2009. The show was on states' rights, or "What redress do states have who are tired of getting kicked around by the federal government?"

29. "Tea Party opposition to bailouts, stimulus packages, and health-care reform is reflected in various proposals to amend the Constitution, including proposals to require a balanced budget, repeal the Sixteenth and Seventeenth Amendments, and give states a veto power over federal laws (the so-called Repeal Amendment)." Elizabeth Price Foley, "Sovereignty, Rebalanced: The Tea Party and Constitutional Amendments," *Tennessee Law Review* 78 (Aug. 3, 2011): 751.

30. Barnett specialized in the closely related Ninth Amendment. The Ninth Amendment reads:

The enumeration in the Constitution, of certain rights, shall not be construed to deny or disparage others retained by the people.

31. Rebecca E. Zietlow, arguing that the Tea Party's constitutional position is a combination of two schools of thought, "popular originalism" and "popular constitutionalism," writes:

Tea Party activists have invoked the Constitution as the foundation of their conservative political philosophy. These activists are engaged in 'popular originalism,' using popular constitutionalism—constitutional interpretation outside of the courts—to invoke originalism as interpretive method.

Rebecca E. Zietlow, "Popular Originalism? The Tea Party Movement and Constitutional Theory," *Florida Law Review* 64 (2012): 483–512.

32. See Christopher W. Schmidt, "Popular Constitutionalism on the Right: Lessons from the Tea Party," *Denver University Law Review* 88, no. 3 (2011): 523–57.

33. Christopher W. Schmidt, "The Tea Party and the Constitution," *Hastings Constitutional Law Quarterly* 39 (2011): 193; Chicago-Kent College of Law research paper, March 18, 2011, 194. The epigraph of Schmidt's article quotes the Hartford Tea Party Patriots mission statement:

We are dedicated to educating, motivating, and activating our fellow citizens, using the power of the values, ideals, and tenets of our
Founding Fathers.

34. www.freerepublic.com/focus/news/2633633/posts. Last viewed August 2013.

35. Michael Lind, "Let's Stop Pretending the Constitution Is Sacred,"
Salon, Jan. 4, 2011, www.salon.com/2011/01/04/lind_tea_party_constitution.

36. The Constitution has been read aloud in the House at the opening of
each Congress ever since.

37. Richard E. Cohen, "Bills Must Cite Constitution," *Politico*, Dec. 17,
2010, www.politico.com/story/2010/12/gop-bills-must-cite-constitution-046
565.

38. Quoted in Eamon Duffy, "The World Split in Two," *New York Review
of Books*, Apr. 18, 2019, 65.

39. Sanford Levinson, "The Constitution in American Civil Religion,"
The Supreme Court Review vol. 1979 (1979): 123–51.

40. Robert N. Bellah, "Civil Religion in America," *Daedalus* 96, no. 1
(Winter 1967): 1–21. Also see Bellah's *Broken Covenant: American Civil Religion in a Time of Trial* (University of Chicago Press, 2nd ed., 1992).

41. Reagan frequently referred to the Winthrop quote in his presidential campaigns, as he pointed out in perhaps his most famous reference to
it, from his election eve address to the nation in 1980:

I know I have told before of the moment in 1630 when the tiny ship
Arabella bearing settlers to the New World lay off the Massachusetts
coast. To the little bank of settlers gathered on the deck John Winthrop said: we shall be a city upon a hill. The eyes of all people are
upon us, so that if we shall deal falsely with our God in this work we
have undertaken and so cause him to withdraw his present help from
us, we shall be made a story and a byword through the world.

Well, America became more than a story, or a byword more than a
sterile footnote in history. I have quoted John Winthrop's words more
than once on the campaign trail this year for I believe that Americans

in 1980 are every bit as committed to that vision of a shining city on a hill, as were those long ago settlers.

Ronald Reagan Presidential Library and Museum, "Election Eve Address a Vision for America," www.reaganlibrary.gov/11-3-80.

The ideological distance between Reagan Republican orthodoxy and the Trump Republican party was quite clear in Reagan's 1989 farewell address, where he went out of his way to tie the "shining city on a hill" to the country's embrace of immigration:

The past few days . . . I've thought a bit of the "shining city upon a hill." . . . I've spoken of the shining city all my political life, but I don't know if I ever quite communicated what I saw when I said it. But in my mind it was a tall, proud city built on rocks stronger than oceans, wind-swept, God-blessed, and teeming with *people of all kinds living in harmony* and peace; a city with free ports that hummed with commerce and creativity. And if there had to be city walls, the walls had doors and *the doors were open to anyone with the will and the heart to get here.* That's how I saw it, and see it still [emphasis added].

Ronald Reagan Presidential Library and Museum, "Farewell Address to the Nation," www.reaganlibrary.gov/research/speeches/011189i.

42. H.Res.397 read:

Affirming the rich spiritual and religious history of our Nation's founding and subsequent history and expressing support for designation of the first week in May as "America's Spiritual Heritage Week" for the appreciation of and education on America's history of religious faith.

[Approximately seven dozen instances are cited here that mention God, spirituality, the Bible, etc., in the course of American history.]

Resolved, That the United States House of Representatives—

(1) affirms the rich spiritual and diverse religious history of our Nation's founding and subsequent history, including up to the current day;

(2) recognizes that the religious foundations of faith on which America was built are critical underpinnings of our Nation's most

valuable institutions and form the inseparable foundation for America's representative processes, legal systems, and societal structures;

(3) rejects, in the strongest possible terms, any effort to remove, obscure, or purposely omit such history from our Nation's public buildings and educational resources; and

(4) expresses support for designation of a "America's Spiritual Heritage Week" every year for the appreciation of and education on America's history of religious faith

See www.congress.gov/bill/111th-congress/house-resolution/397/text.

43. Kristol writes:

[The new class] are the people whom liberal capitalism had sent to college in order to help manage its affluent, highly technological, mildly paternalistic, "post-industrial" society. . . . [The] "new class" consists of scientists, lawyers, city planners, social workers, educators, criminologists, sociologists, public health doctors, etc.—a substantial number of whom find their careers in the expanding public sector rather than the private. . . . in actuality they are acting upon a hidden agenda: to propel the nation from that modified version of capitalism we call "the welfare state" toward an economic system so stringently regulated in detail as to fulfill many of the traditional anti-capitalist aspirations of the Left. . . . Under the guise of nasty "externalities"—[like pollution]—more and more of the basic economic decisions are being removed from the marketplace and transferred to the "public"—i.e., political—sector, where the "new class" by virtue of its expertise and skills, is so well represented. . . . The media, which are also for the most part populated by members of this "new class" who believe—as the Left has always believed—it is government's responsibility to cure all the ills of the human condition, and who ridicule those politicians who deny the possibility . . . of government doing any such ambitious thing.

Irving Kristol, "On Corporate Capitalism in America," *The Public Interest,* 1975, www.nationalaffairs.com/storage/app/uploads/public/58e/1a4/bfd/58 e1a4bfdcb57891670629.pdf.

44. Robert B. Horwitz, *America's Right: Anti-Establishment Conservatism from Goldwater to the Tea Party* (Polity Press, 2013), 16.

45. Angelo Codevilla, *The Ruling Class: How They Corrupted America and What WE Can Do About It* (Beaufort Books, 2010).

46. Horwitz, *America's Right*, 17: "To the Christian right and neoconservatives there was no such thing as disinterested social science; that was simply a mask for liberal social policy."

47. Pierce Nahigyan, "Senator Jim Inhofe: Portrait of a Serial Science-Denier," *Planet Experts*, Nov. 7, 2014, www.planetexperts.com /senator-jim-inhofe-portrait-serial-science-denier.

48. George was the lead author of the "Manhattan Declaration: A Call of Christian Conscience," published just after the 2008 election, which promised civil disobedience in the name of opposition to abortion, same-sex marriage, and infringement of religious freedom. His legal theories, based on Christian-based natural law, have been influential even among liberal judicial thinkers. See his *Conscience and Its Enemies: Confronting the Dogmas of Liberal Secularism* (ISI Books, 2013).

49. Barton's 2012 book, *The Jefferson Lies: Exposing the Myths You've Always Believed About Thomas Jefferson*, was withdrawn by its Christian publishing house, Thomas Nelson, after his misconceptions about Jefferson as a Christian were exposed by a rash of reviewers and professional historians. See Stephanie Simon, "Historian Remains Key Ally of the Right," *Politico*, Sep. 8, 2013, www.politico.com/story/2013 /09/david-barton-historian-right-christian-096443#ixzz2eOsdsS1E. See also Elise Hu, "Publisher Pulls Controversial Thomas Jefferson Book, Citing Loss of Confidence," NPR, Aug. 9, 2012, www.npr.org/sections /thetwo-way/2012/08/09/158510648/publisher-pulls-controversial -thomas-jefferson-book-citing-loss-of-confidence.

50. This was DeLay's answer to the question, "When did people stop doing good for others in the name of God?" The exchange took place on *The Difference*, a talk show on Global Evangelical Television. Cited in talkingpointsmemo.com/livewire/delay-god-wrote-constitution, Feb. 20, 2014.

51. There were a number of variations on this wording. Images of a variety of signs are available at www.google.com/search?q=government+hand s+off+my+medicare&tbm=isch&source=univ&sa=X&ved=2ahUKEwiay_ -G3ufjAhUAFzQIHdbZBR4QsAR6BAgGEAE&biw=1091&bih=629.

52. An exchange at a town hall meeting held by Rep. Robert Inglis (R-SC), as reported in the *Huffington Post*:

Someone reportedly told Inglis, "Keep your government hands off my Medicare."

"I had to politely explain that, 'Actually, sir, your health care is being provided by the government,'" Inglis told the *Post*. "But he wasn't having any of it."

Reported in Bob Cesca, "Keep Your Goddamn Government Hands Off My Medicare!" *Huffington Post*, Sep. 2, 2009, www.huffpost.com/entry/get-your -goddamn-governme_b_252326.

53. "Opening Statement: Sen. Jeff Sessions," NPR, Jul. 13, 2009, www .npr.org/templates/story/story.php?storyId=106540813.

54. This and subsequent quotations from Bork are taken from the transcript of Bork's 1987 hearing before the Senate Judiciary Committee, www .loc.gov/law/find/nominations/bork/hearing-pt1.pdf. Christopher Caldwell has written a recent variation on this argument in *The Age of Entitlement: America Since the Sixties* (Simon and Shuster, 2020), in which he locates the Civil Rights Act of 1964 as the touchstone of what he deems the lamentable pattern of how minority rights (read identity politics and political correctness) have come not merely to infringe on the rights of lunch-counter owners and wedding-cake bakers to choose their own clientele, but has effectively ushered in wholesale abandonment of the prelapsarian Constitution.

55. The slogan was notably backed up by the work of the economist Joseph Stiglitz:

It's no use pretending that what has obviously happened has not in fact happened. The upper 1 percent of Americans are now taking in nearly a quarter of the nation's income every year. In terms of wealth rather than income, the top 1 percent control 40 percent. Their lot in life has improved considerably. Twenty-five years ago, the corresponding figures were 12 percent and 33 percent.

Joseph E. Stiglitz, "Of the 1%, by the 1%, for the 1%," *Vanity Fair*, May 2011, www.vanityfair.com/society/features/2011/05/top-one-percent-201105.

56. Like the Trump movement, though not the Tea Party, OWS was part of something global. Soon after Occupy Wall Street was formed, a wave of Occupy protests swept across cities in Asia, Europe, and the Americas. See

Cara Buckley and Rachel Donadio, "Buoyed by Wall St. Protests, Rallies Sweep the Globe," *New York Times*, Oct. 15, 2011, www.nytimes.com/2011 /10/16/world/occupy-wall-street-protestsworldwide.html.

57. A 2011 Pew Research report showed that "households headed by adults 35 and under have 68% less wealth than those their age a quarter century ago." At the same time, households headed by adults age 65 and older "have seen their wealth increase 42% compared to their counterparts 25 years ago." Consequently, older households are 47 times wealthier than younger households today, compared to only 10 times wealthier in 1984. Eva Pereira, "Wealth Inequality Between Young and Old Generations Reaches Record High," *Forbes*, Nov. 8, 2011, www.forbes .com/sites/evapereira/2011/11/08/wealth-inequality-between-young-and -oldgenerations-reaches-record-high.

58. Mark Lilla, "A Tale of Two Reactions," *New York Review of Books*, May 14, 1998.

59. "Ross Perot in 1992 on NAFTA and the 'Giant Sucking Sound,'" You-Tube video, www.youtube.com/watch?v=xQ7kn2-GEmM.

60. Todd Purdam, "Facets of Clinton," *New York Times Magazine*, May 19, 1996.

61. From Clinton's acceptance speech at the 1996 Democratic National Convention:

My fellow Americans, this must be a campaign of ideas, not a campaign of insults. The American people deserve it.

Now, here's the main idea. I love and revere the rich and proud history of America, and I am determined to take our best traditions into the future. But with all respect, we do not need to build a bridge to the past [this was Clinton's contrast to his Republican opponent Senator Robert Dole of Kansas], we need to build a bridge to the future, and that is what I commit to you to do.

So tonight let us resolve to build that bridge to the 21st century, to meet our challenges and protect our values.

See "Clinton's Speech Accepting the Democratic Nomination for President," *New York Times*, Aug. 30, 1996, www.nytimes.com/1996/08/30/us/clinton -s-speech-accepting-the-democratic-nomination-for-president.html.

62. Francis Fukuyama, "The End of History?," *National Interest* (Summer 1989): 3–18.

See also Fukuyama's book, *The End of History and the Last Man* (Avon, 1992).

63. Fukuyama, "The End of History?," 3.

64. Umberto Eco, "Ur-Fascism," *New York Review of Books*, Jun. 22, 1995.

Interestingly, Eco contrasts this description with the lesser totalitarian nature of Italian Fascism, and agrees with Fukuyama's conviction that Nazism, but not Fascism, represented the only real nationalist challenger to liberal democracy:

Italian fascism was certainly a dictatorship, but it was not totally totalitarian, not because of its mildness but rather because of the philosophical weakness of its ideology. Contrary to common opinion, fascism in Italy had no special philosophy.

65. In this, Trump rhetorically echoed European far-right parties that, unlike the American far-right, typically did not attack their country's programs of social insurance for retirement, health care, child care, and more.

66. It's a small point, but telling: Since at least the 1990s Republicans have disparaged trial lawyers—for their role in prosecuting corporations for harm to individuals or classes of people; and for their support of Democratic politicians. In Trump's takeover of the Republican agenda, this perennial issue seems to have melted away in Republican campaigns. Trump's MO as a businessman employed lawsuits (and the threat of lawsuits) in epic fashion. *USA Today* counted the Trump Organization involved in 4,095 lawsuits over thirty years' time. See "Donald Trump: Three Decades, 4095 Lawsuits," *USA Today*, www.usatoday.com/pages/interactives/trump-lawsuits.

67. See, for example, Masha Gessen, "The Trump-Russia Investigation and the Mafia State," *New Yorker*, Jan. 31, 2019, www.newyorker.com/news/our-columnists/the-trump-russia-investigation-and-the-mafia-state. Gessen cites the Hungarian sociologist Bálint Magyar, who she says "created the concept of the 'post-Communist mafia state.'" Magyar is the author of *Post-Communist Mafia State: The Case of Hungary* (Central European Press,

2018). See also Mark Galeotti, *The Vory: Russia's Super Mafia* (Yale University Press, 2018).

68. Stein Ringen, "Beijing Tightens the Screws," *Open Democracy*, Oct. 2, 2015, www.opendemocracy.net/en/beijing-tightens-screws.

The Fukuyamian expectation that wealth would perforce transform China in the direction of liberalism and the failure of that vision was widespread in the American and international business community. Here it is expressed by a vice president of JP Morgan's corporate investment bank:

> [T]here's a lot of hand-wringing in Washington . . . but there is really a view that China would, that China as it got richer . . . would liberalize. The view that as it was more entrenched in the global system, it would uphold the global existing order. And now it's become more clear that in many ways, they're not. They're definitely not becoming more liberal. And in many ways, they're seeking to upturn the existing order of global trade and existing order of global institutions.

Alex Wolf, interviewed in "Five Things You Need to Know About the Trade War," *JP Morgan Securities*, Aug. 13, 2019, www.jpmorgan.com/securities /insights/five-things-you-need-to-know-about-the-trade-war.

69. See Lewis Hyde's op-ed, "How Nationalism Can Destroy a Nation," *New York Times*, Aug. 22, 2019.

70. Post–Cold War? It is a curious thing that no label has emerged to portray the post–Cold War world. The era going nameless reflects Fukuyama's view that no world-engirdling ideological confrontation seemed to define the age. But perhaps it is not so much the difference as the commonality of what has been on ideological offer that is the era's imprint. One way of looking at that is through a grammatical conceit. All the ideologies on offer, both left and right, have had in common the grammatical first person—so much so that the post–Cold War might reasonably be labeled the Age of the First Person.

The dominant ideology on the right, the one whose triumph seemed to have indicated the "end of history," was a return to laissez-faire principles in political-economic affairs. Here the emphasis is on the first-person singular, the I. The I unfettered, pursuing his or her own interests, brings the most good to the greatest number. Government regulation, taxes, the welfare state—these are all encumbrances that hobble I's pursuit of his/her interests, and ultimately diminish the total good. In the USA, for the first decade and a half of the Age of the First Person this ideology was seriously challenged only by a more radical version of itself—what we've called here free-market fundamentalism.

During this period, the left had little to offer by way of a countering political economic vision. In the USA, the Democratic Party, even in power, had little to offer by way of an alternative political economic vision. In the United States, in short, the Democrats did little to distinguish the party from the Republicans at the level of political economy. Where they did distinguish themselves was on social issues. Social issues—civil rights, gay rights, women's rights—became expressed largely as identity politics. The emphasis here is on the first-person plural, the We.

When the challenge finally came from the right it was through identity politics. Already on the cultural level, the "real American" level, the Tea Party was a counter identity movement. But in leaving behind the Tea Party's free-market absolutist ideology, by 2016 the Tea Party populists were poised to migrate from free-market fundamentalist ideology to anti-immigrant nationalist ideology. They were poised to move from a first-person singular ideology to a first-person plural ideology. Donald Trump would be the agent who effected this transition.

71. Quoted in *Talking Points Memo*, talkingpointsmemo.com/2012/bryan-fischer-today-s-gop-will-be-dead-if-romney-loses. Last viewed November 2012.

72. There was a fourth alternative that would show up with regularity in these exchanges—usually toward the end and usually without much enthusiastic response. It was the argument, as it was often stated, that it was time for "Second Amendment solutions." It is to the Tea Party's credit that neither militia types (nor white supremacists) gained much purchase in the movement. However, it is interesting that Donald Trump, virtually all of whose positions derived from themes and memes he found in his immersion in right-wing media, picked up on this Second Amendment theme. In a campaign rally in August 2016, he aired the idea gunning, as it were, for Hillary Clinton. From the *New York Times* report:

Repeating his contention that Mrs. Clinton wanted to abolish the right to bear arms, Mr. Trump warned at a rally here that it would be "a horrible day" if Mrs. Clinton were elected and got to appoint a tiebreaking Supreme Court justice.

"If she gets to pick her judges, nothing you can do, folks," Mr. Trump said, as the crowd began to boo. He quickly added: "Although the Second Amendment people—maybe there is, I don't know."

Nick Corasaniti and Maggie Haberman, "Donald Trump Suggests 'Second Amendment People' Could Act Against Hillary Clinton," *New York Times*, Aug. 9, 2019.

73. See Michael Scherer, "Trump's Reality Political Show: Will the Donald Really Run for President?," *Time*, Apr. 14, 2011.

74. See Trump's NBC interview in Apr. 2011, www.nbcnews.com/video /nightly-news/42462615.

75. Alexander Mooney, "Trump Sends Investigators to Hawaii to Look into Obama," *CNN Politics* (blog), Apr. 7, 2011, politicalticker.blogs.cnn.com /2011/04/07/trump-sends-investigators-to-hawaii-to-look-into-obama.

76. Glenn Beck's television show trafficked heavily in conspiracy theory. The prevailing background analysis that informed virtually all of his presentation was of a decades-long liberal conspiracy to bring down America, going back to the Progressive period. This would be interspersed with particular conspiracies. For example, he spent months attacking Frances Piven, who, with her late husband, had written a 1966 article, "The Weight of the Poor: A Strategy to End Poverty." The article proposed the poor overwhelming welfare rolls as a strategy to bring about progressive change like a guaranteed income. For Beck, this was a plan to bring about economic collapse and the end of capitalism. His continuing attacks resulted in months of insults and threats—of harm; of death—directed at Piven. (See Brian Stelter, "Spotlight from Glenn Beck Brings a CUNY Professor Threats," *New York Times*, Jan. 21, 2011.) This dynamic of broadcasting conspiracy allegations against "the liberal elite" is a staple of right-wing populism. The Piven case foreshadowed "Pizzagate" and other vigilantism provoked by the broad Trump coalition. Pizzagate involved a 2016 assertion on a variety of alt-right websites that Democratic Party officials were running a human trafficking and child sex ring from the basement of a Washington, DC, pizzeria. This resulted in an armed attack on the pizzeria—three shots were fired from a semi-automatic rifle—by a follower of the conspiracy theory who had taken it upon himself to save the chil-

dren imprisoned in the basement. (See Marc Fisher et al., "Pizzagate: From Rumor, to Hashtag, to Gunfire in D.C.," *Washington Post*, Dec. 6, 2016.)

77. Manchurian candidate theories were everyday discussions on Tea Party websites and blogs. Among the books written proposing Manchurian hypotheses were Aaron Klein and Brenda J. Elliot, *The Manchurian President* (WND Books, 2010), and Webster Griffin Tarpley, *Obama: The Post-Modern Coup—Making of a Manchurian Candidate* (Progressive Press, 2008).

3. The Great Irony: How Trump Split the Tea Party and Won the 2016 Republican Nomination

1. See en.wikipedia.org/wiki/California_Proposition_187.

2. Quoted in Halimah Abdullah, "McConnell Warns GOP Must Broaden Its Appeal or Die," *McClatchy*, Jan. 29, 2009, www.mcclatchydc .com/news/politics-government/article24522688.html.

3. The autopsy report is available online at www.documentcloud.org /documents/624581-rnc-autopsy.html.

4. Benjy Sarlin, "6 Big Takeaways from the RNC's Incredible 2012 Autopsy," *Talking Points Memo*, Mar. 18, 2013, talkingpointsmemo.com/dc/6 -big-takeaways-from-the-rnc-s-incredible-2012-autopsy.

5. Among the report's other recommendations: make openings to minority organizations like La Raza and the NAACP; make openings to young voters, specifically mentioning stepping back from extreme anti-gay positions; find a way to avoid extremist candidates, like some who emerged victorious from state primaries; make the party stop "talking to itself"—including its self-absorbed tendency endlessly to refer back to Ronald Reagan.

6. Cheryl K. Chumley, "Sen. Lindsey Graham: GOP Facing 'Demographic Death Spiral,'" *Washington Times*, Jun. 17, 2013, www .washingtontimes.com/news/2013/jun/17/sen-lindsey-graham-gop-facing -demographic-death-sp.

7. One of Trump's repeated hits at his rallies was reading the lyrics of "The Snake," in which the treacherous reptile turns on its soft-hearted benefactor. Trump was explicit in comparing the snake to immigrants. Trump supporters argue that Trump merely opposes "illegal" immigrants. The snake, whom he simply compared to immigrants (full stop), was one

among any number of explicit expressions that revealed his campaign and his presidency did not limit its opposition to "illegal" immigrants. See his February 2018 rendition of "The Snake" in his appearance at the annual CPAC convention, www.independent.co.uk/news/world/americas /us-politics/the-snake-read-in-full-trump-poem-cpac-anti-immigration -verses-mexican-border-a8225686.html.

The text of "The Snake" is available at www.lyricsfreak.com/a/al +wilson/snake_20276772.html.

8. Educational level seems to be of major significance in determining who within the white working class migrated most heavily to Trump. In "Secular Partisan Realignment in the United States: The Socioeconomic Reconfiguration of White Partisan Support Since the New Deal Era," Herbert P. Kitschelt and Philipp Rehm demonstrate that it was the most economically secure (high income/low education) part of the working class that moved most heavily toward Trump, not their economically more strapped fellows (low income/low education). In *Politics and Society*, Aug. 10, 2019, journals.sagepub.com/doi/full/10.1177/0032329219861215.

9. Rachel Bitecofer, "With 16 Months to Go, Negative Partisanship Predicts the 2020 Presidential Election," Judy Ford Wason Center for Public Policy, Jul. 1, 2019, cnu.edu/wasoncenter/2019/07/01-2020-election -forecast.

Having accurately called the Democratic pickup of forty-two seats in the House of Representatives in 2018, Bitecofer established herself as employing perhaps the most outstanding electoral forecasting model in American academia. The general lack of enthusiasm for Hillary Clinton among the Democratic base was crucial in Trump's path to the presidency. Even more so, Bitecofer suggests, was the great enthusiasm *against* Clinton that drove so much of Trump's electorate. In this, Bitecofer draws on Alan Abramowitz's concept of "negative partisanship" as a fundamental driver of contemporary voting behavior. See his *The Great Alignment: Race, Party Transformation, and the Rise of Donald Trump* (Yale University Press, 2018).

10. John McCormick, "The Election Came Down to 77,744 Votes in Pennsylvania, Wisconsin, and Michigan (Updated)," *Washington Examiner*, Nov. 10, 2016, www.washingtonexaminer.com/weekly-standard/the -election-came-down-to-77-744-votes-in-pennsylvania-wisconsin-and -michigan-updated.

11. Daily Stormer, Nov. 9, 2016. Last viewed November 2016.

12. Nicholas Confessore, "Koch Brothers' Budget of $889 Million for 2016 Is on Par with Both Parties' Spending," *New York Times*, Jan. 26, 2015.

13. Valerie Strauss, "Gov. Scott Walker Savages Wisconsin Public Education in New Budget," *Washington Post*, Jul., 13, 2015, www.washingtonpost.com/news/answer-sheet/wp/2015/07/13/gov-scott-walker-savages-wisconsin-public-education-in-new-budget.

14. In some ways, the 2016 goal of the free-market fundamentalists can be thought of as nationalizing the agenda of ALEC—the American Legislative Exchange Council, which largely drafted the legislation passed in these red trifecta states and proposed them in many other states. With the Washington trifecta they sought, the free-market fundamentalists would be in a position to effect *national* right-to-work laws, *national* abortion restrictions, *national* open-carry gun laws, a neutered EPA, privatizing Social Security, *national* stop-and-frisk policies, and much else.

15. Nicholas Confessore, "David Koch Signals a Favorite: Scott Walker," *New York Times*, Apr. 20, 2015.

See also Joe Nocera, "Scott Walker's Wisconsin Audition," *New York Times*, Jun. 12, 2015.

Also worth noting is an extraordinary prank call in which Walker seems plainly to believe he was talking to David Koch, with whom his ideological lockstep and Koch's supervisory place in Walker's administration are apparent. "Transcript of Prank Koch-Walker Conversation," *Wisconsin State Journal*, Feb. 23, 2011, madison.com/wsj/transcript-of-prank-koch-walker-conversation/article_531276b6-3f6a-11e0-b288-001cc4c002e0.html.

16. Walker also allowed as how he was running because he was called by God to do so. He emailed supporters the following:

As you can imagine, the months leading up to my announcement that I would run for President of the United States were filled with a lot of prayer and soul searching. . . . Here's why: I needed to be certain that running was God's calling—not just man's calling. I am certain: This is God's plan for me and I am humbled to be a candidate for President of the United States.

Quoted in David Badash, "'God's Calling': Scott Walker Tells Supporters Presidential Campaign Is 'God's Plan,'" *New Civil Rights*

Movement, Jul. 13, 2015, www.thenewcivilrightsmovement.com/2015/07/_god_s_calling_scott_walker_tells_his_supporters_his_presidential_campaign_is_god_s_plan. Last viewed August 2019.

17. From Shane Goldmacher, "G.O.P. Embraced Koch Vision, Until Trump Tossed It All Aside," *New York Times,* Aug. 24, 2019:

> The Kochs were perhaps at their peak in 2015, as the last Republican presidential primary was heating up. Koch officials outlined plans to spend as much as $900 million that cycle—possibly as much as the Republican Party itself. In a sign of their influence, Jeb Bush, Ted Cruz, Marco Rubio, Scott Walker and Carly Fiorina all trekked to a luxury hotel in Southern California to pitch the network's donors in person that summer.

18. Kenneth P. Vogel and Cate Martel, "The Kochs Freeze Out Trump," *Politico,* Jul. 29, 2015, www.politico.com/story/2015/07/kochs-freeze-out-trump-120752.

19. Trump took the unusual step of releasing a list of potential nominees to the Supreme Court during the campaign. (See Alan Rappeport and Charlie Savage, "Donald Trump Releases List of Possible Supreme Court Picks," *New York Times,* May 18, 2016.) This was an effective bow toward Republican orthodoxy (the list was compiled by the Heritage Foundation), especially given the unfilled seat following the death of Antonin Scalia and the Senate's refusal, led by Mitch McConnell, to consider President Obama's nominee, Merrick Garland. Perhaps of even greater significance, the list indicated to Christian evangelicals, the largest component of the right populist vote, that Trump was on the right side of their dominant goal, overturning *Roe v. Wade.* Evangelicals would remain the pillar of Trump support well into his presidency, despite his vulgarity, plain lack of religious faith, and flaunting of traditional morality, sexual, and otherwise.

20. Sociology 101 role theory suggests a third stage in the transition from Never Trump to the passionate support that some former passionate Never-Trumpers, like South Carolina senator Lindsey Graham, have come to embody.

> It would be missing an essential aspect of the role if we regarded it merely as a regulatory pattern for externally visible actions. *Acting in*

roles shapes feelings and emotions. We feel more generous when giving gifts and more angry by shaking a fist and yelling. The act not only expresses feelings but *manufactures them.* Roles carry with them both certain actions and the emotions and attitudes that belong to these actions. . . . *Normally, one becomes what one plays at* [emphasis added].

Peter Berger, *Invitation to Sociology* (Anchor, 1963), pp. 97–98.

Emotions can be learned, just as theatrical roles may be learned. And just as theatrical actors learn to experience anger, sorrow, joy, or fear when their roles call for them, so too social actors may learn to experience feelings appropriate to the social settings.

Yiannis Gabriel, "An Introduction to the Social Psychology of Insults in Organizations," *Human Relations* 51, no. 11 (1998): 1330.

One thinks of the last line of George Orwell's *1984*, describing the fate of the one-time rebel Winston Smith: "He loved Big Brother."

21. As Michele Bachmann, leader of the Tea Party Caucus in the House, put it, 2016 would be the "last election" in the USA if immigration reform, in the form of a Hillary Clinton victory, came into office:

"Well, I don't want to be melodramatic but I do want to be truthful. I believe without a shadow of a doubt this is the last election. This is it. This is the last election. And the reason why I say that . . . is because it's a math problem. It's a math problem of demographics and a changing United States. If you look at the numbers of people who vote and who lives [sic] in the country and who Barack Obama and Hillary Clinton want to bring in to the country, this is the last election when we even have a chance to vote for somebody who will stand up for godly moral principles. This is it.

"[Hillary Clinton] has said herself that she is going to grant wholesale amnesty to people from the Third World who are here in the United States and we hear this fake number of 11 million illegal aliens in the United States. Wrong! It's about 30 to 40 million illegal aliens currently in the United States—30 to 40 million!"

David Brody, "Exclusive: Michele Bachmann: This Will Be 'Last Election' If Hillary Wins Presidency," CBN News, Sep. 1, 2016.

Bachmann was reflecting the widespread conviction that straddled from the Republican establishment to its populist fringe that immigration reform was a plot by the Democrats to make themselves a permanent majority party; or as it was sometimes put, to turn the United States into a one-party state. Ann Coulter lamented in September 2018 that Trump, distracted by the Russia investigation, was letting the liberal plot succeed right under his nose. Coulter also illustrates the fluidity this argument has with the alt-right sensibility that immigration is a direct assault on the United States as a white society. (See also Coulter's *Adios America*, Regnery Publishing, 2015).

> The left is very close to having a governing majority due entirely to immigration. Despite the promise of the Trump campaign, there isn't much standing in their way. Now, they're just running out the clock. Soon, we will have admitted so many immigrants that it will be too late to do anything.
>   . . . The very reason the left loathes Trump is that he promised to stop their hostile takeover of our country. . . . The left doesn't care about child rape or human trafficking. They just want an end to America and its infernal *white people.* . . . The whole border surge is a hoax, intended to overwhelm the system and get Democrats their last needed non-American voter. . . . Has anyone ever criticized a black, brown, beige, yellow, red or green nation for wanting to preserve its ethnicity? No, only a white majority is pure evil that must be extirpated.

Ann Coulter, "Liberals Never Sleep (And Neither Does Jeff Sessions)," *Ann Coulter,* Sep. 5, 2018, www.anncoulter.com/columns/2018-09-05.html #read_more.

22. See "I Was Hoping for a *Taller* Honest Man," Jan. 27, 2016. Coulter ridiculed those waiting for a different, more ordinary avatar of the populist anti-immigrant passion.

> Everything we've been begging politicians to talk about . . . Donald Trump has brought up with a roar. . . . The nitpickers are like the cartoon of Diogenes looking over the man before him, and saying: "I was hoping for a *taller* honest man." You're not getting a "taller

honest man." Trump is our only shot to save America, if there's still time.

www.anncoulter.com/columns/2016-01-27.html. Last viewed June 2019.

23. See, for example, Tony Lee, "Mark Levin: Tea Party Only Thing That Stands 'Between Liberty and Tyranny,'" *Breitbart News*, www.breitbart .com/big-government/2012/11/16/mark-levin-tea-party-only-thing-that -stands-between-liberty-and-tyranny.

24. www.teapartynation.com/forum/topics/the-death-of-the-gop?com mentId=3355873%3AComment%3A2182610. Last accessed June 2016.

25. See Justin Sink, "Gingrich: 'I'm Going to Be the Nominee,'" *The Hill*, Dec. 1, 2011.

26. Aaron Couch and Emmet McDermott, "Donald Trump Campaign Offered Actors $50 to Cheer for Him at Presidential Announcement," *Hollywood Reporter*, Jun. 17, 2015.

27. See *Wall Street Journal*, Jun. 16, 2015, for the transcript of Trump's speech, blogs.wsj.com/washwire/2015/06/16/donald-trump-transcript-our -country-needs-a-truly-great-leader.

28. "The Triumph of the Hard Right," *New York Review of Books*, Feb. 11, 2016, www.nybooks.com/articles/2016/02/11/ej-dionne-triumph-of-the -hard-right.

29. Reid J. Epstein, "David Brat Pulls Off Cantor Upset Despite Raising Just $231,000," *Wall Street Journal*, Jun. 10, 2014.

30. Sarah Wheaton et al., "Dave Brat, Accidental Tea Party Leader," *Politico*, nd, www.politico.com/story/2014/06/dave-brat-eric-cantor-virginia -107804_Page2.html.

31. Jay Newton-Small, "How Eric Cantor Lost," *Time*, Jun. 11, 2014, time .com/2854761/eric-cantor-dave-brat-virginia.

32. See "The Case David Brat Made to Voters," *New York Times*, Jun. 11, 2014, www.nytimes.com/interactive/2014/06/11/us/politics/brats-case -against-cantor.html.

33. *Time* magazine's reporting on Brat's victory included this observation from "Virginia Democratic strategist Dave 'Mudcat' Saunders." See Jay Newton-Small, "How Eric Cantor Lost."

34. Jake Sherman, "Cantor Loses," *Politico*, Jun. 10, 2014, www.politico

.com/story/2014/06/eric-cantor-primary-election-results-virginia-107683.

35. Jay Newton-Small, "How Eric Cantor Lost."

36. See Boehner's retirement announcement: www.youtube.com/wa tch?v=rlrp1Cvbono.

37. See Rick Perlstein's analysis of "The New York Values That Shaped Donald Trump" in his "Avenging Angels," *Washington Spectator*, Apr. 18, 2016, washingtonspectator.org/avenging-angels-trump.

38. See the *Wall Street Journal*'s coverage of the "hardhat riots" on May 8, 1970. Reprinted in "After 'Bloody Friday,' New York Wonders If Wall Street Is Becoming a Battleground," chnm.gmu.edu/hardhats/bloody.html.

Also see Rick Perlstein's adoption of the author's term "hardhat populism" in "I Thought I Understood the American Right. Trump Proved Me Wrong," *New York Times Magazine*, Apr. 11, 2017, www.nytimes.com/2017/04 /11/magazine/i-thought-i-understood-the-american-right-trump-proved -me-wrong.html.

39. For an overview of Trump and the Central Park Five, see Jeva Lange, "Donald Trump's 30-Year Crusade Against the Central Park Five," *The Week*, Oct. 7, 2016, theweek.com/articles/653840/donald-trumps-30year -crusade-against-central-park-five.

40. Procaccino was the Democratic candidate, and carried Brooklyn and the Bronx in the election, losing 42 to 36 percent to John Lindsay, who ran on the Liberal Party line, and outpacing Republican John Marchi, who won his home borough of Staten Island. See en.wikipedia.org/wiki /Mario_Procaccino.

Procaccino's *New York Times* obituary highlighted his pro-police combativeness:

"We must stop coddling the criminals and pampering the punks," he would roar. "The do-gooders and bleeding hearts must stop hand-cuffing the police."

Lawrence Van Gelder, "Mario A. Procaccino, 83, Who Lost to Lindsay in 1969, Dies," *New York Times*, Dec. 21, 1995, www.nytimes.com/1995/12/21 /nyregion/mario-a-procaccino-83-who-lost-to-lindsay-in-1969-dies.html. Last viewed September 2019.

41. See Nicholas Fandos, "Donald Trump Defiantly Rallies a New 'Silent Majority' in a Visit to Arizona," *New York Times*, Jul. 11, 2015.

42. See Lawrence Rosenthal, "Trump 2016: Archie Bunker Runs for President," *LA Progressive*, Aug. 12, 2015.

43. See Maria Recio, "Carson Theory on Pyramids Around—and Wrong—for Centuries," *McClatchy*, Nov. 8, 2015.

44. Quoted in Maggie Haberman, "He's 'One of Us': The Undying Bond Between the Bible Belt and Trump," *New York Times*, Oct. 14, 2018.

45. Wolfgang Streeck offers the following observation about the personality oddities Trump shares with other nationalist and populist leaders in the West:

> Strange personalities arise in the cracks of disintegrating institutions. They are often marked by extravagant dress, inflated rhetoric, and a show of sexual power. The first Trumper of the postwar era was the Danish tax rebel, Mogens Glistrup, the founder of the nationalist Progress Party, who, having put his principles into practice, went to prison for tax evasion. Geert Wilders in the Netherlands and Boris Johnson in England are hairstyle Trumpers. Pim Fortuyn and Jörg Haider were both dandies. They died in their finery. Beppe Grillo, Nigel Farage, and Jean-Marie Le Pen, are each one third of a full Trump.

"Trump and the Trumpists," *Inference* 3, no. 1 (Apr. 2017), inference-review .com/article/trump-and-the-trumpists.

46. See *Science Writing Blog*, Sep. 7, 2014.

"Trees cause more pollution than automobiles do"—Former Republican President Ronald Reagan in 1981 and 1979 respectively

thesciencewritingblog.wordpress.com/2014/09/07/ronald-reagan-said-trees -cause-more-pollution-than-automobiles-do-ignoring-trees-conversion-of -co2/comment-page-1.

47. Dylan Byers, "Teflon Don," *Politico*, Aug. 21, 2015, www.politico.com /story/2015/08/teflon-don-121587.

48. See www.economist.com/graphic-detail/2015/12/08/donald-trumps -gravity-defying-poll-ratings.

49. Frank Bruni, *New York Times*, Jul. 18, 2015. See also Rula Jebreal, "Donald Trump Is America's Silvio Berlusconi," *Washington Post*, Sep. 21, 2015.

50. Tobias Jones, *Foreign Policy*, Aug. 21, 2015. The subtitle in Jones's article: "The Italian leader played buffoon, victim, and messiah. Others have followed suit." foreignpolicy.com/2019/08/21/were-all-living-in -berlusconis-italy-world-now-trump-boris.

51. Kathryn Westcott, "At Last—an Explanation for 'Bunga Bunga,'" BBC News, Feb. 5, 2011, www.bbc.com/news/world-europe-12325796.

52. David A. Fahrenthold, "Trump Recorded Having Extremely Lewd Conversation About Women in 2005," *Washington Post*, Oct. 8, 2016.

53. See Gavin Jones, "Berlusconi masterminded tax evasion plan, Italian court says," *Reuters*, Aug. 22, 2013, www.reuters.com/article/us-italy -berlusconi-verdict/berlusconi-masterminded-tax-evasion-plan-italian -court-says-idUSBRE97S0ZN20130829.

In his years of skirting his indictments, Berlusconi's favored tactic to avoid conviction was running out the clock on statutes of limitation with legal maneuvering. It was this 2013 decision by Italy's high court, the Court of Cassation, that barred Berlusconi (who was sentenced to community service) from politics for five years. When he tried to return to his position as the populist head of the coalition of right-wing parties in 2018, he found his populism had been superseded by the nationalist populism of Matteo Salvini and the League. (See chapter 1.)

54. The *Times'* investigation suggested as much as $550 million may have been evaded in taxes by Trump and his family since the 1990s. In addition, the investigation showed that Trump was the heir to "at least $413 million from his father's real estate empire, starting when he was a toddler"—which flew in the face of Trump's self-made man assertions. See David Barstow et al., "Trump Engaged in Suspect Tax Schemes as He Reaped Riches from His Father," *New York Times*, Oct. 2, 2018, www.nytimes .com/interactive/2018/10/02/us/politics/donald-trump-tax-schemes-fred -trump.html.

55. Berlusconi virtually single-handedly introduced the concept of conflict of interest into Italian political discourse.

[Berlusconi] failed to follow through on promises related to his role as a media magnate—putting his assets in a blind trust, for example. In fact, people jested that Berlusconi's entrance into politics was simply a good business move. The only . . . issues to which the Berlusconi government devoted passionate attention were directly related to protecting and advancing Berlusconi's business interests.

Lawrence Rosenthal, "Dateline Rome: The New Face of Western Democracy," *Foreign Policy*, no. 104 (Autumn 1996): 164.

56. Quoted in Alexander Stille, "The Corrupt Reign of Emperor Silvio," *New York Review of Books*, Apr. 8, 2010. Stille also observed another trait Berlusconi shared with Trump. Berlusconi brought "into parliament members of his personal entourage—TV starlets, his personal lawyers, his personal doctor, accountants and executives from his companies, and scores of journalists and TV personalities, all of whom owe almost everything to him."

57. On "executive time" see Alexi McCammond and Jonathan Swan, "Scoop: Insider Leaks Trump's 'Executive Time'-Filled Private Schedules," *Axios*, Feb. 3, 2019, www.axios.com/donald-trump-private-schedules-leak -executive-time-34e67fbb-3af6-48df-aefb-52e02c334255.html.

[Trump's leaked private] schedules, which cover nearly every working day since the midterms, show that Trump has spent around 60% of his scheduled time over the past 3 months in unstructured "Executive Time."

The Washington, DC–based political newspaper *The Hill* estimated that Trump spends at least four and as much as eight hours watching TV daily. See Brandon Carter, "Trump Watches up to Eight Hours of TV per Day: Report," *The Hill*, Dec. 9, 2017, thehill.com/homenews/administration /364094-trump-watches-at-least-four-hours-of-tv-per-day-report.

58. For a case study of Trump dictating policy based on something he sees on Fox News, see Isaac Stanley-Becker, "Trump Tweets the Word 'Africa' for First Time as President—in Defense of Whites in South Africa," *Washington Post*, Aug. 23, 2018.

The episode represented a case study in how the president runs his administration. The apparent basis of Trump's directions to the nation's top diplomat were accusations leveled by Fox—accusations that echo talking points used by white-nationalist groups, including an organization that has referred to "the so-called apartheid" and the "so-called 'historical injustices of the past.'"

www.washingtonpost.com/news/morning-mix/wp/2018/08/23/trump -directs-pompeo-to-investigate-south-african-land-redistribution-after -foxs-tucker-carlson-raises-alarm.

59. Hadas Gold wrote early in Trump's administration, "The new president is the TV watcher-in-chief, so people wanting his attention are clamoring to get on his favorite shows." See her "How to Reach Donald Trump: Go on TV," *Politico*, Feb. 11, 2017, www.politico.com/story/2017/02/trump -watching-tv-cables-news-234914.

For a detailed look at the symbiosis between Trump as president and Fox News, see Jane Mayer, "The Making of the Fox News White House," *New Yorker*, Mar. 4, 2019, www.newyorker.com/magazine/2019/03/11/the -making-of-the-fox-news-white-house.

Mayer writes:

Nothing has formalized the partnership between Fox and Trump more than the appointment, in July, 2018, of Bill Shine, the former co-president of Fox News, as director of communications and deputy chief of staff at the White House.

60. Paolo Cossarini, "The Passion of Populist Politics," *Open Democracy*, Sep. 8, 2019, www.opendemocracy.net/en/transformation/passions -populist-politics.

61. James Hohmann of the *Washington Post* reported on the post-mortem offered by Barry Bennett, Carson's campaign manager:

Bennett fondly recalled the stretch when his client was riding at the top of the polls. In addition to self-inflicted wounds from a power struggle inside the campaign, he believes that the November 2015 terrorist attacks in Paris made it impossible for someone with the retired neurosurgeon's personality to secure the nomination. "We couldn't really believe it, to tell you the truth," Bennett told the group. "The first six weeks of the fourth quarter we raised $22 million. We were going gangbusters, and then we ran into Paris . . . and a couple other issues. In the next six weeks of the fourth quarter, we raised $1.5 million. . . . There was an opportunity for a nice outsider to win until Paris came, and then all of a sudden [voters] needed 'strength' again."

From "The Daily 202: Trump's Pollster Says He Ran a 'Post-Ideological' Campaign," Dec. 5, 2016.

62. Ben Kamisar, "Trump Calls for 'Shutdown' of Muslims Entering US," *The Hill*, Dec. 7, 2015, thehill.com/blogs/ballot-box/presidential-races/262348-trump-calls-for-shutdown-of-muslims-entering-us.

63. See Gideon Resnick, "Trump New Low: Ban All Muslim Immigration to U.S.," *Daily Beast*, Dec. 7, 2015, www.thedailybeast.com/author/gideon-resnick.

In typical fashion, Trump took this idea directly from right-wing media, in this case Frank Gaffney Jr.'s Center for Security Policy. As Resnick reports, "Gaffney Jr. is perhaps best known for his public crusade against the supposedly creeping influence of sharia Muslim law in American politics." This was a daily theme on Tea Party websites, a taken-for-granted peril stalking American society. It was fully part of Trump's armament of right-wing themes and memes that made up the rhetorical substance of his campaign. Resnick continues, pointing out that Gaffney "and his cohorts peddle the conspiracy theory that leading conservative anti-tax warrior Grover Norquist and Hillary Clinton aide Huma Abedin are agents of the Muslim Brotherhood; and that President Obama himself is being advised by radical Islamists." Trump's statement, Resnick points out, "echoes Gaffney almost word for word."

64. Tessa Berenson, "Donald Trump Calls for 'Complete Shutdown' of Muslim Entry to U.S." *Time*, Dec. 7, 2015, time.com/4139476/donald-trump-shutdown-muslim-immigration.

65. Bloomberg Poll: Nearly Two-Thirds of Likely GOP Primary Voters Back Trump's Muslim Ban, *Newsmax*, Dec. 9 2015, www.newsmax.com/Headline/poll-voters-agree-poll/2015/12/09/id/705164.

66. See, for example, Eugene Scott, *Twitter*, Dec. 10, 2015, twitter.com/Eugene_Scott/status/674947367003639808.

67. Ryan Struyk, ABC News, "Donald Trump Hits 41 Percent and Widest Lead Yet in New National Poll," Dec. 14 2015, abcnews.go.com/Politics/donald-trump-hits-41-percent-support-widest-lead/story?id=35758064.

68. Philip Bump, "What Happens If Republicans Face a Brokered Convention?" *Miami Herald*, Dec. 12, 2015, www.miamiherald.com/news/nation -world/national/article49439680.html.

The threat of a brokered convention (Trump had said there would be riots if it happened) brought out a rare publicly stated threat of armed violence on the part of Trump supporters. (See chapter 2 endnote 72 on the public versus private discussion of "Second Amendment solutions.")

We went to the April 20 Donald Trump rally in Ocean City, Maryland, to ask Trump's supporters how they would react if he did not receive the nomination at a contested Republican National Convention. Many told us they were prepared to wage an armed insurrection against the powers that be, or what one Trump fan called "a civil war." Take a look. [Video attached to the report.]

Rebecca Carroll, "Watch: Trump Supporters Threaten Potential Armed Insurrection at Contested GOP Convention," *AlterNet*, Apr. 21, 2016, www .alternet.org/2016/04/trump-supporters-ocean-city-maryland-threaten -potential-armed-insurrection-contested.

69. Simon Maloy, "Ted Cruz's Anti-endorsements: Mitt Romney Clearly Dislikes Cruz, but Will Vote for Him Anyway," *Salon*, Mar. 22, 2016, www.salon.com/2016/03/22/ted_cruzs_anti_endorsements_mitt_rom ney_clearly_dislikes_cruz_but_will_vote_for_him_anyway.

See also Priscilla Alvarez, "Why Did Jeb Bush Endorse Ted Cruz?" *The Atlantic*, Mar. 23, 2016, www.theatlantic.com/politics/archive/2016/03/jeb -bush-endorses-ted-cruz/475008.

70. Michelle Boorstein, "Why Donald Trump Is Tearing Evangelicals Apart," *Washington Post*, Mar. 23, 2016, www.theatlantic.com/politics /archive/2016/03/jeb-bush-endorses-ted-cruz/475008.

71. Steve Mitchell, "Why Evangelicals Support Trump," *Real Clear Politics*, Mar. 6, 2016, www.realclearpolitics.com/articles/2016/03/06/why _evangelicals_support_trump_129864.html.

72. Peter Wehner, "What Wouldn't Jesus Do?," *New York Times*, Mar. 1, 2016, www.nytimes.com/2016/03/01/opinion/campaign-stops/what-would nt-jesus-do.html.

73. Jerry Falwell Jr. on his endorsement of Trump:

God called King David a man after God's own heart even though he was an adulterer and a murderer. You have to choose the leader that would make the best king or president and not necessarily someone who would be a good pastor. We're not voting for pastor-in-chief. It means sometimes we have to choose a person who has the qualities to lead and who can protect our country and bring us back to economic vitality, and it might not be the person we call when we need somebody to give us spiritual counsel.

Sarah Rodriguez, "Falwell Speaks," *Liberty Champion*, Mar. 8, 2016, www .liberty.edu/champion/2016/03/falwell-speaks.

It has been a continuing conundrum for the liberal world trying to understand what seems on the surface an impossible bit of cognitive dissonance—how the world of the "moral majority" countenances support for such a shamelessly corrupt and libertine figure as Trump. The political arguments in this regard are clear, above all Trump's eagerness to appoint judges to the Supreme Court who are likely to overturn *Roe v. Wade*. But more was required to move Trump from merely a hold-your-nose capitulation into the sustained champion that has made evangelical support the enduring rock of Trump's political base. As Falwell's reference to King David above suggests, the needed supercharging has come from biblical analogies. King David in particular has been adduced to justify by analogy such Trump transgressions as the "grab them by the pussy" *Access Hollywood* tape or his affair with Stormy Daniels during his wife's pregnancy.

Evangelical Trump supporters argue that like King David, Trump's sins will not hinder his abilities to act wisely on behalf of his people. If King David can be favored by God even after committing adultery (and murder), so can Trump.

Joan Coasten, "The 'Biblical' Defense of Trump's Affair with Stormy Daniels," *Vox*, Mar. 26, 2018, www.vox.com/policy-and-politics/2018/3/26 /17164268/stormy-daniels-donald-trump-bible-christian.

Already by August 2016, Peter Montgomery, who has followed Christian conservatism over the years for People for the American Way, was able to identify twenty-five biblically based justifications for evangelical support of Trump. See his "'God's Guy': 25 Religious Right Justifications for Supporting Donald Trump," *Right Wing Watch*, Aug. 17, 2016, www

.rightwingwatch.org/post/gods-guy-25-religious-right-justifications-for
-supporting-donald-trump.

One particularly recurrent version of reading Trump back into evangelical theology has been the analogy to King Cyrus of the Persians. As Katherine Stewart explains:

> Cyrus . . . was born in the sixth century B.C.E. and became the first emperor of Persia. Isaiah 45 celebrates Cyrus for freeing a population of Jews who were held captive in Babylon. Cyrus is the model for a nonbeliever appointed by God as a vessel for the purposes of the faithful.

"Why Trump Reigns as King Cyrus," *New York Times*, Dec. 31, 2018, www
.nytimes.com/2018/12/31/opinion/trump-evangelicals-cyrus-king.html.

For a more "insider" view of evangelical support of Trump, see Alex Morris, "False Idol—Why the Christian Right Worships Donald Trump," *Rolling Stone*, Dec. 2, 2019.

74. judsonphillips.com/donald-trump-goes-full-establishment. Last accessed June 2016.

75. judsonphillips.com/donald-and-the-trumpertantrum. Last accessed June 2016.

76. www.teapartynation.com/profiles/blog/show?id=3355873%3ABlog Post%3A3192669&xgs=1&xg_source=msg_share_post. Last accessed June 2016.

Trump vs. Cruz also split the world of radio talk show hosts. See Nick Corasaniti's report, "Donald Trump vs. Ted Cruz Creates a Headache for Talk Radio Hosts," *New York Times*, Mar. 29, 2016.

77. I have altered the sequence of Phillips's paragraphs. For his complete statement, see www.teapartynation.com/a-stunning-defeat.

78. Jacob Heilbronn, "The Neocons vs. Donald Trump," *New York Times*, Mar. 10, 2016, www.nytimes.com/2016/03/13/opinion/sunday/the-neocons -vs-donald-trump.html.

79. See *On the Issues*, www.ontheissues.org/Celeb/Donald_Trump _Health_Care.htm.

80. See Matt Apuzzo and James Risen, "Donald Trump Faces Obstacles to Resuming Waterboarding," *New York Times*, Nov. 28, 2016, www.ny

times.com/2016/11/28/us/politics/trump-waterboarding-torture.html. Ash-ley Ross, "Donald Trump Says He Would 'Take Out' Terrorist Families," *Time*, Dec. 2, 2015, time.com/4132368/donald-trump-isis-bombing.

81. Eli Stokols, "Trump Crosses the 9/11 Line," *Politico*, Dec. 14, 2015, www.politico.com/story/2016/02/trump-9-11-debate-219273.

82. Victor Tan Chen, "All Hollowed Out," *The Atlantic*, Jan. 16, 2016, www.theatlantic.com/business/archive/2016/01/white-working-class -poverty/424341; Gina Kolata, "Death Rates Rising for Middle-Aged White Americans, Study Finds," *New York Times*, Nov. 2, 2015, www.nytimes.com /2015/11/03/health/death-rates-rising-for-middle-aged-white-americans -study-finds.html.

83. Jonathan T. Rothwell and Pablo Diego-Rosell, "Explaining National-ist Political Views: The Case of Donald Trump," Nov. 2, 2016, available at SSRN: ssrn.com/abstract=2822059 or dx.doi.org/10.2139/ssrn.2822059. The authors also found that within the same economic and social classes, low-er educational achievement correlated with higher Trump support, which was the major finding of the Kitschelt and Rehm study mentioned in note 8 in this chapter. The preponderant effect of identity and culture over eco-nomics agrees with the highly researched conclusions of Sides et al. (see note 31 in chapter 1) and others. The authors write:

> Those who favor Trump are dramatically more likely to be Christian (though not Mormon), heterosexual, aged 40 or older, male, and non-Hispanic white. People with these characteristics comprise 35% of those who favor Trump, though just 14% of those who do not. This speaks to the importance of cultural and philosophical issues, as opposed to economic incentives.

Theoretically, the authors trace their conclusions back to Gordon All-port's classic "contact theory." (Gordon Allport, *The Nature of Prejudice*, Addison-Wesley, 1954.)

> This [conclusion] is consistent with contact theory, which has already received considerable empirical support in the literature in a vari-ety of analogous contexts. Limited interactions with racial and eth-nic minorities, immigrants, and college graduates may contribute to

prejudicial stereotypes, political and cultural misunderstandings, and a general fear of not-belonging.

The authors sum up:

Finally, the results concerning race, age, gender, ethnicity, and religion imply that political behavior is not related directly and neatly to economic self-interest or class position. One could argue that blue collar men would disproportionately benefit from Trump's policies on trade and immigration, but as discussed above, these factors are relatively unimportant. As others have found, cultural views and social identity are likely quite important in affecting political preferences.

84. Benedict Anderson, *Imagined Communities* (Verso, 2006), 6.

85. See *Know Your Meme*'s coverage of Eastwooding (including video of Eastwood's speech) at knowyourmeme.com/memes/events/clint -eastwoods-empty-chair-speech-eastwooding-invisible-obama.

86. Hofstadter's essay appeared in the November 1964 issue of *Harper's Magazine*. This was the era in which right-wing extremism had not only made its presence felt in a novel way in American politics, the movement's most well-known organization, the John Birch Society, was instrumental in Arizona senator Barry Goldwater's capture of the Republican presidential nomination. (The Koch brothers followed their father Fred—who was a charter member—into the JBS.) Hofstadter's article can be accessed at harpers.org/archive/1964/11/the-paranoid-style-in-american-politics/7.

87. David Meeks, "Poll: Obama's a Muslim to GOP Voters in Alabama, Mississippi," *Los Angeles Times*, Mar. 12, 2012.

88. Sarah Pulliam Bailey, "A Startling Number of Americans Still Believe Obama Is a Muslim," *Washington Post*, Sep. 14, 2015.

In the Tea Party worldview of Obama as Other, Obama as Muslim added a venomous dimension to his illegitimacy as president owing to his "foreignness." In Tea Party discourse, the Muslim world was the successor to the great American enemies of the twentieth century: Fascism and Communism. In a mind-set that saw the United States engaged in an epic battle against the Muslim world, against an asymmetrical enemy that operates via terrorism, this put Obama (and liberalism generally) on the side of the enemy. They are the enemy on the home front. The domestic Other meets the foreign Other.

89. In his first paragraph Hofstadter points out the ubiquity of conspiracy thinking in the paranoid style of politics: "I call it the paranoid style simply because no other word adequately evokes the sense of heated exaggeration, suspiciousness, and conspiratorial fantasy that I have in mind." In the course of his six thousand–word article he uses the word conspiracy over twenty times, as he surveys American political movements historically. He quotes many assertions of conspiracy, including the famous assertion of conspiracy on the part of Senator Joseph McCarthy in 1951, the projection of foreign policy treason that became the model of projecting domestic policy treason in the Tea Party:

How can we account for our present situation unless we believe that men high in this government are concerting to deliver us to disaster? This must be the product of a great conspiracy on a scale so immense as to dwarf any previous such venture in the history of man. A conspiracy of infamy so black that, which [sic] it is finally exposed, its principals shall be forever deserving of the maledictions of all honest men. . . .

90. See Steve Benen, "Right Falls for 'Thesis' Hoax," *Washington Monthly*, Oct. 24, 2009, washingtonmonthly.com/2009/10/24/right-falls-for-thesis-hoax.

4. Othering Nationalism: The (Bookend) Revolution of 2016

1. Mark Hensch, "Sanders: 'We Need a Political Revolution,'" *The Hill*, May 3, 2015, thehill.com/blogs/ballot-box/presidential-races/240889-sanders-we-need-a-political-revolution.

2. Some observers felt they were viewing a revolutionary scene after the Trump inauguration. A March 2017 *New Yorker* article on Russian interference in the 2016 American election related the following:

"In 1917, armed supporters of Lenin stormed the Winter Palace and arrested capitalist ministers and overthrew the social political order," the lead article in the daily *Moskovski Komsomolets* read. "On January 20, 2017, nobody in Washington planned to storm Congress or the White House and hang prominent members of the old regime from lampposts, but the feeling of the American political élite, especially the liberal part of it, is not different from that of the Russian bourgeoisie one hundred years ago."

E. Osnos et al., "Trump, Putin, and the New Cold War," *New Yorker*, Mar. 6, 2017.

3. Joshua Green gives an excellent and detailed analysis of the pivotal role Bannon played in Trump's election in his 2017 book, *Devil's Bargain: Steve Bannon, Trump, and the Nationalist Uprising* (Penguin).

4. Andrew Zurcher, "Trump's 'Brain' Steve Bannon Emerges from the Shadows," BBC News, Feb. 24, 2017, www.bbc.com/news/world-us-canada -38996534.

5. Michael M. Grynbaum, "Trump Strategist Stephen Bannon Says 'Media Should Keep Its Mouth Shut,'" *New York Times*, Jan. 26, 2017, www .nytimes.com/2017/01/26/business/media/stephen-bannon-trump-news -media.html.

6. "Intellectual or artistic people considered as a social group given to the expression of liberal opinions, [e.g.] *'the politically correct voice of the chattering classes.'*" See en.oxforddictionaries.com/definition /the_chattering_classes.

7. Phillip Rucker and Robert Costa, "Trump's Hard-Line Actions Have an Intellectual Godfather: Jeff Sessions," *Washington Post*, Jan. 30, 2017, www.washingtonpost.com/politics/trumps-hard-line-actions-have -an-intellectual-godfather-jeff-sessions/2017/01/30/ac393f66-e4d4-11e6-ba11 -63c4b4fb5a63_story.html.

8. Bob Dylan, "The Times They Are A-Changin'," bobdylan.com/songs /times-they-are-changin.

9. The cliché, or in this case the internet meme, was known as "Godwin's Law": "As an online discussion grows longer, the probability of a comparison involving Nazis or Hitler approaches 1." In 2012, Godwin's Law became an entry in the Oxford English Dictionary, www.oed.com /view/Entry/340583?redirectedFrom=Godwin%27s+law&.

10. Hannah Arendt, in *The Origin of Totalitarianism*, argues the point

that the prequel to Fascism in Europe was the action of European governments who colonized much of the Third World in the nineteenth century (including the "scramble for Africa"); the Europeans set up regimes with few rights for indigenous people, exploiting them with brutal and often deadly working conditions that approximated slavery. Arendt emphasized the role of "adventurers" who relished the freedom to dominate native populations that colonization offered, and who, as personalities and actors, prefigured Fascism's avant-garde and its militias' most dedicated terrorists.

11. From the inaugural address. Trump added: "This American carnage stops right here and stops right now." See Ed Pilkington, "'American Carnage': Donald Trump's Vision Casts Shadow Over Day of Pageantry," *The Guardian*, Jan. 21, 2017.

12. Mary Ann Georgantopoulos, "Trump Referred to Immigrants as Vermin, Saying They Will 'Infest Our Country,'" *BuzzFeedNews*, Jun. 19, 2018, www.buzzfeednews.com/article/maryanngeorgantopoulos/trump -immigrants-vermin-infest.

13. Kasich's "spot feature[d] retired Air Force Col. Tom Moe speaking at an event in Ohio, the same day Trump held a rally in Columbus. Moe, who the Kasich campaign identifie[d] as a former Vietnam POW," said:

> You might not care if Donald Trump says Muslims should register with their government, because you're not one. And you might not care if Donald Trump says he's going to round up all the Hispanic immigrants, because you're not one. And you might not care if Donald Trump says it's okay to rough up black protesters, because you're not one. And you might not care if Donald Trump wants to suppress journalists, because you're not one. But think about this: If he keeps going, and he actually becomes president, he might just get around to you. And you better hope there's someone left to help you.

14. Ross Douthat, "Is Donald Trump a Fascist?," *New York Times*, Dec. 3, 2015.

15. Robert Kagan, "This Is How Fascism Comes to America," *Washington Post*, May 18, 2016. Kagan followed this up two-and-a-half years into Trump's presidency. Attacking the "Squad," four female and minority

members of Congress in July 2019, Trump told them to "go back" to where they came from. (Only one of the four was born out of the United States.) Kagan responded with an echo of how a charter neoconservative, Nathan Glazer, had earlier reluctantly come to terms with the politics of diversity, publishing in 1998 his book, *We Are All Multiculturalists Now* (Harvard, 1977). See Kagan's "We Are All 'the Squad' Now," *Washington Post*, Jul. 16, 2019.

16. John McNeill, "How Fascist Is Trump? There's Actually a Formula for That," *Washington Post*, Oct. 21, 2016.

17. Umberto Eco, "Ur-Fascism," *New York Review of Books*, Jun. 22, 1995. This URL (last viewed Aug. 14, 2019) lists dozens and dozens of articles citing Eco's fourteen points: www.google.com/search?q=eco%27s+14+poi nts+and+trump&ei=9Z5UXdjMN9H7-gSsuq6IDA&start=30&sa=N&ved= 0ahUKEwiYm6-0x4PkAhXRvZ4KHSydC8E4FBDw0wMIhwE&biw=1200& bih=1006.

In their 1949 study, *Prophets of Deceit: A Study in the Techniques of the American Agitator* (Harper & Brothers), Leo Lowenthal and Norbert Guterman offered a rather exacting preview of Trump, based on close analysis of right-wing American "agitators" of the 1930s and '40s. For example, in their chapter "Social Malaise," the authors enumerate four categories in the agitator's "Catalogue of Grievances" (pp. 11–13):

- Economic: "Not only are foreigners taking our money, they also threaten our jobs."
- Political: "International commitments by the United States government jeopardize political liberties."
- Cultural: "The media of public information are in the hands of enemies of the nation."
- Moral: "While we were praying they had their hands in our pockets."

18. David Frum, "How to Build an Autocracy," *The Atlantic*, March 2017. Also see his book, *Trumpocracy: The Corruption of the American Republic* (Harper 2018).

19. Timothy Snyder, *On Tyranny: Twenty Lessons from the Twentieth Century* (Penguin Random House, 2017).

20. Jason Stanley, *How Fascism Works: The Politics of Us and Them* (Ran-

dom House, 2018). Steven Levitsky and Daniel Ziblatt, *How Democracies Die* (Broadway Books, 2018).

21. Madeleine Albright, *Fascism: A Warning* (HarperCollins, 2018).

22. See *National Review*'s editorial "Against Trump," Jan. 22, 2016, www .nationalreview.com/2016/01/donald-trump-conservative-movement -menace.

23. The quotation is from the entry "Fascism" in the 1932 edition of the *Enciclopedia Italiana* (Italian Encyclopedia). The entry's authorship is attributed to Mussolini. See www.historyguide.org/europe/duce.html.

24. See Belinda Robinson's book review "Italian Forces in WW2 Were Not Soft and Mussolini Wasn't a Clown, Revisionist Historian Claims," *Daily Mail*, Apr. 14, 2014, www.dailymail.co.uk/news/article-2604389 /Italian-forces-WW2-not-soft-Mussolini-wasnt-clown-revisionist-historian -claims.html.

25. The difference in origin between Mussolini's rally style and Trump's is interesting. Mussolini learned his style from the experience of lyric poet and national war hero Gabriele D'Annunzio who, dissatisfied that Italy was not awarded the Dalmatian coast in the World War I settlement at Versailles, took the Croatian town of Rijeka (Fiume) in 1919 with two thousand war veterans and held it for fifteen months, during which time he established his leadership role as the "Duce of the Carnaro." Mussolini's fledgling movement devoted itself to support of D'Annunzio, while Mussolini himself paid close attention to D'Annunzio as he originated the dramaturgy that Mussolini would emulate and make famous around the world.

Trump developed his rally style from his involvement in professional wrestling. Much-viewed YouTube clips (for example, www.youtube.com /watch?v=vVeVcVBW_CE) show Trump and World Wrestling Entertainment chair Vince McMahon confronting one another (and engaging in some physical stunts) in the manner of professional wrestling's over-the-top good and bad characters, provoking and eliciting raucous backing from the crowd during the "Battle of the Billionaires." As ever in professional wrestling, it was a scripted confrontation that nonetheless evoked ritualized crowd fervor as though it were a real competitive sport where one side or the other prevails in a genuine contest. It is notable that Trump learned his live crowd-commanding skills in a context where reality is compromised in this fashion. Despite everyone knowing the outcome is scripted ("rigged," as candidate Trump suggested in undermining the prospect of any election he might not win), whether in the role of protagonist or audience what is "fake" is accorded the same stature as the real. The art of confusing what is real and what is fake, the capacity to manipulate what are, finally, epistemological questions, would be an essential part of Trump's politics and governance and an unending source of frustration for his opposition. (See chapter 6.)

Vince McMahon's wife Linda, who served as CEO of her husband's wrestling empire and was defeated as the Republican senatorial candidate in Connecticut in 2010, served as the administrator of the Small Business Administration in the Trump government.

26. Fascist rhetorical attacks on their opposition were scandalous and sometimes embarrassing. Members of the Italian Socialist Party (PSI) were regularly referred to in print as "*pussisti*," "pus-ists," a play on the anagram of "Official (*ufficiale*) Socialist Party" that suggests pus and pimples and cowardice (*pusillanime*). Members of the *popolari*, the Italian Popular Party, became "*pipisti*," or "pipi-ists." *Fare pipi* is the common Italian term for urinating, like "peeing" in English. In later years a popular motif of Fascist propaganda used precocious ragamuffins (*Balilla*) who dressed and acted like Blackshirts, often club in hand beating sense into their backwards or red cohorts. A particularly satisfying denouement of one of these episodes would show the little heroes peeing on the red flag. Or using it to blow their noses. (See Luigi Villari, *The Awakening of Italy: The Fascista Regeneration*, Methuen & Co., 1924, pp. 16–24.) Mussolini wrote his portion of the *Doctrine of Fascism* in 1932, attempting to give the most serious face he could muster to the ideological history and meaning of his movement. Still, when he had occasion in the *Doctrine* to refer to the convergence of socialism with liberalism, he expressed it in the following form: Italian Socialism in the twentieth century had already "been emasculated and chloroformed by fornication with Giolitti [the leader of the Liberals]." 1932! Ten years after the March on Rome, with liberalism and Marxism shattered, Mussolini, on his best behavior, still presented the issue in such plainly vulgar terms.

27. See Jimmy McCloskey, "'Germophobe' Donald Trump Hates Shaking Hands and Is Obsessed with Using Hand Sanitizer," *Metro News*, Jul. 8, 2019, metro.co.uk/2019/07/08/germophobe-donald-trump-hates-shaking -hands-and-is-obsessed-with-using-hand-sanitizer-10132516.

28. See Gabby Morrongiello, "'In Trump We Trust': Ann Coulter to Release Book About Trump," *Washington Examiner*, May 10, 2016.

29. Dwarfing anything that had been seen before, the First World War caused the combatant nations of Europe to conscript millions and millions of men. This meant tapping huge numbers from what sociologists call the "traditional" sectors of society—those sectors not yet caught up in the industrial world. Men from the countryside were one prime example, men whose lives till then promised to be essentially similar to the lives their fathers had led, and the grandfathers before them. Beyond the family, these men would intersect with a small number of institutions in their lives: the church, the landlord, perhaps a school. They would work hard with their hands, in the fields or a trade, marry from within the village, speak a dialect understood only in their province, and perhaps not understand the national language—German or Italian, for example. They might never travel more than a village or two away from home, and their relationship to their nation-states would be abstract and far away, as if to a foreign country.

Suddenly, millions of these men, still youths, were ripped from their villages, and thrown in with fellows from throughout the nation. In this perverse cosmopolitanism, they were in a fundamental way closer, more intimate, with these fellows than with anyone back home: they depended on one another for their very lives. The young men died in huge numbers, often after months of unfathomable miseries in the trenches. They were maimed in huge numbers. When the war was over, both the villages they had come from and they themselves were altered in ways that could never be undone. Traditional roles no longer existed as they had. The returning veterans could not fit back into civilian life.

From Lawrence Rosenthal, "The Male Fighting Band," in Yiannis Gabriel, *Organizations in Depth* (Sage, 1999), 182.

30. William A. Salamone discusses the revisionist history of the Risorgimento that emerged after the fall of Fascism. See his "The Risorgimento Between Ideology and History: The Political Myth of Rivoluzione Mancata," *American Historical Review* 68, no. 1 (Oct. 1962): 38–56. Antonio Gramsci's analysis of the Risorgimento as failed, as a *rivoluzione mancata*, focused on the liberal forces that successfully challenged the Italian aristocracy and their failure to incorporate the working class and the peasantry into their top-down movement. See John A. Davis, "Modern Italy—Changing

Historical Perspectives Since 1945," in Michael Bentley, *Companion to Historiography* (Routledge, 1997): 593.

31. Rosenthal, "The Male Fighting Band," 182:

> What did it mean to be a fascist in, say, the Po Valley in Italy in late 1921? It meant to dress in a black-shirted uniform, assemble with your fellows at night, ride a truck to another village, lynch the socialist mayor, pour castor oil down the throats of officers and members of labour unions.

The castor oil treatment is portrayed in Federico Fellini's film *Amacord*. The Fascist regime already well established, the young protagonist's father, Aurelio, a construction foreman with an anarchist past, is taken from his home by Blackshirts at night and forced to drink castor oil. See www .youtube.com/watch?v=S6sFMB8nwfA.

32. In his first speech to parliament after the March on Rome, Mussolini brazenly brandished the carrot and the stick:

> Gentlemen! What I am doing now in this hall is a formal act of deference to you, for which I ask no special sign of gratitude. . . .
>
> I could have abused my victory, but I refused to do so. I imposed limits on myself. I told myself that the better wisdom is that which does not lose control of itself after victory. With 300,000 youths armed to the teeth, fully determined and almost mystically ready to act on any command of mine, I could have punished all those who defamed and tried to sully Fascism. I could have transformed this drab, silent hall into a bivouac for my squads. . . . I could have barred the doors of Parliament and formed a government exclusively of Fascists. I could have done so; but I chose not to, at least not for the present.

Quoted in Charles F. Delzell, *Mediterranean Fascism, 1919–1945* (Harper and Row, 1970), 45–46.

33. *Time*, Nov. 28, 2008, content.time.com/time/covers/0,16641,20081124 ,00.html. The *New Yorker* also ran such an Obama-as-FDR graphic: See George Packer, "The New Liberalism," Nov. 8, 2008, www.newyorker.com /magazine/2008/11/17/the-new-liberalism.

34. There is certainly dissent on this matter. See, for example, Michael Grunwald, *The New New Deal: The Hidden Story of Change* (Simon and Schuster, 2012). (It is notable that Grunwald's title—the *hidden* story—alludes to the widespread perception of the promise not kept.) The focus of Grunwald's argument is his insistence on the historically transformative elements of Obama's economic stimulus legislation, which, though widely recognized as having stopped the descent to a full-scale depression, is often derided as having been inadequate.

35. Farhad Manjoo, "Barack Obama's Biggest Mistake," *New York Times*, Sep. 18, 2019.

36. Bhaskar Sunkara, "Barack Obama Is Stuck in the Past. He Represents the Old Democratic Party," *The Guardian*, Apr. 8, 2019.

37. Eli Zaretsky, "Trump's Charisma," *LRB* (blog), Jun. 21, 2019. In his view of the nature of Trump's charisma, Zaretsky recognizes the juvenile, superhero quality that resonates with Trump's base (cf "Magnet Man," chapter 3):

In Trump's case, his charisma rests not so much on having previously beaten his rivals, as on beating them over and over, like a children's superhero. Understanding this is key to understanding his constantly picking fights and engaging in apparently absurd conflicts, especially after he seems to have won a victory—as with the Mueller Report, or immediately after his election. Democrats see this as an expression of personal insecurity, bad temper and bullying. It may well be, but Trump's "insecurity," his unending struggle with those who question his legitimacy, is integral to his charisma.

www.lrb.co.uk/blog/2019/june/trump-s-charisma.

38. Among others, Adrian Lyttleton, the most eminent historian of the rise of fascism in Italy, makes the point that the sine qua non of a fascist movement is the marriage of electoral party and militia. Adrian Lyttleton, *The Seizure of Power: Fascism in Italy, 1919–1929* (Princeton University Press, 1973).

There was nothing casual about Italian Fascism's connection to its militia organs. The movement endured a tremendous internal struggle in its earliest years over whether it was a movement or a party. The struggle climaxed in the summer of 1921, when Fascism officially declared itself a political party as part of a compromise agreed upon to keep the movement from splitting. The charter, published in November 1921, begins: "The National Fascist Party is a militia organized for combat and competence." This is an extraordinary formulation. The militia is not "affiliated" with the party. It is not a "component" of the party. It *is* the party. The party is defined as a militia; party and militia are one and the same.

As fascism is the marriage of a political party and a private militia, its most prefigurative predecessor was the Ku Klux Klan allied with the post–Civil War Democratic Party in the South. The two combined created a one-party electoral monopoly that functioned both overtly and covertly with uniformed vigilantes. With the end of Reconstruction and the coming of Jim Crow, the South's permanent white electoral majority was institutionalized. The "second coming" of the Klan, in the 1920s and '30s coincides with the rise of fascism internationally.

39. Internationally the exception across the range of illiberal parties has been the Golden Dawn movement in Greece. See Helena Smith, "After Murder, Defections and Poll Defeat: The Sun Sets on Greece's Golden Dawn," *The Guardian*, Sep. 21 2019, www.theguardian.com/world/2019/sep/21/greece-sun-has-set-on-far-right-golden-dawn-murder-defections.

40. Yuri Slezkine, *The Jewish Century* (Princeton University Press, 2006), 61.

41. Carl Schorske, *Fin-de-Siècle Vienna* (Knopf, 1980), 119.

42. Tony Judt, "The New Old Nationalism," *New York Review of Books*, May 26, 1994, www.nybooks.com/articles/1994/05/26/the-new-old-nationalism.

43. The National Trade Council was folded into the Office of Trade and Manufacturing Policy in April 2017, over which Navarro was named director.

44. *Scoring the Trump Economic Plan: Trade, Regulatory and Energy Policy Impacts*. Available at assets.donaldjtrump.com/Trump_Economic_Plan.pdf.

45. Stephen K. Bannon, "Steve Bannon: We're in an Economic War with China. It's Futile to Compromise," *Washington Post*, May 6, 2019. Bannon writes: "As Washington and Beijing wrap up months of negotiations on a trade deal this month, whatever emerges won't be a trade deal. It will be a temporary truce in a years-long economic and strategic war with China."

46. See "Prime Minister Viktor Orbán's Speech at the 25th Bálványos Summer Free University and Student Camp," website of the Hungarian Government, Jul. 30, 2014, www.kormany.hu/en/the-prime-minister/the-prime-minister-s-speeches/prime-minister-viktor-orban-s-speech-at-the-25th-balvanyos-summer-free-university-and-student-camp.

47. Two months after losing forty-one seats in the House of Representatives in the 2018 midterm elections, the Republican caucus, after years of indifference and winking at the white supremacist views of Iowa representative Steven King, stripped King of his committee assignments. (Trip Gabriel et al., "Steve King Removed from Committee Assignments over White Supremacy Remark," *New York Times*, Jan. 14, 2019.)

This came three days after the *New York Times* published an interview with King in which he stated, "White nationalist, white supremacist, Western civilization—how did that language become offensive?" In the original article ("A Bullhorn of Anti-immigrant Rhetoric, Long Before Trump Started," *New York Times*, Jan. 11, 2019), *Times* correspondent Trip Gabriel pointed out that King "uses the concepts of either 'culture' or 'civilization' to obfuscate that he is talking about whiteness and race." Gabriel also highlighted that King had developed personal relationships with anti-immigrant and anti-Semitic figures abroad. As the latter article observed, "The condemnations of Mr. King stood in stark contrast to the lawmakers' willingness to tolerate President Trump's frequent offensive and insensitive remarks about migrants, black people, Native Americans and other minorities."

48. Marc Santora, "Poland's Populists Pick a New Top Enemy: Gay People," *New York Times*, Apr. 7, 2019. See also the *Times'* report on the immense influence of Polish radio priest Tadeusz Rydzyk, whose practice resembles that of Father Coughlin in the United States in the 1930s. Rydzyk's connection to the populist and nationalist party in power, Law and Justice, is considerable.

Since Law and Justice came to power in 2015, Father Rydzyk's businesses have received at least $55 million in subsidies from at least 10 ministries and state companies, according to public records.

Marc Santora and Joanna Berendt, "Mixing Politics and Piety, a Conservative Priest Seeks to Shape Poland's Future," *New York Times*, Sep. 21, 2019.

49. See Anton Barbashin and Hannah Thoburn, "Putin's Brain: Alexander Dugin and the Philosophy Behind Putin's Invasion of Crimea," *Foreign Affairs*, Mar. 31, 2014, www.foreignaffairs.com/articles/russia-fsu/2014-03-31/putins-brain.

50. On Mackinder's rediscovery, see Phil Tinline, "The Father of Geopolitics," *New Statesman*, Jan. 30, 2019, www.newstatesman.com/halford-mackinder-father-geopolitics. See also Alfred W. McCoy's "These Five Academics Have Brought Us to the Brink of Geopolitical Disaster," *The Nation*, Dec. 3, 2018, which includes Mackinder in this roll call, www.thenation.com/article/geopolitics-peter-navarro-china-trade-war.

51. This strategy has included support for nationalist and populist movements and parties throughout Europe. See Alina Polyakova, "Putinism and the European Far Right," *Atlantic Council*, Nov. 19, 2015, imrussia.org/images/stories/Russia_and_the_World/Putin-Far-Right/alina-polyakova_putinism-european-far-right.pdf.

In his 2005 annual address to the Federal Assembly of the Russian Federation, Putin famously said, "The collapse of the Soviet Union was the greatest political catastrophe of the twentieth century." While Putin referred to the "drama" of millions of Russians stranded outside the Russian Federation, the more significant geopolitical point was both the felt vulnerability of Western encroachment on Russia's borders, and, most importantly, his conviction that Russia needed to reestablish itself as a world power—and Putin's path to that goal, following Mackinder and Dugin, was again to control the "world island."

52. McFaul calls the transnational counterforce to the West Putin is trying to put together the "Illiberal International." From Matthew Rozsa's interview with McFaul, "What Happens If Putin Wins? Michael McFaul on 'the End of the Liberal International Order,'" *Salon*, Jan. 22, 2019, www.salon.com/2019/01/22/what-happens-if-putin-wins-michael-mcfaul-on-the-end-of-the-liberal-international-order.

McFaul achieved a dubious fame in July 2018 when, at Trump's joint news conference with Putin at their Helsinki summit, Trump spoke approvingly of Putin's proposal to turn McFaul over to Russia for interrogation.

At this week's summit in Helsinki, Russian President Vladimir Putin proposed what President Trump described as an "incredible offer"—

the Kremlin would give special counsel Robert S. Mueller III access to interviews with Russians who were indicted after they allegedly hacked Democrats in 2016. In return, Russia would be allowed to question certain U.S. officials it suspects of interfering in Russian affairs.

One of those U.S. officials is a former U.S. ambassador to Moscow, Michael McFaul, a nemesis of the Kremlin because of his criticisms of Russia's human rights record.

Samantha Schmidt, "Outrage Erupts over Trump-Putin 'Conversation' About Letting Russia Interrogate ex-U.S. Diplomat Michael McFaul," *Washington Post*, Jul. 19, 2018.

Putin's reach for McFaul was an attempt at leverage for him to get hold of Bill Browder, a British businessman who spent several years working in Russia and was also a human rights activist. When Browder's Russian lawyer, Sergei Magnitsky, uncovered a quarter-billion-dollar scam among Putin-favored oligarchs, he was jailed and died in prison. The Magnitsky Act was passed by the U.S. Congress in 2012 and freezes certain oligarchs' U.S. assets. The Magnitsky Act is known to have severely stuck in Putin's craw. For an interview with Browder, see Matthew Rozsa, "Bill Browder Is Putin's Public Enemy No 1—but He Isn't Scared: He's a 'Very Stupid Strategist,'" *Salon*, Jan. 19, 2019, www.salon.com/2019/01/19/putins-public -enemy-no-1-taunts-him-bill-browder-calls-russian-leader-a-very-stupid -strategist.

53. Casey Michel, "US Hate Group Forging Ties with the 'Third Rome,'" *Eurasianet*, Jul. 15, Also see Michel's "International: How the American Right Learned to Love Moscow in the Era of Trump," *Right Wing Watch*, Mar. 2017, www.rightwingwatch.org/report/the-rise-of-the-traditionalist -international-how-the-american-right-learned-to-love-moscow-in-the-era -of-trump.

See also Natasha Bertrand, "'A Model for Civilization': Putin's Russia Has Emerged as 'a Beacon for Nationalists' and the American Alt-Right," *Business Insider*, Dec. 10, 2016, www.businessinsider.com/russia-connections -to-the-alt-right-2016-11; Neil MacFarquhar, "Right-Wing Groups Find a Haven, for a Day, in Russia," *New York Times*, Mar. 22, 2015.

54. Luke O'Brien, "The Making of an American Nazi," *The Atlantic*, Dec. 2017.

55. David Weigel, "Trump Moves Praise for Putin Closer to the Mainstream of the GOP," *Washington Post*, Sep. 9, 2016.

56. archive.adl.org/anti_semitism/duke_russia.html#.WFWZXPkrI2y. Last viewed December 2016.

57. Quoted in Alan Feuer and Andrew Higgins, "Extremists Turn to a Leader to Protect Western Values: Vladimir Putin," *New York Times*, Dec. 3, 2016.

In his excellent article, "The French Origins of 'You Will Not Replace Us': The European Thinkers Behind the White-Nationalist Rallying Cry," Thomas Chatterton Williams discusses Guillaume Faye, a member of France's "Nouvelle Droite"—New Right—in the following terms:

> Not only do thinkers like Faye admire Putin as an emblem of proudly heterosexual white masculinity; they fantasize that Russian military might will help create a "Eurosiberian" federation of white ethno-states. "The only hope for salvation in this dark age of ours," Faye has declared, is "a protected and self-centered continental economic space" that is capable of "curbing the rise of Islam and demographic colonization from Africa and Asia."

New Yorker, Dec. 4, 2017.

58. Paul Gottfried has been a central figure in paleoconservatism for decades. He was also Richard Spencer's most important faculty influence in Spencer's undergraduate years. As the alt-right formed, Gottfried and Spencer went separate ways. Gottfried was unable to understand this white-identity transition, or expansion, in the nature of nationalism. From a 2017 interview with Gottfried:

> Western white people have generally not been "nationalistic" about race. They've been nationalistic about being Frenchmen, Germans, Poles, Russians, etc. Even if all races practice discrimination against racial out-groups, Western identity has centered on other commonalities.

From George Hawley, *Making Sense of the Alt-Right* (Columbia University Press, 2017), 52.

For an interesting background on Spencer and Gottfried, their early convergence, and subsequent divergence, see Jacob Siegal, "The Alt-Right's Jewish Godfather," *Tablet*, Nov. 29, 2016, www.tabletmag.com/jewish-news -and-politics/218712/spencer-gottfried-alt-right. Also worthwhile is Gott-fried's 2007 volume, *Conservatism in America: Making Sense of the American Right* (Palgrave), which includes his attack on neoconservatism.

59. This has corresponded with an astounding rise in the League's pop-ularity. In the 2014 elections for the European Parliament, the then North-ern League won 6.5 percent of the votes and five seats. In the May 2019 European parliamentary election, the League won 34.3 percent of the vote and twenty-eight seats. The League was now the strongest party in Italy; the next highest share of the vote, for the major center-left Democratic Par-ty, was 22.7 percent.

60. Routledge.

61. Rebecca Tan, "Steve Bannon Plans a Far-Right 'Supergroup' in Europe, but Some Key Far-Right Leaders Say They're Not Interested," *Washington Post*, Aug. 14, 2018.

62. Pablo Pardo, "Make Spain Great Again: The Far-Right Vox Party Has Adopted Trump-Style Politics," *Foreign Policy*, Apr. 27, 2019, foreign-policy.com/2019/04/27/vox-spain-elections-trump-bannon. Vox more than doubled its seats, from twenty-four to fifty-two in Spain's November par-liamentary elections of 2019. See Sohail Janniessary, "The Left Will Gov-ern Spain, But the Far Right Is the Real Winner," *Foreign Policy*, Nov. 16, 2019, foreignpolicy.com/2019/11/16/spain-election-vox-far-right-socialists -winner.

63. James Reynolds, "Italy Election: 'White Race' Remark Sparks Row," BBC News, Jan. 18, 2018. (Attilio Fontana, Northern League can-didate: "We need to decide whether or not our ethnic group, our white race, our society should continue to exist, or be wiped out. It's a choice.") "At a rally in Warsaw on November 11th, white-nationalist demonstra-tors brandished signs saying 'Pray for an Islamic Holocaust' and 'Pure Poland, White Poland.'" (Williams, "The French Origins of 'You Will Not Replace Us.'")

"Alberto Testa, an expert on far-right radicalization at the University of West London, told VICE News . . . eastern Ukraine had become a critical staging ground for the international "white jihad struggle" of the far right, where extremists could "train for what some would call racial holy war." Tim Hume, *Vice News*, Jul. 31, 2019, www.vice.com/en_us/article/vb95ma /far-right-extremists-have-been-using-ukraines-civil-war-as-a-training -ground-theyre-returning-home.

64. Moore, *The Social Origins of Dictatorship and Democracy* (Beacon, 1967). Poulantzas, *Political Power and Social Classes* (Verso, 1975). Organski, *The Stages of Political Development* (Knopf, 1973).

65. From Trump's announcement of his candidacy: www.youtube.com /watch?v=SpMJx0-HyOM.

"We're closed!": Between September 2017 and her firing in April 2019, Kirstjen Nielsen was secretary of homeland security in Donald Trump's cabinet. Despite her defense of policies such as the administration's separation of families at the border, Trump grew unhappy with her failure to "secure the border" ("He wants . . . shock and awe") and she became the object of Trump's tirades in cabinet meetings. (See Michael D. Shear and Nicole Perlroth, "Kirstjen Nielsen, Chief of Homeland Security, Almost Resigned After Trump Tirade," *New York Times*, May 10, 2018.) At a particularly fraught cabinet meeting in May 2018, Trump, in a tirade, enunciated in a word his view of how much immigration the United States could absorb:

> As Trump harangued Nielsen for more than 30 minutes in front of the Cabinet this month, other aides grimaced and fidgeted. Nothing she said seemed to calm the president, according to people familiar with the meeting.
>
> "We're closed!" Trump yelled at one point, referring to the border.

Josh Dawsey and Nick Miroff, "The Hostile Border Between Trump and the Head of DHS," *Washington Post*, May 28, 2018.

66. Nick Gass, "Trump Camp Tries to Clarify His 'I Love War' Comment," *Politico*, Sep. 7, 2016, www.politico.com/story/2016/09/trump-i-love -war-comment-227818. Last viewed April 2018.

67. See, for example, Dennis M. Foster, "Would President Trump Go to War to Divert Attention from Problems at Home?," *Washington Post*, Dec. 19, 2016.

5. The Road to the Tiki Torches: The Blurry Convergence of Alienation and White Nationalism

1. A first-hand account of the Battle of Berkeley can be found at Scott Lucas, "Battle of the Bastards," May 9, 2017, www.scottlucas. me/battle-of-the-bastards.

2. Richard Spencer, "What Berkeley Means," Alt-Right.com, Apr. 16, 2017. Spencer opined on the street fighting: "The actual video footage is quite beautiful." altright.com/2017/04/16/what-berkeley-means. Last viewed April 2018.

3. Spencer, was, in effect, raising the so-called Antifa to the level of the organized political parties and opponents of the Nazis. The analogy fails historically for reasons of the utter marginality of Antifa; to the extent Antifa has an ideological point of view, it is made up of anarchists, people who have been showing up at left-wing demonstrations for years with the intent of provoking police violence. See Sean Illing, "'They Have No Allegiance to Liberal Democracy': An Expert on Antifa Explains the Group," *Vox*, Aug. 13, 2018, for an interview with Mark Bray, author of *Antifa: The Anti-Fascist Handbook* (Melville House, 2017).

In the context of the Trump and alt-right era, Antifa functions as a symbiotic consort of right-wing violence. Politically, it gives cover to nonsensical left-right equivalencies, of which perhaps the most famous is Donald Trump's view of Charlottesville—"good people on both sides." Trump has also referred to the Antifa as the "alt-left," as though to draw an equivalence to the violence and extremism of the outer reaches of his political coalition to something which, in effect, must exist on the left. See Linda Qui, "Trump Asks, 'What About the Alt-Left?' Here's an Answer," *New York Times*, Aug. 15, 2017.

4. With guile, Spencer distinguishes himself from white supremacists, arguing that his politics are not about claiming racial superiority so much as they are about according white people the right to nationalism on the basis of whiteness that, for example, Jews get in the state of Israel based on Jewishness.

5. Katie Rogers and Nicolas Fandos, "Trump Tells Congresswomen to 'Go Back' to the Countries They Came From," *New York Times*, Jul. 14, 2019. It is notable that Trump's attack elicited Democratic Speaker Nancy Pelosi's explicit recognition of the white nationalism of Trump's politics:

Pelosi may have offered the bluntest take on Mr. Trump's comments when she said his campaign slogan, Make America Great Again, "has always been about making America white again."

6. See David Neiwert's report, "Neo-Nazi Troll Andrew Anglin's Celebratory Mood Crushed by $14 Million Judgment Against Him," reprinted in *Alternet*, Jul. 16, 2019, www.alternet.org/2019/07/neo-nazi-troll-andrew-anglins-celebratory-mood-crushed-by-14-million-judgment-against-him.

Also see his *Alt-America: The Rise of the Radical Right in the Age of Trump* (Verso, 2017).

7. Richard Spencer, "What Berkeley Means," Apr. 16, 2017.

8. Brett Barrouquere, "Judge Upholds Bulk of Lawsuit Against Alt-Righters in Charlottesville After 'Unite the Right,' Dismisses Peinovich," Jul. 10, 2018. This was a report on the suit in federal court brought against the Charlottesville organizers for conspiracy to commit violence, www.splcenter.org/hatewatch/2018/07/10/judge-upholds-bulk-lawsuit-against-alt-righters-charlottesville-after-unite-right-dismisses.

9. Disrupting government functioning on behalf of an electoral party made a brief appearance in 2000 in American politics. In what came to be known as the Brooks Brothers riot, Republican operatives stormed the offices where Miami-Dade County officials were engaged in a recount of presidential election votes.

Upstairs in the Clark center, several people were trampled, punched or kicked when protesters tried to rush the doors outside the office of the Miami-Dade supervisor of elections. Sheriff's deputies restored order.

When the ruckus was over, the protesters had what they had wanted: a unanimous vote by the board to call off the hand counting.

Several people who attended the demonstration said they had decided to do so after receiving an automated phone message, initiated by local Republican officials, encouraging them.

Dexter Filkins and Dana Canedy, "Protest Influenced Miami-Dade's Decision to Stop Recount," *New York Times*, Nov. 24, 2000.

A modified version of the Brooks Brothers riot occurred on October 22,

2019, when twenty-five Republican congressmen and women stormed a hearing room in the House of Representatives, bringing the impeachment hearing to a halt. (Richard Cowan et al., "Republican Lawmakers Storm Hearing Room, Disrupt Trump Impeachment Inquiry," *Reuters*, Oct. 23, 2019, af.reuters.com/article/worldNews/idAFKBN1X216T.)

10. "Lone wolf" violence is an ambiguous problem in relation to political parties or politicians, but less ambiguous in relation to the alt-right. One lone-wolf example is the case of Cesar Sayoc, the Florida man ("whose white van . . . was covered in stickers celebrating Republicans and denouncing the president's opponents") who sent pipe bombs to opponents of President Trump. (Jon Swaine et al., "Florida Man Charged with Sending 13 Pipe Bombs to Trump Critics," *The Guardian*, Oct. 26, 2018, www.theguardian.com/us-news/2018/oct/26/suspicious-package-pipe -bombs-latest-found-cory-booker-florida.)

The question of "stochastic terrorism" has become deadly serious after attacks in the United States, among other countries, on synagogues in Poway, California, and Pittsburgh, and on Latinos at a Walmart in El Paso. (See Arun Gupta, "Robert Bowers' Synagogue Attack Is Only One of 16 Cases of White-Supremacist Killings Since Trump Was Inaugurated," *Raw Story*, Oct. 28, 2018, www.rawstory.com/2018/10/robert-bowers-synagogue-attack -one-16-cases-white-supremacist-killings-since-trump-inaugurated.) These resemble attacks abroad such as the Christchurch mosque attack in New Zealand, all of which have been tied to alt-right thinking or manifestos citing thinking like "replacement theory."

> Stochastic terrorism is the use of mass communications to incite random actors to carry out violent or terrorist acts that are *statistically predictable but individually unpredictable.* In short, remote-control murder by lone wolf.

stochasticterrorism.blogspot.com.

See Eyal Press, "This Week's Mail Bombs Are No Surprise: They Are Examples of Stochastic Terrorism—Individually Random, but These Days, Statistically Predictable," *New York Times*, Oct. 25, 2018, www.nytimes.com /2018/10/25/opinion/terrorismbombs-democrats-deniro-biden-soros.html.

See also Jonathan Chait, "The (Full) Case for Impeachment," *New York Magazine*, Oct. 14, 2019:

There have been 36 criminal cases nationwide in which the defendant invoked Trump's name in connection with violence; 29 of these cited him as the inspiration for an attack.

nymag.com/intelligencer/2019/10/the-full-case-for-trump-impeachment .html.

11. Much of the planning of Charlottesville took place on a website called Discord.

12. Here is an example of a journalist who was attacked using the gas chamber meme: twitter.com/brodiegal/status/788368180792131584?lang= en. Last viewed October 2017.

13. Joseph Goldstein describes the gathering:

[Spencer] railed against Jews and, with a smile, quoted Nazi propaganda in the original German. America, he said, belonged to white people, whom he called the "children of the sun," a race of conquerors and creators who had been marginalized but now, in the era of President-elect Donald J. Trump, were "awakening to their own identity."

As he finished, several audience members had their arms outstretched in a Nazi salute. Mr. Spencer called out: "Hail Trump! Hail our people!" and then, "Hail victory!"—the English translation of the Nazi exhortation "Sieg Heil!" The room shouted back.

Joseph Goldstein, "Alt-Right Gathering Exults in Trump Election with Nazi-Era Salute," *New York Times*, Nov. 20, 2016. For video of Spencer's speech, see www.youtube.com/watch?v=1o6-bi3jlxk.

At a previous gathering of his movement in Washington, Spencer encouraged his followers: "Let's party like it's 1933," specifying the year Hitler came to power. See John Woodrow Cox, "'Let's Party Like It's 1933': Inside the Alt-Right World of Richard Spencer," *Washington Post*, Nov. 22, 2017.

14. Polls overwhelmingly indicated the American public appears to reject the alt-right's white nationalism and the Nazi motifs of Charlottesville. See, for example, maristpoll.marist.edu/nprpbs-newshourmarist -poll-results-on-charlottesville.

15. Jonathan Berr, "PayPal Cuts off Payments to Right-Wing Extremists," CBS News, Aug. 16, 2017.

[Other] digital platforms have also been increasingly assertive in removing White nationalist and other Far Right accounts. Alex Jones, for example, lost almost all of his mainstream digital accounts. Patreon, a site which manages recurring donations, also became more aggressive in removing Far Right activists, striking an important financial blow against them. Alt-Right attempts to form their own platforms have also largely failed.

From Spencer Sunshine, "Alt-Right and Far Right Mobilization in 2018," *Political Research Associates*, nd, feature.politicalresearch.org/alt-right-and -far-right-in-2018.

16. See Denise Lavoie, "White Supremacist Sentenced to 2nd Life Term for Deadly Charlottesville Car Attack," *Business Insider*, Jul. 16, 2019, www.businessinsider.com/james-alex-fields-sentenced-2nd-life-term -charlottesville-car-attack-2019-7. See also Christine Hauser and Julia Jacobs, "Three Men Sentenced to Prison for Violence at Charlottesville Rally," *New York Times*, Aug. 23, 2018.

17. See Alan Feuer, "Planners of Deadly Charlottesville Rally Are Tested in Court," *New York Times*, Feb. 12, 2018. The case is being argued on the basis of the Reconstruction Acts that undermined the first wave of the KKK—the Civil Rights Act of 1866 and the KKK Act of 1871. See chapter 4, note 38, which points out how twentieth-century fascism was prefigured by the KKK's marriage of a private militia and an electoral party. Feuer quotes one defendant's explicit view of Charlottesville as the attempt to move the alt-right from the web to the streets:

"The goal here is to break us and keep us from taking to the streets," said Jeff Schoep, the leader of the National Socialist Movement.

As Jane Coaston points out ("The Alt-Right Is Going on Trial in Charlottesville," *Vox*, Mar. 8, 2018, www.vox.com/2018/3/8/17071832/alt-right-racists -charlottesville):

[Lead attorney Rebecca] Kaplan's team collected thousands of hours of chats and videos created by the defendants and leaked online—including white nationalist pundit Richard Spencer, rally organizer Jason Kessler, and Andrew Anglin, founder of the neo-Nazi Daily Stormer website—that urged participants to prepare for and commit violence in Charlottesville.

Kaplan's complaint is available online (files.integrityfirstforamerica.org /14228/1567613983-first-amended-complaint-as-filed.pdf) and is well worth consulting. In addition to a complete list of the defendants, the complaint cites absolutely exhaustive evidence of planning for violence among the defendants, largely accumulated by following their posts on Discord.

An excellent discussion of the complaint is available at Dahlia Lithwick, "Can the Organizers of the Alt-Right Be Held Responsible for the Violence in Charlottesville," *Slate*, Oct. 12, 2017, www.slate.com /articles/news_and_politics/jurisprudence/2017/10/two_new_lawsuits _against_the_organizers_of_charlottesville_s_unite_the_right.html. Last viewed April 2018.

Richard Spencer, one of the defendants, acting as his own lawyer, unsuccessfully moved to dismiss the case against him on the grounds that he was unable to find a lawyer willing to defend him. (See Zoe Tillman, "Richard Spencer Said He Couldn't Find a Lawyer to Defend Him Against a Lawsuit About the Violence in Charlottesville," *BuzzFeed*, Jan. 30, 2018, www.buzzfeednews.com/article/zoetillman/richard-spencer-says-he -couldnt-find-a-lawyer-to-defend-him.)

This was a far cry from his exhilaration in the immediate aftermath of the Charlottesville demonstration, when he opined that some of the video from the march was beautiful; that it was fun and established a model that would be repeated; that it was well known that the alt-right was a non-violent movement—and even that the murderer of Heather Heyer, in his automobile, was acting in self-defense. (See Brandi Bushman, "Charlottesville Lawsuit Aims to Stop White Nationalist Militias," *Courthouse News Service*, Oct. 12, 2017, www.courthousenews.com/charlottesville-lawsuit -aims-stop-private-militia-groups. And Alt-right.com, Aug. 13, 2017. Last viewed December 2017.)

18. See German Lopez, "Unite the Right 2018 Was a Pathetic Failure," *Vox*, Aug. 12, 2018.

19. The complaint is available at www.law.georgetown.edu/icap/wp -content/uploads/sites/32/2018/02/lawsuit-charlottesville.pdf.

20. See "Kessler Settles Lawsuit over Militia Groups at Unite the Right Rally," NBC 29, Jul. 12, 2018, www.nbc29.com/story/38630548/kessler-set tles-militia-lawsuit-7-12-2018.

21. Luke O'Brien, "The Making of an American Nazi," *The Atlantic,* December 2017.

22. Roger Eatwell, "Fascism," in *The Oxford Handbook of Political Ideologies,* Michael Freeden et al., eds., 478.

23. *Il Popolo d'Italia,* Nov. 15, 1919.

24. *The Futurist Manifesto* is available online at www.societyforasianart .org/sites/default/files/manifesto_futurista.pdf.

25. Quoted in Jacob Siegel, "The Alt-Right's Jewish Godfather," *Tablet,* Nov. 29, 2016, www.tabletmag.com/jewish-news-and-politics/218712 /spencer-gottfried-alt-right.

26. See Sarah Posner, "How Donald Trump's New Campaign Chief Created an Online Haven for White Nationalists," *Mother Jones,* Aug. 22, 2016, www.motherjones.com/politics/2016/08/stephen-bannon-donald-trump -alt-right-breitbart-news.

27. See Marcia Clemmitt, "'Alt-Right' Movement," *CQ Researcher,* Mar. 17, 2017, library.cqpress.com/cqresearcher/document.php?id=cqresrre2017 031700&abstract=false. And Josh Harkinson, "White Nationalists See Trump as Their Troll in Chief. Is He with Them?" *Mother Jones,* Jan.–Feb. 2017, www.motherjones.com/politics/2016/11/trump-white-nationalists-hate -racism-powerteh.

28. See www.youtube.com/watch?v=AXDXJQxbVkY. Bannon also tied his agenda to undermining the "mainstream media" he saw as the natural ally of the "administrative state."

They're corporatist, globalist media that are adamantly opposed to an economic nationalist agenda like Donald Trump has . . . there's a new political order that's being formed out of this. . . . We're a nation with an economy, not just an economy in some global marketplace with open borders. But we're a nation with a culture.

Essentially, what Bannon called the administrative state Donald Trump came to call the "deep state" as president, and argued over and over again it acted as a cabal to undermine his administration.

29. I calculate that fully 19 percent of Trump's 2019 State of the Union dealt either with dreadful criminal behaviors of "illegal aliens" or with security threats and solutions—like a wall—at the southern border. Some excerpts:

As we speak, large, organized caravans are on the march to the United States. We have just heard that Mexican cities . . . are getting trucks and buses to bring them up to our country. . . .

One in three women is sexually assaulted on the long journey north. Smugglers use migrant children as human pawns to exploit our laws and gain access to our country. Human traffickers and sex traffickers take advantage of the wide open areas between our ports of entry to smuggle thousands of young girls and women into the United States and to sell them into prostitution and modern-day slavery.

Tens of thousands of innocent Americans are killed by lethal drugs that cross our border and flood into our cities—including meth, heroin, cocaine, and fentanyl.

The savage gang, MS-13, now operates in 20 different American States, and they almost all come through our southern border. Just yesterday, an MS-13 gang member was taken into custody for a fatal shooting on a subway platform in New York City. Here tonight is Debra Bissell. Just three weeks ago, Debra's parents, Gerald and Sharon, were burglarized and shot to death in their Reno, Nevada, home by an illegal alien.

30. Nate Silver calculates that "the shift among union voters was enough to swing the 2016 election to Trump."

Hillary Clinton's loss of Union support in 2016 compared to
    Obama in 2012
All Union members: 64.8%–55.2
White male Union members: 52.3%–40.7
Nonwhite male Union members: 81.4%–73.2

White female Union members: 64.5%–55.7

Nonwhite female Union members: 88.5%–83

According to the CCES [Cooperative Congressional Election Study], Obama won union voters by 34.4 percentage points in 2012, but Clinton did so by only 16.7 points in 2016. That roughly 18-point swing was worth a net of 1.2 percentage points for Trump in Pennsylvania, 1.1 points in Wisconsin, and 1.7 points in Michigan based on their rates of union membership—and those totals were larger than his margins of victory in those states.

FiveThirtyEight, May 2, 2019, fivethirtyeight.com/features/silver-bulletpoints-the-union-vote-could-swing-the-election.

31. Bannon bet heavily on backing senatorial candidate Roy Moore for the 2017 special election in Alabama to replace Jeff Sessions, who was moving on to become the U.S. attorney general. Bannon stuck with the candidate despite the emergence of news stories of his sexual abuse of underage young women. Moore lost to the first Democratic senator from Alabama in a generation. This was Bannon's major domestic political initiative after his dismissal from the Trump administration. Moore's loss severely undermined Bannon's stature within the Republican Party, and seemed in no small part a motivation to take his political consulting skills abroad to Trumpian candidates and parties. See Andrew Procop, "Steve Bannon's Republican Critics Are Gleefully Dunking on Him for Roy Moore's Shocking Loss," *Vox,* Dec. 12, 2017, www.vox.com/2017/12/12/16770678/roy-moore-loses-steve-bannon; and Maxwell Tani, "Republicans Blame Steve Bannon for Roy Moore's Shocking Loss in Alabama," *Business Insider,* Dec. 12, 2017, www.businessinsider.com/republicans-blame-steve-bannon-for-roy-moores-loss-2017-12.

32. The "Tax Cut and Jobs Act of 2017" lowered the corporate tax from 35 percent to 21 percent and cut the top rate of taxation (for married couples filing jointly) from 39.6 percent to 37 percent. The tax cut was a real test of the limits of the administration's commitment to "economic populism": Steve Bannon argued for *increasing* the top rate to 44 percent. See Anna Edgerton, "Bannon's Plan to Tax Top Earners 44% to Be Considered by GOP," *Bloomberg,* Jul. 26, 2017, www.bloomberg.com/news/articles/2017-07-27/bannon-s-plan-to-tax-top-earners-is-said-to-be-considered-by-gop.

Bannon was fired as White House advisor after seven months, and had his major financial backers drop him a few months later. Maggie Haberman et al., "Bannon, Key Voice of Populist Right, Exits White House," Aug. 19, 2017; Kenneth P. Vogel et al., "Donors and Candidates Abandon Bannon After His Break with Trump," *New York Times*, Jan. 5, 2018.

33. "Donald Trump has now had more turnover in his Cabinet in the first two-and-a-half years of his presidency than any of his five immediate predecessors did in their entire first terms." Madeleine Joung, "Trump Has Now Had More Cabinet Turnover Than Reagan, Obama and the Two Bushes," *Time*, Jul. 12, 2019, time.com/5625699/trump-cabinet-acosta.

34. Miller seems almost uniquely able to channel Trump. During the 2016 campaign, Miller often opened for Trump at rallies, where he specialized in delivering the red meat of immigrant criminality—feeding images of the Imagined Other. Miller is noted for his extreme confrontational attitude in interviews and news conferences. He has also been Trump's speech writer for his most important addresses, like the inaugural address and the State of the Union.

35. In effect, Navarro is arguing that China has successfully undercut the United States' comparative advantage in its exports of high valued-added goods and services, like aeronautics and tech and financial services. ideasandinsights.jpmorgan.com/ipbonline-tl/api/attachments/2409/en /macro_markets_2018_07_11.pdf.

Navarro's policies in action have not produced. See Ana Swanson, "Trump Vowed to Shrink the Trade Deficit, but It Keeps Getting Wider": "The overall trade deficit continued to widen in the first nine months of 2019, suggesting that the global trade wars haven't had the desired effect," *New York Times*, Nov. 6, 2019.

Navarro has also brought into his militarized notion of trade the conservative bias of zero-sum thinking.

Navarro [is] a zero-sum economist, who, like Trump, believes that every item not made in the U.S. represents the theft of an American job.

Jacob Heilbrunn, "The Most Dangerous Man in Trump World?," *Politico*, Feb. 12, 2017.

36. See Linda Gordon's excellent *The Second Coming of the KKK: The Ku*

Klux Klan in the 1920s and the American Political Tradition (Liveright, 2017). Gordon's study makes clear that, with Jim Crow firmly established in the South, the Klan's second coming was aimed at immigrants and was especially strong in northern cities. The rhetoric against "immigrant hordes" is remarkably reminiscent of Trumpian warnings about immigrant "invasions." Also worthwhile is Archie Mayo's 1937 film, *Black Legion*, starring Humphrey Bogart, which portrays an actual Detroit-based group of that name that had its origins in the KKK.

37. Belew, *Bring the War Home* (Harvard University Press, 2019), 120. Belew also attributes the beginnings of national militia solidarity to the 1979 Greensboro Massacre, which resulted in the deaths of four members of the Communist Workers' Party who were holding a "Death to the Klan" march. "The Greensboro shooting had the effect of consolidating and unifying the white power movement," p. 75. For the early history of white nationalism, also see Leonard Zeskind, *Blood and Politics: The History of the White Nationalist Movement from the Margins to the Mainstream* (Farrar Straus Giroux, 2009).

38. "Timothy Snyder, a historian and professor at Yale University, said 'alt-right' is a term . . . meant to provide a fresh label that would sound more attractive than 'Nazi,' 'neo-Nazi,' 'white supremacist,' or 'white nationalist.'"

Kurtis Lee, "President Trump Says the 'Alt-Left' Was Partly to Blame for the Violence at Charlottesville. Wait: What's the Alt-Left?," *Los Angeles Times*, Aug. 16, 2017, www.latimes.com/nation/la-na-pol-alt-left-20170816 -story.html.

39. Kat Chow, "What the Ebbs and Flows of the KKK Can Tell Us About White Supremacy Today," NPR, Dec. 8, 2018, www.npr.org/sections /codeswitch/2018/12/08/671999530/what-the-ebbs-and-flows-of-the-kkk -can-tell-us-about-white-supremacy-today. Blee is the author of *Women of the Klan* (University of California Press, 1992) and *Inside Organized Racism: Women in the Hate Movement* (University of California Press, 2003). See also Caroline Kitchener, "How the KKK Resonates Today," *The Atlantic*, Oct. 31, 2017:

Before the alt-right, the 1920s KKK was the last white supremacist group to engage seriously in national politics, according to Blee. Sixteen Klansmen became senators, 11 became governors, and approximately 75 became congressmen. Far more were sympathetic to the Klan's agenda. "By taking over the political parties, the Klan sought to institutionalize the organization," said Blee. "They had a big influence on the presidential level."

www.theatlantic.com/membership/archive/2017/10/how-the-kkk -resonates-today/544565.

40. Alan Blinder, "David Duke, Ex-K.K.K. Leader, to Seek Senate Seat in Louisiana," *New York Times*, Jul. 23, 2016.

41. James Oliphant and Steve Holland, "After Firing, Bannon Returns to His 'Killing Machine,'" *Reuters*, Aug. 18, 2017, www.reuters.com/article /us-usa-trump-bannon-right/after-firing-bannon-returns-to-his-killing -machine-idUSKCN1AY2JQ.

42. From Joshua Green's *Fresh Air* interview with Dave Davies, NPR, Oct. 9, 2019, www.npr.org/2019/10/09/768556474/how-a-political-hit-job -backfired-and-led-to-trumps-impeachment-peril.

"Looking at it from their point of view," the liberal strategist David Brock told me of Schweizer and GAI, "the Times is the perfect host body for the virus."

There was a New York Times story based on Schweizer's report-ing. . . . And, as Bannon intended, a whiff of corruption attached itself to Hillary Clinton. . . . The book really succeeded in what Bannon had set out to do. And that was to raise doubts about the ethics and mor-als and fitness for the presidency of Hillary Clinton.

Bannon's critique of how Republicans deal with the media goes back to the 1990s and Bill Clinton's impeachment, when he thought that Republicans really just wound up talking to themselves in an echo chamber. . . . Voters didn't listen to them.

See also Joshua Green, "Trump's Impeachment Saga Stems from a Politi-cal Hit Job Gone Bad," *Bloomberg*, Oct. 2, 2019, www.bloomberg.com/news /articles/2019-10-02/trump-s-impeachment-saga-stems-from-a-political -hit-job-gone-bad. Green offers an intriguing hypothesis in this article: Trump's impeachment vulnerability owing to his call to the Ukraine president asking for the favor (in exchange for delivery of $400 million in military material) of investigating Joe Biden's son Hunter's activities in the Ukraine was an attempt to have Bannon's *Clinton Cash* lightning strike twice. Schweizer published *Secret Empires: How the American Political Class Hides Corruption and Enriches Family and Friends* in 2018, which casts innuendo about Hunter Biden's work in Ukraine. But discussion of the book failed to break out of right-wing media into the mainstream. Trump, whose dedication to consuming right-wing media is unflagging as president, decided to use Bannon tactics to move it into the mainstream, and enlisted Giuliani in an adventure to get the Ukraine government to openly and publicly announce an investigation into Hunter Biden, which would perforce land in the mainstream press.

43. See Tim Gosling, "The Nationalist Internationale Is Crumbling: Steve Bannon Is Trying to Sell Trumpism to Eastern Europeans—but Shared Ideologies Die Hard When They Run into Economic and Military Realities," *Foreign Policy*, Jul. 20, 2018, foreignpolicy.com/2018/07/20/the -nationalist-internationale-is-crumbling-steve-bannon-eastern-europe -hungary-czech-republic-slovakia-trade.

44. See www.ebizmba.com/articles/political-websites. After Breitbart at number 2, there are Drudge (3); Infowars (7); Blaze (10); Daily Caller (11); WND (12); Newsmax (13); Washington Times (14). Last referenced October 18, 2017.

45. Vintage, 1960.

46. The Statler Brothers' 1965 song, "Flowers on the Wall," is a virtual anthem of the alienated young man, circa the 1950s and '60s, when TV ("Smokin' cigarettes and watchin' Captain Kangaroo") anticipated the media role that the internet would supplant—and make interactive—in the twenty-first century. The Statler Brothers' performance of the song, and the lyrics, may be found at www.google.com/search?q=smoking+cigarett es+and+watching+captain+kangaroo&oq=smoking+cigarettes+an&aqs=ch rome.1.69i57j0l5.11862j1j1&sourceid=chrome&ie=UTF-8.

47. Garret Keizer, "Nihilist Nation: The Empty Core of the Trump Mystique," *New Republic*, Oct. 25, 2018, newrepublic.com/article/151603/nihilist -nation-empty-core-trump-mystique.

48. Throwing out an alternative to Russian hacking emails in the 2016 election, Donald Trump referenced an image of the shut-in young man at his internet keyboard in his first presidential debate with Hillary Clinton:

She's saying Russia, Russia, Russia, but I don't—maybe it was. I mean, it could be Russia, but it could also be China. It could also be lots of other people. It also could be somebody sitting on their bed that weighs 400 pounds, OK?

Transcript of the first debate, www.nytimes.com/2016/09/27/us/politics /transcript-debate.html.

49. See M. Ambedkar, "The Aesthetics of the Alt-Right," *Post-Office-Arts Journal*, Baltimore, February 2017, baltimore-art.com/2017/02/11/the -aesthetics-of-the-alt-right.

50. www.pokemon.com/us/pokedex/pikachu.

51. www.imdb.com/title/tt0083658. The film is based on a Philip K. Dick story "Do Androids Dream of Electric Sheep?" Along with Ursula K. Le Guin, Dick is perhaps the most prominent writer of the New Wave science fiction movement of the 1960s, which marked a movement from outer-space stories, and otherwise the imagining of nonterrestrial worlds, to imagining life on earth fundamentally changed by largely sinister developments, both technological and political.

52. Lawrence Person, "Notes Toward a Postcyberpunk Manifesto," *Slashdot*, nd, news.slashdot.org/story/99/10/08/2123255/notes-toward-a-post cyberpunk-manifesto. Last viewed October 2019.

53. From "Massively Multiplayer Online Game (MMOG)," on the Technopedia website:

A massively multiplayer online game (MMOG) refers to videogames that allow a large number of players to participate simultaneously over an internet connection. These games usually take place in a shared world that the gamer can access after purchasing or installing the game software.

In addition to RPGs and real-time strategy (RTS) games, the online gameplay has become an essential feature in many first person shooters (FPS), racing games and even fighting games. For many gamers, the ability to compete with players from all over the world in a variety of online-only game modes overshadows the single player mode that many of these games were originally designed around.

www.techopedia.com/definition/27054/massively-multiplayer-online
-game-mmog.

54. M. Stephanie Murray, *Arizona Daily Wildcat*, Oct. 8, 1997. Accessed at *Arts Ground Zero* ("Bethke crashes the cyberpunk system"), wc.arizona .edu/papers/91/32/13_1_m.html.

55. Joshua Green, *Devil's Bargain: Steve Bannon, Trump, and the Nationalist Uprising* (Penguin, 2017), 145.

56. Green, *Devil's Bargain*, 145. See also Mike Snider, "Steve Bannon Learned to Harness Troll Army from 'World of Warcraft,'" *USA Today*, Jul. 18, 2017, www.usatoday.com/story/tech/talkingtech/2017/07/18/steve -bannon-learned-harness-troll-army-world-warcraft/489713001.

57. Jonathan Rauch writes:

Trolls attack real news; they attack the sources of real news; they disseminate fake news; and they create artificial copies of themselves to disseminate even more fake news. By unleashing great quantities of lies and half-truths, and then piling on and swarming, they achieve hive-mind coordination. Because trolling need not bother with persuasion or anything more than very superficial plausibility, it can concern itself with being addictively outrageous. Epistemically, it is anarchistic, giving no valence to truth at all; like a virus, all it cares about is replicating and spreading.

Jonathan Rauch, "The Constitution of Knowledge," *National Affairs*, no. 41 (Fall 2019), www.nationalaffairs.com/publications/detail/the-constitution -of-knowledge.

58. See, for example, Sarah Jeong's harrowing first-person account of her own and others' harassment around Gamergate. Sarah Jeong, "When the Internet Chases You from Your Home," *New York Times*, Aug. 15, 2019. Similar battle lines have been drawn in almost every form of popular culture over the last decade, but perhaps most virulently in the world of comic books—see the right-wing Comicsgate movement—and superhero films, whether from the Marvel or DC Comic Universe. Over and over again young men's morbid fear of the modest entry of women and queer voices into a space they had once regarded as a "safe space" for them has produced hysterical fits of outrage, in several cases leading to the

organized effort to lower the ratings of a film on Rotten Tomatoes because of the perception that a film had too many women or diverse characters. This reached its apotheosis with the release of the Star Wars movie, *The Last Jedi*. See www.vox.com/culture/2017/12/18/16791844/star-wars-last-jedi -backlash-controversy.

59. Henry Farrell, "The 'Intellectual Dark Web' Explained: What Jordan Peterson Has in Common with the Alt-Right," *Vox*, May 10, 2018.

60. BuzzFeed tells the story of Bannon's cultivation of Yiannopoulos based on an extraordinary cache of emails between them and with others. See Joseph Bernstein, "Here's How Breitbart and Milo Smuggled White Nationalism into the Mainstream," Oct. 5, 2017, www.buzzfeednews.com /article/josephbernstein/heres-how-breitbart-and-milo-smuggled-white -nationalism. The emails tell the story of Steve Bannon's grand plan for Yiannopoulos, whom the Breitbart executive chairman transformed from a charismatic young editor into a conservative media star capable of mag- netizing a new generation of reactionary anger.

61. From Yiannopoulos's "Full Text: Milo on How Feminism Hurts Men and Women," Breitbart, Oct. 7, 2016.

[Yiannopoulos] told angry young men that they were being terror- ized by "an army of sociopathic feminist programmers and cam- paigners, abetted by achingly politically correct American tech bloggers," and gave his young followers permission to embrace the politics of destruction.

Excerpted from Amanda Marcotte, *Troll Nation: How the Right Became Trump-Worshipping Monsters Set on Rat-F*cking Liberals, America, and Truth Itself* (Skyhorse Publishing, 2018), www.alternet.org/heres-how-us-became -troll-nation-gamergate-rise-trump.

62. Marcotte, *Troll Nation*.

63. Megan Condis, "From Fortnite to Alt-Right," *New York Times*, Mar. 28, 2019. See also her study, *Gaming Masculinity: Trolls, Fake Geeks, and the Gendered Battle for Online Culture* (University of Iowa Press, 2018).

Gamergate united men's rights activists, white nationalists, and neo- reactionaries around indignation over the inroads that women and minorities had made into video game culture, previously dominated by young white men.

Henry Farrell, "The 'Intellectual Dark Web' Explained: What Jordan Peterson Has in Common with the Alt-Right," *Vox*, May 10, 2018.

April Glaser reports on the website Discord, which melds "150 million gamers" with virulent white supremacy.

> What's common among most of these groups is that they blur juvenile-seeming, semi-ironic meme making with outright racism— that is, they're what experts on white supremacy recognize as on-ramps to indoctrination. This isn't a new tactic for the far right. . . . The tactic was pioneered on Stormfront, the largest and oldest white-supremacist community on the internet, which was started in 1995 by Don Black, a former grand wizard of the Ku Klux Klan. "On Stormfront, they would sometimes have paid moderators that are waiting there for when someone shows up and asks things like, 'What is white nationalism? What do you guys really believe in?' And then there were moderators there waiting to engage them when they showed interest in having a more serious discussion," said [Joan] Donovan [the lead researcher on media manipulation at the Data & Society Research Institute].

"White Supremacists Still Have a Safe Space Online: Discord Is a Hub for 150 Million Gamers—as well as Some of the Worst People on the Web," *Slate*, Oct. 9, 2018, slate.com/technology/2018/10/discord-safe-space-white -supremacists.html.

64. "Pepe the Frog Meme Branded a 'Hate Symbol,'" BBC News, Sep. 28, 2018, www.bbc.com/news/world-us-canada-37493165.

65. Incels are "involuntary celibates," and their websites traffic in rhetoric about violence and rape posed as revenge for incels' sexual deprivation. Like white nationalism, incel sites raise the issue of stochastic terror. (See note 10, this chapter.) Lone wolf attacks on women have included those at École Polytechnique in Toronto (1989), at Virginia Tech (2007), at Collier Center women's fitness center outside Pittsburgh (2009), and at Isla Vista (2014). Like a number of white nationalist shooters including Breivik in Norway (2011) and Bowers in Pittsburgh (2018), Elliot Rodger, the shooter

in Isla Vista, left behind a manifesto (others, including Rodger, have left videos, even real-time videos of the shootings), which is frequently cited in positive terms on incel sites.

> "The Incel Rebellion has already begun! . . . We will overthrow all the Chads and Stacys! All hail Supreme Gentleman Elliot Rodger!"

Niraj Chokshi, "What Is an Incel? A Term Used by the Toronto Van Attack Suspect, Explained," *New York Times*, Apr. 24, 2018. (Chads are hunky young men understood by incels to be successful with voluptuous hyper-feminine women, known as Stacys.)

See Zack Beauchamp, "Our Incel Problem: How a Support Group for the Dateless Became One of the Internet's Most Dangerous Subcultures," *Vox*, Apr. 23, 2019, www.vox.com/the-highlight/2019/4/16/18287446/incel-definition-reddit. See also Jeff Sharlet, "Are You Man Enough for the Men's Rights Movement?," *GQ*, Feb. 4, 2014, www.gq.com/story/mens-rights-activism-the-red-pill.

66. Michael Anton, "Are the Kids Al(t)Right?," *Claremont Review of Books* 19, no. 3 (Summer 2019). Anton's article is a review of the book, which, he argues, "has struck a chord with younger people—especially men—who are dissatisfied with the way the world is going and have no faith in mainstream conservatism's efforts to arrest, much less reverse, the rot."

Bronze Age Pervert, *Bronze Age Mindset* (Independently published, Jun. 6, 2018), www.amazon.com/Bronze-Age-Mindset-Pervert/dp/1983090441.

67. On "cuckservative" see George Hawley, *Making Sense of the Alt-Right* (Columbia University Press, 2017), 94–99. See also Alan Huhas, "'Cuckservative': The Internet's Latest Republican Insult Hits Where It Hurts," *The Guardian*, Aug. 13, 2015, www.theguardian.com/us-news/2015/aug/13/cuckservative-republicans-conservatives-jeb-bush. See also Alan Rappeport, "From the Right, a New Slur for G.O.P. Candidates," *New York Times*, Aug. 13, 2015.

6. (Grayed-Out) Illiberalism: The Road Taken

1. See coverage of the marches in Susan Chira and Yamiche Alcindor, "Defiant Yet Jubilant Voices Flood U.S. Cities," *New York Times*, Jan. 21, 2017; and Perry Stein et al., "Women's Marches: More Than One Million Protesters Vow to Resist President Trump," *Washington Post*, Jan. 21, 2017.

2. See Lauren Gambino et al., "Thousands Protest Against Trump Travel Ban in Cities and Airports Nationwide," *The Guardian*, Jan. 29, 2017, www.theguardian.com/us-news/2017/jan/29/protest-trump-travel-ban -muslims-airports.

3. See Elana Schor and Rachel Bade, "Inside the Protest Movement That Has Republicans Reeling," *Politico*, Feb. 10, 2017, www.politico.com /story/2017/02/protest-movement-republicans-234863.

4. On January 30, 2005, 58 percent of the Iraqi electorate defied threats of violence to vote in the first elections since Saddam's ouster. After reaching the polls, Iraqis proudly displayed their ink-dipped purple fingers as indications that they had voted. In Washington, Republican congressmen flaunted purple fingers as a sign of solidarity with Bush and pride at how the United States had brought democracy to Iraq.

In his 2005 State of the Union address on February 2, President Bush proudly saluted the Iraqi voters. . . .

The speech also showed that Bush had been reading from the neo-con handbook; he proclaimed to the world that his administration's goal was the promotion of "democratic movements and institutions in every nation and culture, with the ultimate goal of ending tyranny in our world."

"This is real neoconservatism," Robert Kagan, a leading neocon, told the *Los Angeles Times*. "It would be hard to express it more clearly."

Craig Unger, *American Armageddon*, originally published as *The Fall of the House of Bush* (Scribner, 2007, 327).

In the Republicans' pre-Trump ideological orthodoxy, foreign policy was essentially farmed out to neoconservatism. Despite the claim that the aim of invading Iraq was the nonexistent threat of weapons of mass destruction ("WMD"), the invasion was really the long-awaited realization of a pre-existing "regime change" agenda, spelled out in the 2000 report "Rebuilding America's Defenses," published by the Project for the New American Century (PNAC). Infamously, the report lamented that the project of regime change might have to await a "catastrophic and catalyzing event—like a new Pearl Harbor"—which September 11, 2001, provided as the needed pretext. web.archive.org/web/20130817122719/http://www

.newamericancentury.org/RebuildingAmericasDefenses.pdf. Last viewed November 2019.

PNAC had proposed a military invasion to depose Saddam to the Clinton administration, without success. At least ten members of the project held high positions in the Bush administration. Only when the WMD *causus belli* had been discredited was the "freedom agenda"—which accurately tracked neoconservative thinking—rolled out into the light of day as the administration's goal of imposing democracy, oxymoron notwithstanding.

5. On the fifth-year anniversary of "Mission Accomplished," May 2008, during the final year of the Bush presidency,

> the war in Iraq ha[d] claimed the lives of at least 4,058 members of the U.S. military—3,924 of whom have died since Mr. Bush landed on the deck of the USS Abraham Lincoln.

"'Mission Accomplished,' Five Years Later," CBS News, May 1, 2008, www .cbsnews.com/news/mission-accomplished-5-years-later.

6. I deliberately use the word "unitary" here. In the long historical debate about presidential, or executive, power under the Constitution, the case for relatively unrestricted presidential power—independent of oversight by legislative or judicial power—has been made in the form of the theory of the "unitary executive." In pre-Trump Republican orthodoxy, legal theory and jockeying for sway in judicial appointments fell to the Federalist Society, which grew up as a conservative counterweight to the American Bar Association. The strong theory of the unitary executive was argued by Federalist Society legal theorists and became prominent during the George W. Bush administration, which claimed unrestricted freedom of action above all in its prosecution of military action. Trump has vulgarized the "unitary executive" considerably, arguing that "I have an Article 2 [of the Constitution, which defines executive power] where I have the right to do whatever I want as president." www.c-span.org/video/?c4809509 /user-clip-trump-constitution-i-president.

See Michael Brice-Sadler, "While Bemoaning Mueller Probe, Trump Falsely Says the Constitution Gives Him 'the Right to Do Whatever I Want,'" *Washington Post*, Jul. 23, 2019. And Jason Lemon, "Trump Insists the Constitution's Article II 'Allows Me to Do Whatever I Want," *Newsweek*,

Jun. 16, 2019, www.newsweek.com/trump-insists-constitution-allows-do
-whatever-want-1444235.

Trump's third attorney general, William Barr, comes out of the Federalist Society's unitary executive wing and has stood out for opinions and
policies that so defend the president against submitting to congressional
oversight he seems to hew to a Trumpian ideal that the Justice Department
is more a legal arm of the executive—Trump's lawyers, in effect—than an
independent agency. (Note that in most states, attorneys general are independent elective positions, rather than executive appointments.) Trump's
Justice Department conjures up Sarah Churchwell's observation that
locates in "both American populism and European fascism" a "willingness to sacrifice the rule of law to defeat those whom it views as enemies."
Sarah Churchwell, "America's Original Identity Politics," *New York Review
of Books*, Feb. 7, 2019.

7. These issues were raised by some Democrats as justification for
Trump's impeachment in the years before the party's leadership decided
in September 2019 to proceed with impeachment based on Trump seeking
to blackmail Ukraine's president into "investigating" Joe Biden and his son
Hunter. Vermont Representative Peter Welch wrote his constituents a letter
in this regard in July 2019, which is articulate in citing these issues:

I wanted to let you know that I have concluded President Donald
Trump should be impeached.

I do not arrive at this conclusion lightly. The power of impeachment granted to Congress by our Founding Fathers should not be
casually employed. In our democracy, every deference should be
given to the outcome of every election.

However, after 30 months in office, President Trump has established a clear pattern of willful disregard for our Constitution and
its system of checks and balances. His presidency has wrought an
unprecedented and unrelenting assault on the pillars and guardrails
of our democracy, including the rule of law on which our country
was founded.

Instead of embracing the fundamental responsibility of every
American president to unite our country, this president has unleashed
a torrent of attacks on fellow citizens based on their race, gender, religion and ethnic origin.

Instead of respecting the constitutional principle that no person, including the President of the United States, is above the law or beyond accountability, this president attacks our courts and judges and stonewalls Congress in the exercise of its Article 1 oversight responsibility.

Instead of strengthening the institutional pillars of our democracy, this president is methodically tearing them down. He fired the FBI Director and made every effort to derail the Mueller investigation. He calls for the jailing of political opponents and pardons political allies. And at every turn, he demeans, attacks and discredits the free press, dangerously labeling it as the enemy of the people.

And instead of ensuring fair elections, this president and his administration have labored to limit the fundamental right of Americans to vote and welcomed the assistance of hostile foreign powers in his campaigns.

America's democracy is resilient, but it is also fragile. Its stability and progress depend on the consent of the governed, a respect for the rule of law, and the capacity of our leaders to inspire trust and confidence in each other and in the federal government.

On January 20, 2017, President-elect Donald Trump stood on the West Front of the United States Capitol, placed his left hand on two Bibles, raised his right hand, and swore to "preserve, protect and defend the Constitution of the United States." I have concluded that he has failed to honor that solemn oath which, in my view, merits impeachment under our Constitution.

8. Yascha Mounk, *The People Vs. Democracy: Why Our Freedom Is in Danger and How to Save It* (Harvard University Press, 2018). See Mounk's four-fold table of exemplars on p. 36.

9. Mussolini was particularly proud of Fascism's invention of the term "totalitarian." In its essence, it meant the virtual erasure of civil society. In Mussolini's well-known formula: "Everything within the state, nothing outside the state, nothing against the state."

10. Quoted in Eliah Bures, "Don't Call Donald Trump a Fascist," *Foreign Policy*, Nov. 2, 2019.

11. In the 1970s, when Italy was experiencing incidents of domestic terror from both its far right and its far left, there were threats of a coup d'état

from the right—for example, the alleged Borghese coup plot of 1970. A bulwark against a coup was Italy's membership in the EU, which would be threatened if the country's parliamentary system was overthrown. Italy's founding membership in the European Coal and Steel Community, the predecessor of the European Common Market and the EU, was widely popular in Italy. Having emerged from Fascism only six years before the community's 1951 founding, being a "normal" nation was nothing short of a source of national pride. That both upstart winners of Italy's 2018 national elections, the Five Star Movement and, especially, the League, are anti-Europe speaks volumes of the galloping advances populist nationalism has made in Italy since 2015.

12. Quoted in *Wikiquotes*, en.wikiquote.org/wiki/Benito_Mussolini.

13. "The Doctrine of Fascism" was composed by Mussolini in collaboration with Giovanni Gentile, the regime's chief ideologist and legal theorist who came to Fascism from the Italian Nationalist movement. The article was prepared for the 1932 edition of the *Enciclopedia Italiana* (Italian Encyclopedia), and can be read in its entirety at www.worldfuturefund .org/wffmaster/Reading/Germany/mussolini.htm. Last viewed November 2019.

14. Randall Collins, "Trump and the Sopranos," *Sociological Eye*, Dec. 1, 2016, sociological-eye.blogspot.com/2016/12/trump-and-sopranos.html.

15. See Neil Siegel, "Political Norms, Constitutional Conventions, and President Donald Trump," *Indiana Law Journal*, Vol. 93, 2017.

16. See video at www.theguardian.com/us-news/video/2017/may/25 /trump-appears-to-push-aside-montenegro-pm-at-nato-photocall-video. See also Niraj Chokshi, "Trump Appears to Push Aside the Leader of Montenegro," *New York Times*, May 25, 2017, www.nytimes.com/2017/05/25/us /politics/trump-push-aside-leader-montenegro-nato-summit.html.

17. See John Haltiwanger, "Trump Gave a Thumbs-Up in a Photo with a Baby Orphaned by El Paso Mass Shooting," *Business Insider*, Aug. 9, 2019, www.businessinsider.com/trump-gave-thumbs-up-photo-baby-orphaned -el-paso-shooting-2019-8.

18. See Julie Hirschfeld Davis and Eileen Sullivan, "Trump Praises Manafort, Saying 'Unlike Michael Cohen' He 'Refused to Break,'" *New York Times*, Aug. 22, 2018, www.nytimes.com/2018/08/22/us/politics/trump -cohen-manafort.html.

19. See Dareh Gregorian and Ali Vitali, "Lawmakers React to Text of Trump's Ukraine Call: 'A Classic Mob Shakedown,'" NBC News, Sep. 25, 2019, www.nbcnews.com/politics/donald-trump/classic-mob-shakedown-lawmakers-react-summary-trump-s-ukraine-call-n1058631.

Randall Collins's article, "Trump and the Sopranos," published in the *Sociological Eye* on December 1, 2016, before Trump's inaugural, was prescient on this score. He pointed out that the Trumps were a "family in the pre-modern mold," with their businesses "family held, avoiding bureaucratic strings . . . stay[ing] as far as possible from the formal rules and record-keeping of big corporations, publically-traded companies, and government regulations. Like the Mafia, it is based on the opposite of transparency—which means open to formal oversight and outside interference."

On the cultural level, Trump's candidacy also recalls Charles Foster Kane's run for New York governor in Orson Welles's movie *Citizen Kane*. Like Kane (*"He never gave himself away. He never gave anything away. He just left you a tip. . . . He never believed in anything except Charlie Kane. He never had a conviction except Charlie Kane in his life."*), Trump was a narcissistic silver-spoon trust-fund baby who fancied himself the hero of the "common man." Like Trump, after developing fame in media, Kane suddenly enters politics at the level of high office, promising to throw his opponent into jail when he wins. Unlike Trump's *Access Hollywood* pussy-grabbing tape, the exposure of Kane's sexual misconduct—pre–World War II America was culturally far from 2016 America on such issues—dooms his campaign at the last moment. Recalling Trump's repeated assertions of the vote being "rigged," and his suggestions of not accepting an electoral defeat, Kane's newspaper prepares two headlines for election night: one, "Kane Elected"; the other "Fraud at Polls!" See film clip at www.youtube.com/watch?v=9iMy0969BTw.

Trump uses his dogged insistence that he was the victim of voter fraud to explain away defeat in the 2016 popular vote. See Abby Phillip and Mike DeBonis, "Without Evidence, Trump Tells Lawmakers 3 Million to 5 Million Illegal Ballots Cost Him the Popular Vote," *Washington Post*, Jan. 24, 2017, www.washingtonpost.com/news/post-politics/wp/2017/01/23/at-white-house-trump-tells-congressional-leaders-3-5-million-illegal-ballots-cost-him-the-popular-vote.

20. Much has been written about Orbán and his party, Fidesz, which

is sometimes called a party of lawyers. An excerpt from *The Economist's* coverage of their methods for dominating the judiciary:

> The party quickly set about using its two-thirds supermajority to change the constitution. It raised the number of justices on the constitutional court from 11 to 15, appointing four of its own to the new places. It then lowered the compulsory retirement age for judges and prosecutors, freeing up hundreds of posts for Fidesz loyalists. It set up a National Judiciary Office run by Tunde Hando, a college contemporary of Mr Orban's. Her nine-year term, which is due to end next year and under current laws could not be renewed, makes her unsackable by parliament. Ms Hando can veto judicial promotions and influence which judges hear which cases. Fidesz now enjoys control of prosecutors' offices, the constitutional court and the Curia (the highest court of appeals).

"How Viktor Orban Hollowed Out Hungary's Democracy," *The Economist*, Aug. 29, 2019, www.economist.com/briefing/2019/08/29/how-viktor -orban-hollowed-out-hungarys-democracy. More generally, see also Kim Lane Scheppele, "Autocratic Legalism," *University of Chicago Law Review* 85 (2018): 545–83, lawreview.uchicago.edu/publication/autocratic-legalism. For an assessment of the state of Trump's grayed-out shadow of an illiberal regime, see historian of Nazi Germany Christopher Browning's "The Suffocation of Democracy," *New York Review of Books*, Oct. 25, 2018.

21. Rick Klein, "Clinton, Trump Aides Angrily Clash at Election Forum," ABC News, Dec. 1, 2016, abcnews.go.com/Politics/clinton-trump -aides-angrily-clash-election-forum/story?id=43913148.

22. "Fake News: Trump Golf Resorts Display Fake Time Magazine Cover," BBC News, Jun. 28, 2017, www.bbc.com/news/world-us-canada -40427357; Vivian Yee, "By Fudging Math, Trump Takes His Towers to Greater Heights," *New York Times*, Nov. 2, 2016.

23. See Glenn Kessler et al., "President Trump Has Made 13,435 False or Misleading Claims over 993 Days," *Washington Post*, Oct. 14, 2019, www .washingtonpost.com/politics/2019/10/14/president-trump-has-made-false -or-misleading-claims-over-days.

24. Hannah Arendt, "Truth and Politics," *New Yorker*, Feb. 25, 1967.

25. See   www.nbcnews.com/meet-the-press/video/conway-press-secre
tary-gave-alternative-facts-860142147643.

26. Lori Robertson and Robert Farley, "The Facts on Crowd Size," Fact-
Check.org, Jan. 23, 2017. The administration edited its versions of photos
as part of its claims on crowd size. See Chris Riotta, "Trump Inauguration
Photos Edited to Make Crowd Look Bigger After President Intervened,
Documents Reveal," *The Independent,* Sep. 6, 2018.

27. See Jacob Carter, "Sharpiegate and 120 Other Trump Attacks on
Science," *The Hill,* Sep. 11, 2019, thehill.com/opinion/energy-environment
/460937-sharpiegate-and-120-other-trump-attacks-on-science.

28. The term was introduced in Ron Suskind's "Faith, Certainty and the
Presidency of George W. Bush," *New York Times Magazine,* Oct. 17, 2004.
The step between "reality-based community" and "post-truth" America
was the emergence of the term "truthiness," which was Merriam-Webster's
2006 "word of the year." See Caroline McCarthy, "Merriam-Webster's
Word of the Year: Truthiness!," CNet, Dec. 11, 2006, www.cnet.com/news
/merriam-websters-word-of-the-year-truthiness.

George W. Bush's political mastermind, Karl Rove, came up with the
remarkable phrase *reality-based community.* . . . A year later, *The Colbert Report* went on the air. In the first few minutes of the first episode, Stephen Colbert, playing his right-wing-populist commentator
character, performed a feature called "The Word." His first selection:
truthiness. "Now, I'm sure some of the 'word police,' the 'wordinistas'
over at *Webster's,* are gonna say, 'Hey, that's not a word!' Well, any-
body who knows me knows that I'm no fan of dictionaries or reference books. They're elitist. Constantly telling us what is or isn't true.
Or what did or didn't happen. Who's *Britannica* to tell me the Panama
Canal was finished in 1914? If I wanna say it happened in 1941, that's
my right. I don't trust books—they're all fact, no heart . . . Face it,
folks, we are a divided nation. . . . divided between those who think
with their head and those who know with their heart. . . . Because
that's where the truth comes from, ladies and gentlemen—the gut."

From Kurt Andersen, "How America Lost Its Mind, *The Atlantic,* Sep. 20,
2017.

29. Suskind, "Faith, Certainty and the Presidency of George W. Bush."

30. Anonymous, *New York Times*, Sep. 6, 2018. See Sabrina Siddiqui, "Trump Calls for Investigation of New York Times over Op-ed 'Treason,'" *The Guardian*, Sep. 7, 2018, www.theguardian.com/us-news/2018/sep/07 /trump-calls-for-investigation-new-york-times-op-ed-treason.

31. David Jackson, "Donald Trump Now Accuses Nancy Pelosi of 'Treason' (and Wants to Impeach Her)," *USA Today*, Oct. 7, 2019. See also Katie Rodgers, "As Impeachment Moves Forward, Trump's Language Turns Darker: "Treason" is a word the president has increasingly used when talking about his critics," *New York Times*, Oct. 1, 2019, www.nytimes .com/2019/10/01/us/politics/trump-treason-impeachment.html.

32. See Philip Bump, "Trump, Not Understanding Treason, Names People He Thinks Committed the Capital Crime," *Washington Post*, May 23, 2019, www.washingtonpost.com/politics/2019/05/23/trump-not-understanding -treason-names-people-he-thinks-committed-capital-crime.

33. The deep state is more or less equivalent to Steve Bannon's notion of the "administrative state" he promised to smash. (See chapter 5.)

34. Quoted in Elizabeth Chuck, "Trump Names Tillerson as Nominee for Secretary of State," NBC News, Dec. 13, 2019, www.nbcnews.com /politics/politics-news/trump-names-rex-tillerson-nominee-secretary -state-n695281.

35. Allan Smith, "Trump Lashes Out at Rex Tillerson for Saying Putin Out-Prepared Him," NBC News, May 23, 2019, www.nbcnews.com/politics /donald-trump/trump-lashes-out-rex-tillerson-saying-putin-out-prepared -him-n1009156.

36. See "Trump and Kim in Quotes: From Bitter Rivalry to Unlikely Bromance," *Aljazeera*, Feb. 27, 2017.

37. Michael Shear et al., "Strikes on Iran Approved by Trump, Then Abruptly Pulled Back," *New York Times*, Jun. 21, 2019.

38. Paradigmatic example: "Trump Revives Year-Old Insult for House Intel Chair Adam 'Schitt,'" Eileen A.J. Conelly, *New York Post*, Nov. 16, 2019, nypost.com/2019/11/16/trump-revives-year-old-insult-for-house-intel -chair-adam-schitt.

39. Jonathan Rauch, "The Constitution of Knowledge," *National Affairs*, no. 41 (Fall 2019). Rauch adds, "Trump's signature claim to be 'a

counter-puncher' is simply an act of gaslighting. *He* is always the victim, according to his account. So he's always 'counter-punching,' even if he throws the first five, 10 or 20 blows." www.nationalaffairs.com/publications /detail/the-constitution-of-knowledge.

This parallels Mussolini's characteristic and nonsensical claim that the Fascist movement's punitive expeditions were always defensive in nature—not proactive but responses to aggression by their enemies. In his news conference the day after Charlottesville, Richard Spencer argued that James Fields, who drove his car into counter-protesters, killing one and injuring others, was acting in self-defense. Spencer added the nonsensical assertion that everyone knows the alt-right is nonviolent.

40. From "Donald Trump on Social Media," *Wikipedia*, en.m.wikipedia .org/wiki/Donald_Trump_on_social_media. Viewed Nov. 29, 2019.

41. Trump's calls for violence against opponents, the occasional dissenter in his rally crowds, and the press are legion. An early summary as a candidate may be found in Kate Sommers-Dawes, "All the Times Trump Has Called for Violence at His Rallies," *Mashable*, Mar. 11, 2016, mashable .com/2016/03/12/trump-rally-incite-violence. On Trump's continuation of this behavior as president, see David Leonhardt, "It Isn't Complicated: Trump Encourages Violence," *New York Times*, Mar. 17, 2019. And Jonathan Chait, "Trump Isn't Inciting Violence by Mistake, but on Purpose. He Just Told Us," *New York Magazine*, Nov. 5, 2018, nymag.com/intelligencer/2018/11 /trump-isnt-inciting-violence-by-mistake-he-just-told-us.html.

42. See, for example, John Wagner, "Trump Takes Aim at Obama, Clinton, Judges, Election Officials, Reporters and a Host of Others Before Leaving the Country," *Washington Post*, Nov. 9, 2018, www.washingtonpost .com/politics/trump-takes-aim-at-obama-clinton-judges-election-officials -reporters-and-a-host-of-others-before-leaving-the-country/2018/11/09 /bd52140a-e435-11e8-b759-3d88a5ce9e19_story.html.

43. From Michael Shaw, "Six Rare Images That Capture Trump's TV Addiction," *Columbia Journalism Review*, May 31, 2017, www.cjr.org/politics /trump-tv-addiction.php.

See Elaine Godfrey, "Trump's TV Obsession Is a First," *The Atlantic*, Apr. 3, 2017, www.theatlantic.com/politics/archive/2017/04/donald-trump -americas-first-tv-president/521640.

See also Brandon Carter, "Trump Watches up to Eight Hours of TV Per

Day: Report," *The Hill*, Dec. 9, 2017, thehill.com/homenews/administration /364094-trump-watches-at-least-four-hours-of-tv-per-day-report.

44. For example, former Fox TV host Lawrence Kudlow was made director of the National Economic Council in March 2018; and John Bolton was named national security advisor the following month—he lasted five months in the position.

45. A perhaps extreme example: Trump spent fifty-three minutes on the phone with *Fox and Friends* the morning of November 22, 2019. (See *Axios*, www.axios.com/trump-fox-and-friends-call-impeachment-ukraine -e1739c65-33d3-4c35-a723-7a31abb488ef.html.)

46. See Jessica Kwong, "Fox News's Sean Hannity Basically Has a Desk at White House as President's Most Influential Counselor: Trump Advisor," *Newsweek*, Sep. 5, 2019, www.newsweek.com/sean-hannity-white -house-desk-counselor-donald-trump-1457917.

47. For example, see Chris Cillizza, "Why Donald Trump Feels Betrayed by Fox News," CNN, May 21, 2019, www.cnn.com/2019/05/20/politics/fnc -fox-news-donald-trump/index.html.

48. One (quite painful) example of Trump buying into the conspiracy fevers on the right was the case of the death of Seth Rich.

> Fox News played an instrumental role in helping push the conspiracy theory that the 27-year-old Rich, who was murdered in a botched robbery in July 2016, had contact with WikiLeaks, which released thousands of Hillary Clinton campaign emails during the 2016 presidential race.

Ari Berman, "Seth Rich's Family Just Won a Legal Victory Against Fox News, *Mother Jones*, Sep. 14, 2019, www.motherjones.com/politics/2019 /09/seth-richs-family-just-won-a-legal-victory-against-fox-news. See also Ed Pilkington, "The Strange Case of Fox News, Trump and the Death of Young Democrat Seth Rich," *The Guardian*, Aug. 7, 2017, www.theguardian .com/media/2017/aug/07/seth-rich-trump-white-house-fox-news.

In "Exclusive: The True Origins of the Seth Rich Conspiracy Theory," Michael Isikoff traces the chain of Rich conspiracy thinking through the populist right media and its path to Fox News and to Donald Trump. An excerpt illustrating that passage:

Along the way, the idea that Rich was murdered in retaliation for leaking DNC emails to WikiLeaks was championed by multiple allies of Trump, including Roger Stone. The same day [WikiLeaks head Julian] Assange falsely hinted that Rich may have been his source for DNC emails, Stone tweeted a picture of Rich, calling the late DNC staffer in a tweet "another dead body in the Clinton's wake." He then added: "Coincidence? I think not."

Yahoo News, Jul. 9, 2019.

49. From Matthew Gertz, "I've Studied the Trump-Fox Feedback Loop for Months. It's Crazier Than You Think," *Politico,* Jan. 5, 2018, www.politico .com/magazine/story/2018/01/05/trump-media-feedback-loop-216248.

From Daniel Moritz-Rabson, "Video Compilation Shows Thirty Times Trump Repeated 'Fox and Friends' Talking Points in 2018," *Newsweek,* Dec. 28, 2018:

A video compiled by news monitor Media Matters shows 30 times President Donald Trump repeated talking points from *Fox & Friends* in 2018, illuminating the close connection between the president and the morning show.

www.newsweek.com/trump-fox-and-friends-influence-video-twitter -tweets-fox-news-1274231.

50. F.W. Deakin, *The Brutal Friendship: Mussolini, Hitler and the Fall of Italian Fascism,* vol. 1 (Doubleday, 1966), 41–42.

51. Murray Kempton, "A Genius of Journalism," *New York Review of Books,* Oct. 7, 1982. Kempton notes that half of Fascism's Grand Council in 1930 consisted of journalists.

52. See Jessica Estepa, "Reporter Says Donald Trump Used Alter Ego 'John Barron' to Get onto Forbes 400 List," *USA Today,* Apr. 20, 2018, www .usatoday.com/story/news/politics/onpolitics/2018/04/20/reporter-recalls -trumps-alter-ego-amazed-didnt-see-through-ruse/537312002.

As John Cassidy pointed out:

These days, when Trump has a self-serving whopper to spread around, he goes on Twitter and attaches his own name to it. In the age of @realDonaldTrump, there is no longer any need for John Barron.

"Trump's History of Lying, from John Barron to @realDonaldTrump," *New Yorker*, Apr. 23, 2018, www.newyorker.com/news/our-columnists/trumps -history-of-lying-from-john-barron-to-realdonaldtrump.

53. In this Trump most resembles his British counterpart Boris Johnson.

"Boris Johnson is more of a journalist than he is a statesman by a considerable margin," said David Yelland, a former editor of The Sun, a tabloid. "His instincts are those of a newspaper columnist, and his consistency is that of a British newspaper columnist, in the sense that he says one thing on a Monday and another on a Tuesday and it doesn't matter."

Benjamin Mueller, "For Pro-Brexit Press, Boris Johnson Is Already a Winner," *New York Times*, Oct. 21, 2019, www.nytimes.com/2019/10/21/world /europe/brexit-newspapers-boris-Johnson.html.

54. The Putin quote is from a *Financial Times* interview with him in June 2019. See Lionel Barber et al., "Putin Says Liberalism Has 'Become Obsolete,'" *Financial Times*, Jun. 27, 2019, www.ft.com/content/670039ec-98f3 -11e9-9573-ee5cbb98ed36.

55. Patrick J. Buchanan, "Is Putin Right? Has Liberalism Lost the World?," Patrick J. Buchanan Official Website, Jul. 2, 2019, buchanan.org /blog/is-putin-right-has-liberalism-lost-the-world-137223#more-137223.

Buchanan's embrace of Trumpism includes lionizing Trump's tariff policies. See his "Tariffs: The Taxes That Made America Great," Buchanan Official Website, May 13, 2019.

Tariffs were the taxes that made America great. They were the taxes relied upon by the first and greatest of our early statesmen, before the coming of the globalists Woodrow Wilson and FDR.

That is economic patriotism, putting America and Americans first.

Once a nation is hooked on the cheap goods that are the narcotic free trade provides, it is rarely able to break free. The loss of its economic independence is followed by the loss of its political independence, the loss of its greatness and, ultimately, the loss of its national identity.

As he did with World War II in his book *Churchill, Hitler, and "The Unnecessary War": How Britain Lost Its Empire and the West Lost the World* (Crown,

2008), Buchanan was attempting to recast *tout court* a pillar of received liberal thinking—in this case on the New Deal and the causes of the Great Depression:

> That the Smoot-Hawley Tariff caused the Depression of the 1930s is a New Deal myth in which America's schoolchildren have been indoctrinated for decades. The Depression began with the crash of the stock market in 1929, nine months before Smoot-Hawley became law. The real villain: the Federal Reserve.

buchanan.org/blog/tariffs-the-taxes-that-made-america-great-136986.

56. Gottfried decried what he called "multicultural totalitarianism." With some reluctance he increasingly understood the inherent connection between anti-liberal nationalism and race that would become the hallmark of the alt-right:

> In a 2009 essay, Gottfried wrote: "To the extent that anything resembling the historic right can flourish in our predominantly postmodernist, multicultural and feminist society—and barring any unforeseen return to a more traditionalist establishment right—racial nationalism, for better or worse, may be one of the few extant examples of a recognizably rightist mind-set."

Jacob Siegel, "The Alt-Right's Jewish Godfather," *Tablet*, Nov. 29, 2016, www.tabletmag.com/jewish-news-and-politics/218712/spencer-gottfried -alt-right.

57. VDARE was named in honor of Virginia Dare, the first white child born on the American continent.

58. Roy Beck, *The Case Against Immigration* (Norton, 1996).

See Jason DeParle, "The Anti-Immigration Crusader," *New York Times*, Apr. 17, 2011, for the place of John Tanton as a pioneer of establishing the modern field of anti-immigrant pressure groups. Also see Nicholas Kulish and Mike McIntire, "Why an Heiress Spent Her Fortune Trying to Keep Immigrants Out," *New York Times*, Aug. 14, 2019, for the unique role of Cordelia Scaife May, who bankrolled the movement to the tune of $180 million over the years.

59. See chapter 5, note 34. Also notable in expounding the nationalist point of view prefiguring Donald Trump was the radio talk show host Michael Savage, who used the phrase "borders, language and culture" to summarize his views. Racist anti-immigrant views were expressed popularly throughout this period. One notable instance was the case of the Atlanta Braves pitcher John Rocker. Rocker was vocal about his extreme distaste for the diversity of New York, and in particular what he encountered on the subway ride out to Shea Stadium in Queens or walking the streets in Manhattan:

> The biggest thing I don't like about New York are the foreigners. I'm not a very big fan of foreigners. You can walk an entire block in Times Square and not hear anybody speaking English. Asians and Koreans and Vietnamese and Indians and Russians and Spanish people and everything up there. How the hell did they get in this country?

Jeff Pearlman, "At Full Blast," *Sports Illustrated*, Dec. 23, 1999, web.archive .org/web/20000817193712/http://sportsillustrated.cnn.com/features/cover /news/1999/12/22/rocker.

60. As for the white nationalist dimension of paleoconservative and anti-immigrant nationalism:

> The heart of where these guys differ from neoconservatives and Republican orthodoxy is basically: "What is the American nation and what is the nature of American nationhood?". . . It's not based on "We hold these truths to be self-evident." It's based on "What were the color of the people who wrote those words?"

Lawrence Rosenthal, quoted in Katie Rogers and Jason DeParle, "White Nationalists' Websites Influenced Miller," *New York Times*, Nov. 18, 2019.

61. See George Hawley, *Making Sense of the Alt-Right*, 97.

62. Publius Decius Mus, "The Flight 93 Election," *Claremont Review of Books*, Sep. 5, 2016, www.claremont.org/crb/basicpage/the-flight-93-election.

Anton began the argument for the creation of a new "national conservatism" that would continue after Trump's election. Conservatism had lost its way in the globalist consensus it had come to share with liberalism:

If conservatives are right about the importance of virtue, morality, religious faith, stability, character and so on in the individual;
if they are right about sexual morality or what came to be termed
"family values"; if they are right about the importance of education
to inculcate good character and to teach the fundamentals that have
defined knowledge in the West for millennia; if they are right about
societal norms and public order; if they are right about the central-
ity of initiative, enterprise, industry, and thrift to a sound economy
and a healthy society; if they are right about the soul-sapping effects
of paternalistic Big Government and its cannibalization of civil society and religious institutions; if they are right about the necessity
of a strong defense and prudent statesmanship in the international
sphere—if they are right about the importance of all this to national
health and even survival, then they must believe—mustn't they?—
that *we are headed off a cliff*.

All of Trump's 16 Republican competitors would have ensured
more of the same—as will the election of Hillary Clinton. . . . Most
important, [that means] the ceaseless importation of Third World foreigners with no tradition of, taste for, or experience in liberty means
that the electorate grows more left, more Democratic, less Republican,
and less traditionally American with every cycle.

63. See Jennifer Schuessler's report on the "Claremonsters" at "'Charge
the Cockpit or You Die': Behind an Incendiary Case for Trump," *New York
Times*, Feb. 20, 2017. See also Jon Baskin, "The Academic Home of Trumpism," *Chronicle of Higher Education*, Mar. 17, 2017, www.chronicle.com/article
/The-Academic-Home-of-Trumpism/239495.

64. "Fact Sheet: Immigrants in California," *American Immigration
Council*, Oct. 4, 2017, www.americanimmigrationcouncil.org/research
/immigrants-in-california.

65. Jeremy W. Peters takes up the problem of California as the center
of Trumpian intellectual ferment in "In the Heart of 'The Resistance,'
California Conservatives Are Invigorated," *New York Times*, Oct. 31, 2017,
www.nytimes.com/2017/10/31/us/california-republicans-bannon-miller
-conservative.html.

This California reverse effect—that immigrant proximity inflamed
anti-immigrant feeling among ideologues—was also reflected in Califor-

nia having contributed disproportionately to the militant leaders of the alt-right, including the violent characters of Charlottesville, the Battle of Berkeley, and elsewhere.

66. Daniel Luban, "The Man Behind National Conservatism," *New Republic*, Jul. 26, 2019, newrepublic.com/article/154531/man-behind-nati onal-conservatism.

See also Jacob Heilbrunn's report on the conference at "National Conservatism: Retrofitting Trump's GOP with a Veneer of Ideas," *New York Review of Books*, Jul. 18, 2019, www.nybooks.com/daily/2019/07/18/national -conservatism-retrofitting-trumps-gop-with-a-veneer-of-ideas.

Anne Applebaum covered a February 2020 National Conservatism conference in Rome. See her report, "This Is How Reaganism and Thatcherism End," *The Atlantic*, Feb. 10, 2020, www.theatlantic.com/ideas/archive/2020 /02/the-sad-path-from-reaganism-to-national-conservatism/606304.

67. Yoram Hazony, *Virtue of Nationalism* (Basic Books, 2018). According to Luban, Hazony, who was raised in the United States, was reportedly "mesmerized" by meeting ultranationalist rabbi Meir Kahane as a young man, and participated in Benjamin Netanyahu's early inner circle.

Other significant texts related to the conference include: Michael Anton's "The Trump Doctrine," *Foreign Policy*, Apr. 20, 2019, foreignpolicy .com/2019/04/20/the-trump-doctrine-big-think-america-first-nationalism; Senator Josh Hawley's speech at the National Conservatism Conference, www.hawley.senate.gov/senator-josh-hawleys-speech-national-conser vatism-conference; and Rich Lowry's *The Case for Nationalism: How It Made Us Powerful, United, and Free* (HarperCollins, 2019). (It is also worth noting Charles King's response to Lowry, "America's Original Identity Politics: Rich Lowry's Flawed Case for Nationalism," *Foreign Affairs*, Nov. 7, 2019, www.foreignaffairs.com/reviews/review-essay/2019-11-07/americas -original-identity-politics.)

68. Yoram Hazony, "Conservative Democracy," *First Things*, Jan. 2019, www.firstthings.com/article/2019/01/conservative-democracy. It is notable how significantly this privileging of the ethnic and spiritual basis of conservatism over the words of the U.S. foundation documents contradicts the "originalism" that has characterized conservative thought since the 1980s and has established itself as the cornerstone of right-wing and right populist notions of jurisprudence.

See also Hazony's (with Ofir Haivry) "What Is Conservatism?,"

American Affairs 1, no. 2 (Summer 2017), which notably expands the dramatis personae of American conservatism beyond the received thinking of neoconservative and orthodox Republican thought.

> The emergence of the Anglo-American conservative tradition can be identified with the words and deeds of a series of towering political and intellectual figures, among whom we can include individuals such as Sir John Fortescue, Richard Hooker, Sir Edward Coke, John Selden, Sir Matthew Hale, Sir William Temple, Jonathan Swift, Josiah Tucker, Edmund Burke, John Dickinson, and Alexander Hamilton. Men such as George Washington, John Adams, and John Marshall, often hastily included among the liberals, would also have placed themselves in this conservative tradition rather than with its opponents, whom they knew all too well.

69. Hazony, "Conservative Democracy."

70. Daniel Luban, "The Man Behind National Conservatism." From Michael Anton's "The Trump Doctrine":

> While traditional empires may have gone out of fashion, globalization has taken its place as the imperialism of our time. Globalization represents an attempt to do through peaceful means—the creation of transnational institutions, the erosion of borders, and the homogenization of intellectual, cultural, and economic products—what the Romans (and Cyrus and others) achieved through arms.
>
> Globalism and transnationalism impose their highest costs on established powers (namely the United States) and award the greatest benefits to rising powers seeking to contest U.S. influence and leadership.

71. Schmitt defines sovereignty as the power to invoke the state of exception. He wrote, "The Sovereign is he who decides on the exception." See Quinta Jurecic, "Donald Trump's State of Exception," *Lawfare*, Dec. 14, 2016, www.lawfareblog.com/donald-trumps-state-exception.

Agamben argues that the whole of the Nazi era was a state of exception imposed by Hitler as the executive. See Giorgio Agamben, *State of Exception* (University of Chicago Press, 2004).

72. Ed Pilkington and Martin Pengelly, "Trump Proposed Sending Migrants to Guantánamo, Claims Book by Anonymous Author," *The Guardian*, Nov. 14, 2019.

73. Lauren Suken, "The United States Treats Migrants Worse Than Prisoners of War," *Foreign Policy*, Jul. 26, 2019, foreignpolicy.com/2019/07/26/the-united-states-treats-migrants-worse-than-prisoners-of-war.

Today, U.S. Immigration and Customs Enforcement (ICE) detention centers have custody of approximately 54,000 refugees, asylum-seekers, and migrants. An additional 20,000 are being held in the custody of Customs and Border Protection, with 11,000 more children held by the Department of Health and Human Services. That's a higher number of detainees than there were U.S. prisoners of war (POWs) in the Gulf War, Vietnam War, Korean War, and the Pacific Front of World War II combined.

Suken illustrates numerous violations of the standards for detainees set by the Geneva Convention. She points out among other violations that "in some facilities, babies are being fed with unwashed bottles; there are no diapers, soap, or toothpaste. Showers are unavailable or too few, as are laundry facilities and clean changes of clothes"—all violations; and that among the consequences, "approximately 26 people have died in the centers—seven of whom were children."

74. The text of the State of Emergency Declaration may be found at www.whitehouse.gov/presidential-actions/presidential-proclamation-declaring-national-emergency-concerning-southern-border-united-states.

75. Julian De Medeiros, "The Wall Isn't a State of Emergency but a State of Exception," *openDemocracy*, Feb. 16, 2019.

76. James Vincent, "Watch Jordan Peele Use AI to Make Barack Obama Deliver a PSA About Fake News," *The Verge*, Apr. 17, 2018, www.theverge.com/tldr/2018/4/17/17247334/ai-fake-news-video-barack-obama-jordan-peele-buzzfeed. See also Hilke Schellmann, "The Dangerous New Technology That Will Make Us Question Our Basic Idea of Reality," *Quartz*, Dec. 5, 2017, qz.com/1145657/the-dangerous-new-technology-that-will-make-us-question-our-basic-idea-of-reality.

77. This is from Schiff's January 24 closing argument. For a transcript

see https://www.rev.com/blog/transcripts/adam-schiff-closing-argument -transcript-thursday-impeachment-trial.

78. Mueller's report disappointed Blue America because it effectively left legal action based upon it to either the Justice Department or Congress. According to a federal judge, William Barr purposely "distorted" and "misled" in his handling of the report, causing "the court to seriously question whether Attorney General Barr made a calculated attempt to influence public discourse about the Mueller report in favor of President Trump." (Charlie Savage, "Judge Calls Barr's Handling of Mueller Report 'Distorted' and 'Misleading,'" *New York Times*, Mar. 5, 2020.)

Mueller had explained both his inclination to leave prosecution to others and his passively stated belief in Trump's guilt as follows:

> *Because we determined not to make a traditional prosecutorial judgment, we did not draw ultimate conclusions about the President's conduct.* The evidence we obtained about the President's actions and intent presents difficult issues that would need to be resolved if we were making a traditional prosecutorial judgment. At the same time, *if we had confidence after a thorough investigation of the facts that the President clearly did not commit obstruction of justice, we would so state.* Based on the facts and the applicable legal standards, *we are unable to reach that judgment. Accordingly, while this report does not conclude that the President committed a crime, it also does not exonerate him.* [emphasis added]

From the Justice Department's heavily blacked-out publication of the *Report on the Investigation into Russian Interference in the 2016 Presidential Election*, Volume II of II, p 8 and p 182, https://www.justice.gov/storage/report.pdf.

79. Michael Cohen was convicted of campaign finance violations for hush-money payoffs to porn star Stormy Daniels and Playboy Playmate Karen McDougal. Cohen's indictment in the Southern District of New York cited "Individual-1" ("who was elected President") as his accomplice in the crime. (Glenn Fleishman, "Feds Accuse Individual-1—Also Known as Trump—of a Crime in Michael Cohen's Sentencing Memo," *Fortune*, Dec. 7, 2018, fortune.com/2018/12/07/feds-accuse-trump-crime-cohen-campaign -finance.)

As Cohen made clear at his sentencing:

I pled guilty in federal court to felonies for the benefit of, at the direction of, and in coordination with "Individual 1" . . . And for the record: "Individual 1" is Donald J. Trump.

Dara Lind, "Michael Cohen: 'Individual 1 Is Donald J. Trump,'" *Vox*, Feb. 27, 2019, www.vox.com/2019/2/27/18243038/individual-1-cohen-trump-muell er.

80. In its purest form, Trump's tic was on display in one of his presidential debates with Hillary Clinton:

Clinton: That's because he'd [Putin] rather have a puppet as president . . .
Trump: [interrupting] No puppet. No puppet. You're the puppet.

See www.youtube.com/watch?v=UaVWRetR4jg.

Charles Blow captured the central role of psychological projection in Trump's "tic" when he wrote:

Trump is like the unfaithful spouse who constantly accuses the other of infidelity because the guilt of his or her own sins has hijacked their thinking and consumed their consciousness. The flaws he sees are the ones he possesses.

Charles M. Blow, "America's Whiniest 'Victim,'" *New York Times*, Aug. 7, 2017.

81. For Blue America, there was a bellwether in watching the Republican Party go Full Trump. In September 2018, the Senate Judiciary Committee held hearings for Brett Kavanaugh's nomination to the Supreme Court. A Stanford research psychologist, Christine Blasey Ford, alleged that "a drunken young Mr. Kavanaugh pinned her to a bed, tried to rip off her clothes and clapped his hand over her mouth to muffle her cries for help."

Kavanaugh responded with seething fury. He followed Trump's two-step formula of denial and projection. In addition, he appended a conspiracy theory alleging motivations based on avenging Trump's election. Along with alleging "hoaxes," conspiracy thinking was a commonplace in how projection played out in right-wing media and among Republican spokespersons. Kavanaugh:

This whole two-week effort has been a calculated and orchestrated political hit, fueled with apparent pent-up anger about President Trump and the 2016 election, fear that has been unfairly stoked about my judicial record, revenge on behalf of the Clintons and millions of dollars in money from outside left-wing opposition groups.

From Brett Kavanaugh's opening statement: Full transcript, *New York Times*, Sep. 26, 2018, www.nytimes.com/2018/09/26/us/politics/read-brett -kavanaughs-complete-opening-statement.html.

Senator Lindsey Graham followed Kavanaugh's statement with a furious and snarling attack on the Democratic members of the committee: "What you want to do is destroy this guy's life, hold this seat open and hope you win in 2020." Striking here is how blatant the psychological projection has become: Graham is accusing the Democrats of attempting to do precisely what the Republicans had done in 2016 with Barack Obama's Supreme Court nomination of Merrick Garland—"hold[ing] the seat open and hop[ing] you win in 2016." The illiberal mentality rejects professionalism and objectivity; at the heart of their projection is the conviction, judging from themselves, that all behavior is intrinsically self-interested.

See Ian Swartz, "Sen. Graham Explodes at Kavanaugh Hearing: 'Most Despicable' Thing in Politics, I Hope You Never Get This Seat," *Real Clear Politics*, Sep. 27, 2018, which includes video of Graham's outburst, www.realclearpolitics.com/video/2018/09/27/sen_graham_explodes _on_dems_at_kavanaugh_hearing_most_despicable_thing_ive_seen_in _politics.html.

82. See chapter 3, note 9.

83. See the following:

- McKay Coppins, "The Billion Dollar Disinformation Campaign to Reelect the President," *The Atlantic*, Mar. 2020, www.theatlantic.com/magazine/archive/2020/03/the-2020 -disinformation-war/605530.
- Arthur Ituassu, "Digital Media and Public Opinion in Brazil After Trump 2016," *Open Democracy*, Dec, 6, 2019, www .opendemocracy.net/en/democraciaabierta/public-opinion -in-brazil-after-the-campaigns-of-trump-and-bolsonaro.

- Philip N. Howard, "How Political Campaigns Weaponize Social Media Bots," *IEEE Spectrum*, Oct. 18, 2018, spectrum .ieee.org/computing/software/how-political-campaigns -weaponize-social-media-bots.

84. The anti-sheltering movement offered the contrast between Trumpian populist supporters out on the streets and the backing of right-wing money like Americans for Prosperity and the DeVos family. In this it raised the question much debated about the Tea Party: was it an Astroturf or a grass-roots movement? (See chapter 2, note 12; also see Adam Gabbatt, "Thousands of Americans Backed by Rightwing Donors Gear Up for Protests," *The Guardian*, Apr. 18, 2020, www.theguardian.com/us-news/2020 /apr/18/coronavirus-americans-protest-stay-at-home.)

Trump gave his support to this movement in tweets that exhorted "Liberate Minnesota/Virginia/Michigan." His Virginia tweet was particularly volatile since he included the suggestion that gun rights were at stake to a movement where individuals frequently appeared conspicuously carrying automatic weapons. ("LIBERATE VIRGINIA, and save your great 2nd Amendment. It is under siege!" See Colby Itkowitz, "'Liberate': Trump Tweets Support of Protests Against Stay-at-Home Orders," *Washington Post*, Apr. 17, 2020, washingtonpost.com/politics/2020/04/17/liberate-trump -tweets-support-protesting-against-stay-at-home-orders.) Trump's implicit call to arms was particularly incendiary since it came at a time when "civil-war chatter" (the moment seemed ripe for the "boogaloo"—the militia uprising) was florid on militia blogs. See Devin Burghart, "Coronavirus and the Militia-Sphere," *IREHR*, Mar. 20, 2020, www.irehr.org/2020/03/26 /coronavirus-militia-sphere.

85. See chapter 2 on the Tea Party's popular-originalist constitutionalism—the view that interpretation of the Constitution must adhere word-for-word to its text, and that interpretation of the Constitution should not be left solely in the hands of judges and lawyers and trained professionals, but was best practiced by ordinary citizens. A relatively sober statement of the populist epidemiological case was offered by "ReOpen Maryland":

Government mandating sick people to stay home is called quarantine. However, the government mandating healthy citizens to stay home, forcing businesses and churches to close is called tyranny.

(Quoted in Gabbatt, "Thousands of Americans Backed by Rightwing Donors Gear Up for Protests".)

Populist epidemiology reached perhaps its high point in "Lysolgate" when Trump, who had taken to daily two-hour-long sessions with the press that often turned belligerent, mused that "injecting" disinfectant might be worth investigating as a way to wipe out coronavirus infections. See Katie Rogers et al., "Trump's Suggestion That Disinfectants Could Be Used to Treat Coronavirus Prompts Aggressive Pushback," *New York Times*, Apr. 24, 2020.

The anti-shutdown movement was rife with conspiracy theories. The usual suspects, the deep state and the globalists, were seen to be attempting to inculcate permanent mass dependency on government; plotting the overthrow of capitalism and the triumph of socialism; trying to collapse the economy to bring down Trump. China was another candidate, seen as having tried to weaponize the virus in its Wuhan lab. Bill Gates, who foresaw the pandemic in a much-viewed Ted Talk, was another candidate. So was the World Health Organization.

86. See the earlier discussion in this chapter of an Enabling Act's potential role as a kind of Rubicon to cross from illiberalism to institutionalizing the total shutdown of democracy that was effected in the historical fascist states of the twentieth century. For a report on this development in Hungary see Silvia Amaro, "Hungary's Nationalist Leader Viktor Orban Is Ruling by Decree Indefinitely Amid Coronavirus," CNBC, Mar. 31, 2020, www.cnbc.com/2020/03/31/coronavirus-in-hungary-viktor-orban-rules-by -decree-indefinitely.html.

For a view indicating the gravity with which Europe viewed this development, see Renata Uitz, "The EU Needs to Stop Funding Viktor Orbán's Emergency Rule," *euronews*, Apr. 7, 2020, www.euronews.com/2020/04/07 /the-eu-needs-to-stop-funding-viktor-orban-s-emergency-rule-view.

87. "When somebody is president of the United States his authority is total." "Total," one is tempted to note in this context, is the root of "totalitarian." This statement, plus a number of similar statements Trump made in his coronavirus sessions with the press, may be seen at www .youtube.com/watch?v=r3QXrQDTDYo.

For an overview of the broadly based pushback on Trump's assertion of "total" power, see Charlie Savage, "Trump's Claim of Total Authority in Crisis Is Rejected Across Ideological Lines," *New York Times*, Apr.14, 2020.

88. A strong late April statement of this point of view came from a sheltering-in-place Joe Biden, who had already established himself as the Democratic Party's presumptive nominee for president: "Mark my words, I think [Trump] is going to try to kick back the election somehow, come up with some rationale why it can't be held."

See Amanda Holpuch, "Joe Biden Warns That Donald Trump May Try to Delay November Election," *The Guardian*, Apr. 24, 2020, www.theguardian .com/us-news/2020/apr/24/joe-biden-donald-trump-delay-election.

INDEX

ABOUT THE AUTHOR

Dr. Lawrence Rosenthal is chair and lead researcher of the Berkeley Center for Right-Wing Studies. He has taught at the University of California, Berkeley, in the sociology and Italian studies departments and was a Fulbright professor at the University of Naples in Italy. He lives in Berkeley.

PUBLISHING IN THE PUBLIC INTEREST

Thank you for reading this book published by The New Press. The New Press is a nonprofit, public interest publisher. New Press books and authors play a crucial role in sparking conversations about the key political and social issues of our day.

We hope you enjoyed this book and that you will stay in touch with The New Press. Here are a few ways to stay up to date with our books, events, and the issues we cover:

- Sign up at www.thenewpress.com/subscribe to receive updates on New Press authors and issues and to be notified about local events
- Like us on Facebook: www.facebook.com/newpress books
- Follow us on Twitter: www.twitter.com/thenewpress

Please consider buying New Press books for yourself; for friends and family; or to donate to schools, libraries, community centers, prison libraries, and other organizations involved with the issues our authors write about.

The New Press is a 501(c)(3) nonprofit organization. You can also support our work with a tax-deductible gift by visiting www.thenewpress.com/donate.